1936

1934

1933

1942

1944

Yehudi Menuhin

Robert Magidoff

Yehudi Menuhin
The Kremlin vs. The People
In Anger and Pity
Rye and Nettle (Verse)

Yehudi Menuhin

THE STORY OF THE MAN AND THE MUSICIAN

Robert Magidoff

DOUBLEDAY & COMPANY, INC., GARDEN CITY, NEW YORK, 1955

From the Author

I was a very young man working my way through high school and college when a small boy named Yehudi Menuhin was being universally hailed as the greatest child prodigy since Mozart. That boy became a legend to me, as to many others, as miraculous as the other legends of those faraway days— Charles Lindbergh, Charlie Chaplin, or Babe Ruth—except that Menuhin was more real and magical because music and literature were a greater reality to me than aviation, films, or sports.

Many years later, I met him in Moscow, of all places, where I was serving as correspondent for the National Broadcasting Company and where Menuhin, already in Europe on one of his periodic wartime visits, had been invited by the Soviet Government to give a series of concerts. We met, had several meals together, and talked long past midnight after two of his concerts; and soon he departed from Russia as precipitously as he had come, leaving me fascinated by his simplicity and artistry and wondering about the "chemical composition" of a legend and about what being a legend does to a person. Among other things, for instance, he said, apropos a remark I had made on his hectic solitary travels: "You might never guess that not until after my eighteenth birthday did I cross the street unescorted for the first time. It was a strange, awkward, and exhilarating experience, as was my first contact with the telephone. All the telephoning had been done for me, so that the phone had become a symbol of intrusion by the outside world and had remained so for many years, although now that instrument is almost as natural a 'biological' part of me as is the violin."

Nearly five years were to pass before we met again, this time in London. I told Menuhin on that occasion of how I had kept wondering about him and what an unusual subject he'd make

7

for a book, a book I'd like to write. He smiled: "Why don't you?" I made the start two years later, in December 1952, and all too soon discovered the truth of Boswell's words: "Biography occasions a degree of trouble far beyond that of any other species of literary composition."

As I was launching the work on this biography, Menuhin said in response to a request of mine: "Here are the names and addresses of persons who have known me and my family for many years. Some are more recent friends. Speak to them all and report what you believe to be true." I have since spoken to about one hundred persons in six countries of Europe and in a dozen cities in the United States, who gave me generously of their time and placed at my disposal diaries, letters, and photographs. My debt to them is enormous.

As to his own contribution, Menuhin promised to speak freely and answer all my questions (which he has done with rare objectivity), but only if, when, and as his concert schedule allowed time for discussion. It did not take me long to become convinced that he was not being coy: his daily practice, rehearsals with accompanists and orchestras, press interviews, and the demands made upon him by various individuals and organizations all proved to be so time-consuming that I was able to complete my interviews with him only after I had traveled with him for five months in Europe and had made four trips to his home in California.

Few, if any, lives of concert artists have been more extensively covered by the world press as has been Menuhin's, but rarely has the printed word told so little of the inner life and growth of a man as in his case. This narrative is an attempt to bring the real person and the legendary one into alignment.

R. M.

CONTENTS

PROLOGUE: *Chaconne* 13

ONE: *Moshe and Marutha* 17

TWO: *Growing Pains* 29

THREE: *The First Steps* 37

FOUR: *San Francisco—Hail and Farewell!* 51

FIVE: *Paris and Georges Enesco* 65

SIX: *Carnegie Hall* 87

SEVEN: *Fame and Discipline* 99

EIGHT: *The "Prince Khevenhüller"* 121

NINE: *Berlin and Adolf Busch* 135

TEN: *Ville d'Avray* 149

ELEVEN: *Elgar, Toscanini, and a Battle Lost* 169

TWELVE: *"Mother's Year"* 189

THIRTEEN: *"The Marrying Menuhins"* 209

FOURTEEN: *The War Years* 223

FIFTEEN: *Retooling* 239

SIXTEEN: *The Submerged Part of the Iceberg—I* 253

SEVENTEEN: *The Submerged Part of the Iceberg—II* 269

EIGHTEEN: *"What's Past Is Prologue"* 289

LIST OF RECORDINGS 299

INDEX 309

Yehudi Menuhin

Chaconne

On a hot September afternoon in 1927, a little boy and his father were riding in a two-horse carriage along a road running through a green valley. The road led from Sinaia, the summer capital of Rumania, to Villa Luminish—"villa of light"— home of the violinist and composer Georges Enesco. On either side of the valley rose the thickly wooded Carpathian Mountains, their rugged summits cleft here and there with dense shadow. Sunlight played upon the foliage already beginning to glow with the rich tints of autumn, and only the unyielding evergreens clung to their original colors amid the red, brown, gold, and rust of birches, oaks, maples, and poplars. Directly overhead the sky was a clear, unsuspecting blue, but clouds were gathering in the west, and the driver, who knew the ways of late summer storms, kept prodding his well-fed horses.

The boy was bareheaded, and his fair hair was ruffled in the wind. He wore blue flannel shorts, a white blouse open at the neck, white socks, and square-toed boys' shoes. His feet dangled above the floor of the droshky, and now and again he kicked his heels back in time with the clop-clop of the trotting horses. He was a chubby, sunburned lad, with eyes of a dark, clear blue and a delicate, slightly aquiline nose. The small boyish chin was round and firm. All in all, he looked like any eleven-year-old, except for his eyebrows, which were darker than his hair and met across the forehead, giving him a curious maturity of expression.

His father, sitting beside him, was a lightly-framed man,

small and wiry, with bespectacled, dusty-blue eyes. He wore a dapper summer suit and hat and sported a mustache brown as his hair. At his feet lay a violin case.

They were silent, the father deep in thought, the boy absorbed by the plaintive songs of shepherds tending their herds in the valley. The road wound ahead past scattered villas, each in its clearing cut out of the stiff pinewoods, surrounded by a neat garden ablaze with color that outshone even the abandon of the turning foliage.

As the sound of distant thunder overtook them, the father roused himself, anxiously scanning the sky. Unfolding a blanket he said:

"That storm is catching up with us, Yehudi. You'd better cover your head and shoulders."

"Oh, but, *Aba*,[1] it's such fun to get wet in the rain!"

But when Aba swung the blanket behind the boy's back, Yehudi obediently helped to wrap it round his shoulders.

The first drops of rain began to fall as they drew up at the back door of the turreted, whitewashed villa. Georges Enesco, who came down to hurry them inside, was a tall, broad-shouldered man with a massive, handsome head and an open face—a very unusual face, the forehead smooth and strikingly broad, the amber-green eyes set wide apart, the mouth firm and generous.

"Come in, come in, my friends!" he exclaimed, "I've been watching the sky for the past half hour."

"No storm can keep Yehudi from the farewell lesson with you," said Moshe Menuhin, as he shook hands with Enesco.

The boy smiled at his teacher and took his hand as they started climbing up the steep spiral staircase leading to the studio. It was a large room, simply furnished, with books and music overflowing from the shelves onto the desk, the stand, and piano. The windows gave on to a sweeping view of the Carpathian Alps. The thunderstorm had at last broken, and, on reaching the studio, Yehudi ran to the window to look out at the mountains standing grim and forbidding in the down-

[1]*Aba*—father in Hebrew.

pour as the lightning played round their summits and the thunder echoed and rolled.

The father took a chair into a far corner of the room and settled there, remaining silent and motionless until the end of the session.

Enesco sat in his accustomed place near the desk, waiting for Yehudi to play the composition he had been studying— Bach's *Chaconne.* The boy started almost reluctantly, but the opening bars sounded full, organlike, and, as the variations succeeded each other on the immutable bass, the storm seemed to blend with the music, punctuating and stressing the passion, the suffering, the faith, and the hope in the *Chaconne.* Yehudi played with such power and penetration that Enesco looked up at him with incredulity. His eyes shut, the boy betrayed no emotion, but from time to time he opened them, and Enesco could then see that their blue color had almost disappeared, for the pupils had expanded until the eyes appeared black.

He approached the moment toward the end of the *Chaconne* where the music returns to D minor. That was the passage which Enesco had described to him as resembling the petrified yet infinitely compassionate face of a medieval Madonna carved in wood, and now, as if in response to the master's words, Yehudi's Madonna was stylized, and strangely alive and beautiful.

He finished and looked at his teacher with eager, boyish eyes, but Enesco was silent. Finally, in his soft, clear voice he asked for the work once more, and again there took place the miracle of the *Chaconne,* to the accompaniment of the unflagging storm.

Yet a third time Enesco repeated his request, and with unabated intensity Yehudi again played the immortal work of Johann Sebastian Bach.

This episode was described to me by Georges Enesco twenty-six years later in his small, crowded Paris apartment, when he was reminiscing about his first years as teacher of

Yehudi Menuhin. It was a much older Enesco who spoke. One of the grand old men of music, he had paid a heavy toll to age, affliction, and suffering,[2] but his hands, with their long, powerful fingers, had retained their chiseled beauty and expressiveness, and his voice remained soft and clear. Speaking slowly, he said:

"That was the strangest, the most exalted experience in my entire life as a musician. The *Chaconne* is one of man's truly sublime monuments, a veritable cathedral, the amazing architecture of which obscures for most violinists the emotional life seething within its walls. Whoever penetrates its tragedy and its faith has won the battle for Bach and, through him, for the understanding of the human soul. It is incomprehensible, but at the age of eleven Yehudi seemed to have understood it. It was as if he had lifted the enormous weight of human tears and hopes and, unbruised, carried it through that thunderstorm.

"I beg you, do not press for details or explanations. Can you describe the mystery of creation? Can anyone? I certainly cannot, and I believe no mortal can. One senses the creative force and stands in awe, but one cannot explain or describe it. There are, of course, rules to the writing of music and to its performance, but the miracle of music happens independently of the rules. Genius is a miracle about which one can say: I know not the whys and wherefores of it, but it could not have been otherwise.

"It would be futile also to question Yehudi about this, because he will not know how to speak of it. All he can do is perform the miracle again from time to time, and that is more than is given to most mortals.

"He is a performing artist, not a composer, and yet there has always been a creative force in his playing, which communicates itself to audiences despite his reserve and seeming withdrawal. Yehudi is like a vineyard on the top of Vesuvius. There lies the vineyard, all peaceful and still, thriving in the warm sun and the blue skies. But under that lovely vineyard is the volcano."

[2]Georges Enesco died on May 4, 1955.

ONE

Moshe and Marutha

The violinist's father, Moshe Menuhin, was born in the Russian ghetto city of Gomel, a direct descendant of a long line of illustrious Chassidic rabbis. Poor and deprived of civil rights, as were most Russian Jews at the time, the numerous members of the Chassidic religious group found ecstasy and release from worldly cares in the devotional songs and dances, which they executed with the abandon of gypsies and the dedication of saints.

Although music was in their blood, the Chassidic Jews, and especially the elite among them, to whom Moshe belonged, looked down upon fiddlers and the rest of the musicians. Eagerly sought after to bring cheer and merriment to weddings and other celebrations, they were relegated to a very low rung on the social ladder, regarded as welcome yet inferior beings, frivolous, wandering do-nothings without kith or kin who would even stoop to playing for the cruel and unpredictable goyim,[1] accepting their hospitality and enlivening their pagan festivities.

Moshe's family passed on from generation to generation the story of one of his ancestors named Benjamin, who excelled in Talmudic studies and sang the glory of Jehovah in a voice "so golden that one's heart melted in sweetness and adoration." But Benjamin had also learned to play the fiddle, and, although he studied under his uncle, the great Rabbi Joseph of Lubavich, he often disappeared from the rabbi's court to play

[1]Gentiles.

and sing at weddings and birthdays. One night, so the story goes, the richest landowner of the district, a gay young blade who had neither God nor mercy in him, sent for Benjamin and his fellow musicians to entertain his guests at a bacchanalian party that lasted for several days and nights. Toward the end of the third day, they dragged Benjamin out on the lawn, dressed him up in a bearskin, and demanded that he do the dance of the bear. Then they threw him into a huge barrel, poured water into it, and ordered him to go on singing. Benjamin, who was like a fish in the water, not only kept himself afloat but also sang and even put on a show of pretending that he enjoyed the game.

Amazed by this resilience and sportsmanship, the revelers cheered Benjamin and presented him with a fine brick house, but upon returning to the rabbi's court the young man, in his disgust, smashed the violin to smithereens, forsook playing at parties, and devoted the rest of his life to Talmudic studies and to the singing of holy prayers.

Like Benjamin in his youth, Moshe was drawn to the violin and secretly took six lessons, but one day his grandfather overheard him practice and spoke to him in anguish: "It does not become a true Jew to fiddle while his people are in exile." Moshe put his violin away but soon earned more stern words when he was caught flying a kite on the eve of the Sabbath. So the kite joined the abandoned violin, and Moshe had nothing to do with either until many years later, when he encouraged his own son Yehudi to play the violin, and when they flew kites happily together in the parks of San Francisco.

Moshe's father had died when the boy was only four years old. His mother remarried, and he was so unhappy with his stepbrothers and stepsisters that, at the age of nine, he was taken to Jerusalem to live with his grandparents. His kind but fanatically religious grandfather compelled Moshe to spend twelve to fourteen hours a day in prayer and in the study of the Bible, but the boy's thoughts were far away in a land of which most Russian Jews dreamed, where all people were equal and free, and where he could earn his bread by working on the soil, a land called America.

Moshe was fourteen when his grandfather died, leaving him a fortune of exactly one hundred dollars, large enough for the youth to buy a transatlantic ticket, but upon reaching Paris he was told that he was too young to travel unescorted to the States and was promptly packed off back to Palestine. A bright and studious lad, he entered the secular Herzlia Gymnasium[2] on a scholarship, where he found new and absorbing interests in mathematics and science.

Moshe roomed with strangers in a small, dark apartment in Tel Aviv's twin city of Jaffa, prepared his own breakfasts and suppers on a tiny kerosene stove, and studied hard. Upon graduation he had the choice of scholarships in ancient Constantinople or in the New World's New York. Not for a moment did he hesitate over the choice, although it was hard for him to part with Marutha Sher, the lovely, frail girl with enormous blue eyes and honey-colored hair he knew at school.

Marutha had gone to Palestine with her mother at the age of fifteen from the Black Sea resort of Yalta, where she was born. Her father, estranged from his family some years previously, had emigrated to America, where he settled down somewhere in the Middle West. Twice during the time when Moshe knew Marutha in Palestine her father had sent for her and she had gone, each time for several unbearable months. She was sweet-voiced but proud and unapproachable, and she seemed as indifferent to Moshe as to her many other suitors.

After an agonizing period of indecision, he finally left for New York with a heart torn between happiness over being bound at last for the land of his dreams and the longing for his first love. Upon arrival, he was enrolled, because of his brilliant record, in the sophomore year at New York University, where he studied mathematics and pedagogy. To supplement his modest scholarship, he taught afternoons and evenings in a Hebrew school in the Bronx.

Between his studies, teaching, and writing letters to Maru-

[2]The leading high school in Tel Aviv.

tha, Moshe had little time for social life. The only private
home he frequented during that period was that of Lubarsky,
a wealthy tea merchant and one of the founders of the Zionist
movement in Russia and later in the United States. Along
with other scholarship students from Palestine, and just as
underfed and ill-clothed as they, Moshe drifted to the Lubarsky home, where every Friday night they found awaiting
them a good meal and good talk. Not the least attraction was
the host's handsome daughter Rachel, who had lost her mother
when still a child and who, upon coming of age, had taken
over the duties of hostess in her father's spacious, hospitable
home. She paid little attention to the shy and shabbily clad
Moshe until one night he asked eagerly and with pride for
permission to bring a friend of his, a girl who had recently
arrived from Palestine. That happened forty-odd years ago,
in November 1913, and to this day the face of Rachel (now
Mrs. Garbat) lights up when she recalls her first meeting with
Marutha: "She came into the room like a ray of sunshine dis-
guised as a girl in a white dress."

A year later Moshe and Marutha were married. Neither of
the two young people, whose joint age did not add up to
forty, had any money to spare. Indeed, all they had was just
sufficient for modest meals and a room in a boarding house.
In the carefree way of young people in love, they had no fear
of the future, and spent most of their free evenings taking
walks in Bronx Park and singing Hebrew songs to their
hearts' content. To help make ends meet and give themselves
the luxury of occasional concert tickets, Marutha gave private
Hebrew lessons, but when their first child was on the way
they denied themselves even that modest pleasure, which
Marutha, an amateur pianist, missed greatly.

Proud and uncomplaining, they refused offers of help and
in the end decided to take a large apartment and rent out
rooms. They found one such place on 165th Street, where the
superintendent assured them that his was a fine, exclusive
house, in which no apartments were let out to Jews.

"But we are Jews!"

"You don't look it, and we could make an exception for you."

They walked away in indignation, Marutha saying to her husband:

"We must find a name for our child which will leave no room for doubt or misunderstanding!"

On April 22, 1916, a boy was born to the Menuhins, whom they named Yehudi, which in Hebrew means "the Jew."

Moshe and Marutha were becoming increasingly attached to their new homeland, finding peace and happiness in it, but, after the years they had spent in sun-baked Palestine, they were ill adapted for life in the eastern part of the United States. To them, inadequately clad and chilled to the bone, the East meant cold wet sidewalks and depressing rides in poorly lit subways. California loomed as the golden land of sun and promise. Sparsely settled as it was at that time, it also meant to Moshe the land of the pioneers where he could at last realize his dream of living and working on a farm.

He graduated from the university soon after Yehudi's birth and was free for the trek westward, but, with not a dollar to his name and an extra mouth to feed, Moshe hunted for a job instead. After many a disappointment, the Menuhins settled in Elizabeth, New Jersey, where they were engaged as teachers at the Jewish Community Center Hebrew school. On the day they were to meet their classes, the Menuhins were unable to arrange for anyone to take care of their infant, so they simply took Yehudi along, leaving him peacefully asleep in his basket on a large billiard table that dominated the recreation room of the center.

Here, as in all orthodox Hebrew schools, only boys were enrolled. From the very beginning they loved their new teachers, brimming over as they were with youthful enthusiasm and vitality. One boy, Sam Marantz, a quiet, serious lad of twelve, became particularly attached to the Menuhin family and never tired of helping them in small ways, running errands, carrying kindling wood, or baby-sitting with Yehudi. By way of reward, he had an occasional meal with his adored teachers in their small home cluttered with furniture and books. In the living room stood an old Matushek upright, and a cello rested patiently in a corner, waiting for the time when Marutha could afford to take lessons.

Both Menuhins were in sharp and welcome contrast to the other teachers, all old men with long beards who, it seemed to the schoolboys, derived a wicked joy in keeping them from their outdoor games in order to cram Hebrew prayers into them. The ancient language was sacred to their orthodox parents, but to the American-born children it was utterly alien. What the boys liked about the Menuhins was their approach to Hebrew as a living tongue, giving it vitality and meaning by linking it with the history of the Jewish race and with the life of the pioneer settlers in Palestine. Moreover, the Menuhins held their classes outdoors whenever weather permitted, either in the play yard of the community center or in the park. The idyll, however, soon ended, because the conservative elements among the teachers and the parents rose up in arms against the unorthodox methods of the Menuhins and their iconoclastic approach to the Hebrew language. In vain did the young couple cite the progress made by their pupils in a few brief months, the excellent discipline, and the happiness of the children. Moshe again found himself pitted against the same crushing force that had so injured his childhood, robbing him of fresh air, of his harmless kite, of his violin lessons. The clash was irreconcilable, and the Menuhins resigned.

Moshe counted his savings and resolved, with Marutha's acquiescence, that this was as good a time as any to pack up and go to California. The momentous decision arrived at, he went straight to New York's Grand Central Station and asked for two tickets to San Francisco by the cheapest way possible. As he was about to pay for them, he discovered to his chagrin that he was six dollars short, even for travel by coach. But fate was smiling on him that day, for the ticket agent, touched by the anguish of the young foreigner, loaned him the six dollars and handed him the precious tickets. Moshe hurried back to Marutha with the unbelievable news that their dream had come true, and she at once set to packing. As the ancient upright represented their greatest capital investment, she decided that the rest of the furniture would be sold in order to pay for shipment of the piano to California and to furnish them with food en route. Without a word to Aba, she went straight out to the nearest secondhand dealer and, bringing him back to the small apartment, told him with unprofessional candor that she had to get rid of the furniture immediately. This superb salesmanship brought in a flat and final offer of sixteen dollars, which she accepted there and then, blandly impatient at Moshe's despair when, on returning to the apartment, he found it nearly stripped, and Marutha with the paltry sum in her hand. After this, it did not take them long to get ready, and they set off for the West, accompanied as far as New York by the faithful Sam.

They arrived in San Francisco with exactly thirty-two cents left to their name and found shelter with a relative of Moshe's living near by, and the latter made repeated attempts to settle on the land. Without capital or backers, however, he found it impossible to make a real start, so that he responded with relief and alacrity to an invitation to establish a modern Hebrew school in San Francisco.

Like all newcomers, they yielded to the charm of the Golden Gate city and spent many happy hours walking along its hilly streets, riding the cable cars, seeing the sights of Chinatown, or eating crab with their farmer friends on Fisherman's Wharf, noisy, crowded, and smelling deliciously of fish. The friendliest and gayest of these farmers was Natia Kavin, a burly Russian with flaming red hair and childlike but shrewd blue eyes, who ran a chicken farm in Petaluma, then a tiny settlement which proudly called itself "The Egg Basket of the World." The little family's greatest pleasure during those years were the drives to the Kavins'. Yehudi remembers sitting in the back of the farmer's Dodge with the two little Kavin girls, looking through the small round back windows at the road running away from them. The farm itself was a medley of cheerful sounds and smells dominated by the cackling of hens and the fragrance of fresh-mown grass. An overnight stay at the Kavin farm was for Yehudi the height of bliss, filled with the excitement of sleeping in a strange bed, waking up in the morning to the singing of birds, playing hide-and-seek among the prickly haystacks, and building houses out of fruit crates.

He was always keyed up and tense with happiness on the eve of a trip to the Kavins', so that Marutha had to remain at his bedside longer than usual, telling him tales of the Cherkess tribe in the Caucasus, men of fierce pride and great strength who fought off invaders to keep their land free and happy. And she always sang a Russian lullaby:

> *"Sleep, my pretty, pretty baby,*
> *Bayushki-bayu,*
> *Moonlight shines into the cradle*
> *Which I built for you.*
>
> *I shall tell you lovely stories,*
> *I shall sing for you,*
> *Sleep, my pretty, pretty baby,*
> *Bayushki-bayu."*

The merriest moments of the visits to the Kavins' were provided by the eating contests between Moshe and Natia. Both had enormous appetites and little discrimination, albeit their particular greed was for strawberries. Yehudi still remembers his amazement at the speed with which heaps of strawberries would disappear from the plates of the two men. The short, skinny Moshe usually got far ahead of Natia in the beginning, but he inevitably lost each contest, because his energies and capacity were consumed by the initial effort, while the bulky Kavin went on devouring the berries in his slow, methodical way long after Moshe had given up in exhaustion.

Yehudi attributes to these visits his lifelong fondness for fruits and berries, for the Menuhins invariably found waiting for them at the Kavins' huge bowls filled with apples, oranges, plums, bananas, and, especially, the favorite fruit of Yehudi's infancy and childhood, cherries. He disliked walking, and, even when he was four, tried to get one of his parents to carry him, but, resorting to the principle of the donkey with a carrot to his nose, they ensured his exercise by means of cherries doled out one by one from a paper bag.

The drives to the Kavins', which ran like a gay thread through Yehudi's entire childhood, awakened in him a love for the California landscape which neither the ruggedness of the Swiss Alps nor the quiet beauty of the English countryside nor the exotic vistas of India were ever to overshadow. "As we drove along in the ancient Dodge," he recalls, "Aba sang old Chassidic songs. The motion of the automobile, California's landscape, and my father's singing curiously blended into one sensation that has left a lasting impression on me. Aba sang with a joy and an abandon that seemed to give him release from all his cares and the problems of coping with me and, very soon, my two sisters, as well as with our immeasurably sweet and just as immeasurably strong-willed mother. Even the Kavins, to whom the world of these songs was completely alien, were moved by them. Later, our changed circumstances, the concert tours all over the globe, and new associations conspired to relegate these songs to the background until they completely disappeared from our lives, but they are a living thing within me, and this is why, perhaps, the *Kaddisch* by Maurice Ravel and the *Nigun* and *Abodah* by Ernest Bloch have meant so much to me. My pre-violin days were idyllic, containing not a cloud, no hint of the trials to come. My parents were completely happy with each other and were proud of me and treated me as an equal, while the few friends we had were, like our pleasures, modest and simple."

Yehudi spent much of his early childhood playing with adults or listening to grown-up talk, so that whenever he found himself with other children he felt at a loss. Once in the swing of things, he played their games with enthusiasm, but he never knew how to begin. It was strange the way grownups always seemed to know, so sure of themselves as they guided him into all sorts of exciting activity, while children so often waited for him to take the initiative, a thing he hated to do. He also hated playing games to order, something he was told to do at certain hours every day. Somehow, this injunction offended and bewildered him, but he never said anything about it and his parents did not know.

By a curious coincidence, practically all of the Menuhin friends, then and later, had daughters, so that there were very few boys in Yehudi's life until after he had outgrown his adolescence. Occasional attempts by his parents to bring boys of his own age into the home invariably failed, for, as he had never gone to school and indeed was destined never to go, he had little common ground on which to make friends with them.

Having settled down in San Francisco, Moshe and Marutha were able to return to an old source of pleasure—music. A great cultural and educational center, the city prided itself particularly on the fullness of its musical life. There was a large symphony orchestra which attracted some of the world's most celebrated soloists, and others came for recitals. Moshe's meager but steady income at last allowed Marutha to take weekly lessons from the leading cellist of the orchestra, Dr. Arthur Weiss, and enabled the young couple to attend concerts regularly. At first even this little outing was impossible, for they could not afford to hire someone to sit with the baby in their absence, but one day, soon after Yehudi's second birthday, the idea occurred to them that, with his sweet, even temper and capacity for sleep, he might slumber through a performance or, if awakened, sit quietly through it.

An understanding usher helped them to smuggle the sleeping child into the Curran Theater, where the orchestra gave its concerts, and showed them their seats, much to the puzzlement and annoyance of their neighbors. At the first sounds of music Yehudi awoke, but he did not cry. He sat up straight on his mother's lap and watched the orchestra, a smile on his face, his little body swaying in rhythm. Thus he became a regular attendant of the symphony series and soon began to realize that the appearance on the stage of a big, bald-headed, black-bearded man (conductor Alfred Hertz) with a small stick in his hand, meant that funny noises would soon stop and in their stead would come wonderful, exciting sounds.

The seats which the Menuhins occupied afforded a clear view of the orchestra, and Yehudi, whose attention was early attracted by the violin section, singled out in the front row a medium-sized man with a gentle face and a restrained manner who occasionally played a brief solo part. This was Louis Persinger, the first violinist of the San Francisco Symphony Orchestra and a concert artist of considerable reputation. Along with his colleagues, Persinger soon noticed the child who listened with an owl-like earnestness, pointing a finger in his direction from time to time. If the little boy occasionally failed to show up at a concert, the musicians noticed his absence and wondered if he were in bed with the measles, an event which, incidentally, caught up with Menuhin only some thirty years later.

On the eve of his fourth birthday, Yehudi announced in the middle of a piece that he wanted to play the violin and, his finger directed at Louis Persinger, appointed "that man" as his teacher. The parents, trying to keep him quiet, made a hasty promise, but later, as they recounted the episode to their friends, laughed it off as a child's fancy. One of them, however, Cantor Reuben Rinder, took the incident seriously. He had noticed other straws in the wind. For the last few months, Yehudi had been singing himself to sleep with a one-line song he made up in Hebrew about a little girl he knew: "*Lily alcha lishon, Lily alcha lishon* [Lily went to sleep, Lily went to sleep]." He remembers to this day the words and the music, and how he kept singing the phrase to himself over and over again until his eyes would close with sleep. The cantor's trained ear caught the faithfulness with which the child kept repeating the tune, embellishing it with little variations.

Rinder received further confirmation of Yehudi's musical gifts during the modest celebration of the boy's fourth birthday. The one thing the boy had especially asked for as a birthday gift was a violin, and someone brought in a little toy instrument. Ignoring the other presents, Yehudi took the violin, tucked it under his chin and drawing the bow across the strings, produced an ugly, screeching sound. Puzzled, he tried again, then threw the tin toy to the ground and trampled it underfoot, crying:

"It won't sing! It won't sing!"

Marutha described the incident in a letter to her mother in Palestine, treating it in a somewhat humorous vein, but the old lady wrote back that she had a feeling the boy was in earnest, and enclosed a check for twenty-five dollars for the purchase of a real instrument. Still, the Menuhins were reluctant to launch their little son on serious studies and postponed the purchase until he had reached the solid age of five. They paid twelve dollars for the instrument, using the rest of the grandmother's money as part of a down payment on their first car, a new Chevrolet.

The first tone which Yehudi produced on his longed-for fiddle gave him immense satisfaction, and forthwith he reminded his parents of their promise of violin lessons from "that man." Cantor Rinder talked to Persinger, but the concert-master, having spent many fruitless hours listening to children hailed by parents and friends as prodigies, declined. Marutha then recalled a sign, "Violin Lessons," hung over the entrance to a small, dilapidated house in the neighborhood, and with her customary, somewhat casual directness, took Yehudi there. The teacher proved to be a broken-down old man defeated by drudgery and smelling unpleasantly of tobacco and wine. His fee was reasonable enough but, after watching the child struggle through two lessons, Marutha withdrew him and began looking for a teacher of repute.

And so, in May 1921, aged five, the boy was taken to the studio of Sigmund Anker. Yehudi Menuhin's life work had begun.

TWO

Growing Pains

Moshe's teaching abilities, his energy and flair for administration, were gradually forging a career for him. The model school which he had established grew and thrived, attracting the best Hebrew teachers and the support of wealthy patrons, with whose help he founded seven similar institutions and was in the end appointed superintendent of San Francisco's Hebrew schools. He also became a landlord of a kind with the purchase of a two-story house on Steiner Street and the renting out of the upper floor. The Menuhins themselves occupied the lower half of the house, which opened on to a cement backyard and a rectangular garden boasting clumps of flowers, two palm trees, and a swing. Fresh-air devotees that Moshe and Marutha were, they built a screened bungalow in the yard, which, while relieving the congestion in the house, provided the whole family with additional and very pleasant bedrooms.

To supplement his income, Moshe converted the basement, which opened on to the street, into a garage for five cars in addition to his own. Even so, the Menuhins were far from affluent, and Marutha had to scrape and skimp in order to pay for Yehudi's violin lessons. For one thing, the family was getting larger. A little girl was born in April 1920 and named Hephzibah—Hebrew for "the desired one"—and in October 1921 came another girl, Yaltah, so named in honor of Marutha's home town in the Crimea. The young mother had her hands full feeding the family, keeping the house clean, looking after the roomers, and soon had to give up her cello lessons but doggedly continued to play the piano. Her favorite piece was Chopin's *Valse in B minor,* so it became the first musical work Yehudi memorized in its entirety. Because of the children and the house, Marutha could not even consider an outside job, but she helped her husband with some of the extra work he undertook, such as coaching boys for the celebration of their thirteenth birthdays, a particularly festive occasion for orthodox Jews. She received her young pupils in the kitchen, where she punctuated her tuition with journeys to and from the stove and with occasional lightninglike flights to succor or scold her little girls in the bedroom or to admonish the practicing Yehudi for producing scratchy sounds.

Hebrew was the language of the Menuhin household at the time, the only language Yehudi spoke during the first three years of his life. Thereafter, English and other tongues came in quick succession, crowding the Hebrew out of his memory. Nonetheless, during a few weeks in Israel many years later, he recaptured it with great ease. It was from his mother that Yehudi first learned to read and write Hebrew, and it was she who launched him in the study of English, German, Italian, and Russian. She also taught him to read music.

One day, shortly before Yehudi had started his violin lessons with Sigmund Anker, he was resting with his mother on a park bench after a walk when she suddenly announced that she was going to show him a new game. Taking a blank sheet of paper from her bag, she drew five lines across the page and superimposed notes on them, one by one. As she wrote each note, she sang it, then asked him to repeat the sound, which the boy found no hardship at all, the game growing more and more complicated as he was called upon to identify the notes by name and sing them without any help from his mother. It was a fascinating game, whether they sang together or separately, and whether she praised him or laughed at his mistakes. He so loved to hear her laugh that he would sometimes make mistakes on purpose, watching her out of the corner of his eye. They went on playing the game even after he had started taking music lessons, at which she was always present, and she also kept an eye on him as he practiced. She did not possess deep insight into music, but had a genuine feeling for it and loved a fine, clean sound. At the first hint of a scratch she would burst into Yehudi's room, saying that he played like a shoemaker and that he was unworthy of such a noble instrument. Yehudi would lower his eyes, red-faced and silent, then go back to his practice the moment Marutha closed the door behind her.

He was an even, sweet-tempered child, almost placid. Plump, fair-haired, with a frank boyish look in his blue eyes, he kept asking incessant questions, like most children, betraying an inquisitive mind of an unruffled and practical nature. He was not articulate, and words or the play of words did not interest him, but he was fascinated with the way his toys were designed and wanted to know exactly what it was that made them roll, unfold, or squeak. When he saw his first rainbow, he hastened to inquire about its exact size, where it came from, and why it had to go away. The simple miracle of the mirror early aroused his curiosity, and he wondered over the mystery of the firefly and the glowworm. Whenever taken for a walk or a ride, he demanded to know exactly where a street began and ended; where the city began and ended, and the state, and the country. Above all, why?

Neither his appearance nor the questions betrayed any hint of emotional disturbances, but they were there, nevertheless. During the day, they would usually be dissipated in play or, later on, in study. But at times they would not let go of him until he escaped them in a wild, aimless toss of a ball, or a sudden mad dash round and round the small backyard, or in the futile slamming of a door. At night, these vague, unbidden moods were aggravated by fears. The fear that came first, as with most children, was terror of the dark after he had been put to bed and remained alone. He was ashamed of being afraid and kept repeating to himself Marutha's stories of the brave Cherkess. If he wanted to be one of them, she had said, he must be as fearless as those lionhearted people of the mountains, who never cried and who ate well and slept soundly.

Before long, another fear assailed Yehudi—the thought that something terrible was about to happen to his parents. The dismay inspired by this thought grew with the realization that they were nearing the decrepit age of thirty. He then became convinced that he was going to lose them, for he was certain that few people lived much longer. He would wake up in the middle of the night with the shattering thought that he might never see them again, and he would sit up in his narrow cot, surrounded by a dark silence punctuated by the creaking of wood in the old house. There he sat, tense and cold, straining his ears for sounds to come out of his parents' room, and when he thought he had heard them stir or whisper, he knew they were still alive, near him, and he would sigh happily and fall asleep.

Yehudi so hated to part with his parents at night that he worked out a system of complaints to keep them at his bedside for as long as possible or bring them back after they had gone. To make the complaints sound alarming and plausible, he usually began with a groan caused by "a pain in my leg." There would follow the comforting feel of his parents' fingers on his leg, the request to stand and walk, and then the discovery of the fatal truth—nothing was wrong with his leg. He would be scolded and left again abandoned to the darkness and his fears. Of them he dared not complain, for he could not bear the thought that his mother might think him unworthy of being a Cherkess, and would instead produce a story of a stomach-ache. This was harder to verify, and he would in the end be given a hot-water bottle, the reassuring warmth of which would finally lull him to sleep.

Like his dread of the dark, the thought of losing his parents was something very big and very private. All day long he was busy studying, eating, riding his scooter up and down the cement courtyard or walking with his mother, baby Hephzibah asleep in her carriage. He was usually busiest at week ends, when Aba was free and the family went on all-day outings.

There were as yet no bridges in San Francisco, so that among Yehudi's most vivid early memories are gay crowds of holiday-makers, knapsacks on their backs, crossing the bay on ferries and disappearing into the countryside. Sometimes the Men-uhins went by car to the Kavins' or took trips to Muir Woods, of the giant sequoia; or they would drive out to Mt. Tamalpais, where small locomotives ran them up to the summit from where they could start walking to their favorite picnic grounds.

Every now and then, even during those festive hours, Yehudi suddenly recalled the fears that haunted him at night, but the adults around him rarely noticed his forlornness, for it lasted only a brief moment as he shrugged off the memory, strong and unscared in the light of day, resolved to train himself to be proud and unafraid at all times. Beset with the desire to prove once and for all his indomitable courage, he was often driven to strange expedients, one of which has remained engraved in his memory all these years. On that afternoon, barely five, he was taken to see his first film. Walking between Moshe and Marutha, Yehudi felt quite grown-up at the thought of his first movie. Indeed, he felt so secure and strong that he decided to prove his courage to himself right there and then by sticking out his tongue at the first acquaint-ance they met along the way. His heart beat faster each time he thought he recognized someone approaching them, and he would steel himself for his brave deed, but each time he proved to be mistaken and had to gather his courage all over again. He had almost reached the cinema when, to his horror, none other than Cantor Rinder came out of some doorway, beaming at the sight of Yehudi and his parents. Why did it have to be dear old Rinder, his good friend and playmate? But the heart of a Cherkess is made of steel, and he never falters! Yehudi dismally stuck his tongue out at the baffled man. Embarrassed and angry, the parents ordered the boy to apologize, but he stood silent, flushed and unhappy, praying that Rinder would somehow understand. Maybe he did, for he looked tenderly at the boy and treated his action as a joke. But

Marutha was furious and, having failed to extract an apology from Yehudi, took him straight home.

This incident coincided with the boy's transition from help-less and carefree babyhood to that of self-assertion which, as with other children, frequently clashed with the discipline im-posed by adults, precipitating misunderstandings, humiliation, pain, and rebellion. The parents, hitherto a patient source of care, protection, and love, began to impose an authority and to demand obedience to complicated, often baffling rules of social behavior. So many places became out of bounds, so many things forbidden, others suddenly made obligatory. One is expected to preface every request by a "please," follow each act of attention or care with a "thank you," and apologize for every failure to live up to the rules, despite the galling fact that adults so often failed to observe them!

There had been few formalities in the Menuhin home, where meals were served in the kitchen and friends were entertained on rare occasions; but now, as Yehudi was changing from child to boy, Marutha began to insist upon manners. It was then that his stubbornness began to assert itself. A kind and easygoing boy, he did not normally mind saying "thank you" or "please," but at times he'd forget, and then his mother's face would darken and her voice carry a threat. It had seemed to him that only the loneliness and the dark were menacing, and he rebelled against the very thought of yielding to fear in the middle of the day. However much he hated to test his strength by defying his mother, of all people, he somehow felt at times impelled to do so, and on such occasions, he recalls, "wild horses couldn't drag an apology out of me." But his childish stubbornness was no match for Marutha's rocklike determination, and he would capitulate in the end with a grudging "I am sorry" scribbled on a scrap of paper and stealthily handed to his mother.

Sometimes his pride was wounded so deeply or his commit-ment to rebellion had gone so far that he would find himself unable to make even this small gesture. He would then be punished by being deprived of an ice cream or a toy, or by being sent to his room. Like his father, Yehudi tended to forget each incident the moment it was resolved, but Marutha would brood, her face drawn and her laughter gone, spreading a pall of gloom over the household. For days thereafter, everyone "moved about in shrouds." When she would finally emerge from her mood and start laughing again, her husband and son would be practically wild with relief, and the boy would make a secret vow always to behave according to *Imma's*[1] expectations and would be both surprised and mortified each time he failed—and fail he inevitably did, as children will.

Yehudi's most memorable failure took place at a time of great rejoicing, a trip to Yosemite National Park, of which his parents had been dreaming for years. Yehudi must have been six when Moshe took a ten-day vacation and off they went in their Chevvy, taking little Hephzibah with them. They settled down for their holiday in a tent colony at the foot of Inspiration Point, their tent standing under a large, shady tree which sheltered a picnic table, benches, and a fine fireplace for barbecuing; Yehudi brought his violin with him and practiced every day a De Bériot concerto, the slow movement of which Aba christened "the Yosemite." A man living alone in a nearby tent took to the boy, played games with him, told him stories of the conquest of the West, and made wonderful whistles out of the thick green stems of bushes.

One morning Marutha invited Yehudi's new friend to join them for a real Sunday breakfast of fruit and pancakes and maple syrup. It was a fairy-tale morning, with the mist lifting before their eyes, like a curtain rising, uncovering the craggy peaks of the surrounding mountains. Yehudi, stuffed to his heart's content, rose from the table and started to walk away.

"Yehudi," Marutha called him back, "you must ask to be excused before you may leave."

The boy turned around to apologize and say "May I be excused?" but something in him rebelled at the last second, and the words stuck in his throat, big and lumpy. That was the first time he had been called upon to ask permission before leaving

[1]*Imma*—mother in Hebrew.

the table. And why today of all days? Why in this simple pic-nic atmosphere under a tree and in the presence of his new friend, who was watching, alert and amused? The wretched boy lowered his eyes and could not utter a word.

Marutha ordered him back to his place on the bench. He sat down obediently but still refused to break his silence. The breakfast guest, no longer amused, rose and left amid general embarrassment. Moshe, flustered and unhappy, as always on such occasions, began to reason with the boy and ended up with a compromise suggestion that all he had to do was to say that he was sorry. But it was too late. Yehudi could say nothing at all, not even for the sake of his mother, sitting across the table from him. If need be, he was ready to lay down his life for her, but he could not bring himself to say those simple words: "May I be excused?" or even "I am sorry." They sat thus in complete silence for over three hours, maybe four. It was Yehudi who finally broke down. He grunted a few words which neither parent could make out but which Marutha accepted as an apology, and he was forthwith permitted to rise and go about his own affairs.

From that day on, so far as he remembers, he never failed to ask to be excused whenever ready to rise after a meal. Also from that day on, the very mention of Yosemite Valley brings back the memory of the scene under the tree. Inspiration Point follows as an afterthought.

THREE

The First Steps

During his first few months with Sigmund Anker, Yehudi made no more progress than any ordinary pupil, much to the disappointment of his teacher, whom the boy's eagerness had led to expect miracles. Marutha, who sat through the lessons with an air of resignation, reported on her return home the sad news of Anker's dissatisfaction, while Moshe looked at Yehudi sorrowfully, shook his head, and said nothing. The disillusionment of the adults, however, did not begin to match the intensity of the boy's heartbreak. Carrying in his memory the magnificence of the music he had heard, and overcome by a powerful urge to make music, Yehudi was miserable with his helplessness. The incessant drilling of those first few months infuriated and frustrated him, crushing his elation, even as the toy violin of the previous year had crushed his expectation of drawing beautiful sounds out of it.

The difficulties that beset Yehudi were those that baffle all beginners. How does one draw a straight bow? How does one hold the violin? How should one distribute the weight of the instrument, giving it proper support between the shoulder and the head, and in a way that leaves the hand in perfect control while it executes the fingering?

Yehudi kept falling into trap after common trap as he persisted in tucking in the little finger of his left hand, practically hiding it under the neck of the violin. He held onto the instrument like grim death, grasping the neck between the inbent thumb and the base of the first finger with a force that made free and easy motions of the joints impossible, thus further blocking the flow of sound. To make things worse, his right arm was too short for the length of the bow, and he kept "going around the corner," as violinists say, each time the down stroke of the bow approached the tip.

Yehudi's problems multiplied tenfold when he began to work on the fingering and the vibrato. He had no trouble with producing clear and true sounds by drawing the bow across the open strings, but then, to make music, he had to find the right notes with the right fingers. Compared with playing the piano, it is not unlike the difference between flying and walking. When you walk, the earth supports your weight, and, provided you do not try to run too fast, you are on firm ground or, at least, close enough to it to be safe. In flying, however, you must develop a certain speed before you can soar upward. Correct fingering is that speed. With the vibrato, you really begin to fly, as it transforms what the French call the *blanc* tone into one that is alive and quivering with color. In his initial efforts to control the vibrato, it seemed impossible to Yehudi to combine the elementary essential of a firm grip on the violin with the needed free play of the finger joints; the one seemed to preclude the other. He was greatly handicapped, as are so many beginners, by his teacher's unwillingness or inability to analyze the necessary technique step by step. Instead of showing how every finger joint is trained to be loose and free to move in all directions, how the opposing sets of joint muscles are to balance each other, how support of the violin is to become dependent solely on the prop of the thumb and the contact of fingertip on string, the exasperated Anker merely shouted:

"Vibrate! Vibrate! Shake your hand! No, no! A thousand times, no! Try again! Vibrate!"

The bewildered Yehudi did try; he tried until he was ready to burst into tears. Day after day he stumbled through sounds that pained him and seemed to jeer at him, until finally, after endless hours of anguished practice, he acquired a vibrato of sorts. The achievement was hard-won but it opened up a whole new world to him. He could now, at long last, respond to that compelling urge within him to make music, which had alone enabled him to survive the ordeal by drill.

From this point on, his progress was astounding, and on November 26, 1921, only six months after he had started taking violin lessons, Yehudi made his first public appearance at the annual Anker studio recital with a short, tuneful piece called *Remembrance*. He was still two months short of six on February 11, 1922, when he played Paderewski's *Minuet* before the wider audience of the Pacific Musical Society, accompanied by his mother. Eight months later, he played the Accolay concerto at the Annual Music Week sponsored by the Pacific Musical Society. Reviewing the performance, Redfern Mason predicted in the San Francisco *Examiner* that the boy, then scarcely emerged from babyhood, "would one day be a master among masters."

Two other public appearances followed, at one of which Yehudi played De Bériot's difficult *Concerto Number Nine*, with piano accompaniment, causing the San Francisco *Chronicle* reviewer to write:

"His attack on the first note made the audience sit up in wonderment; he played without hesitation and with marvelous accuracy of expression."

However, Yehudi learned that a musician's path is not all smoothness when he entered the annual student Gold Medal Contest at the Fairmont Hotel. His main rival was a lovely girl of twelve named Sarah Krindler who dashed off Sarasate's *Gypsy Airs* with such gusto and assurance that she easily won the coveted medal, completely eclipsing his rendition of Beethoven's *Minuet in G*. Cantor Rinder was in the hall, armed for just such an emergency with a delightfully illustrated children's book about Mozart which he forthwith presented to Yehudi. The little boy thanked him courteously, displaying no outward sign of disappointment, but his failure to win the medal was a wound which took long to heal. He ignored the *Minuet* in either practice or performance until the score was mislaid and eventually lost. Some thirty years later, when

Menuhin was gathering material for the recording of a large group of short pieces, he came across the composition and, as the childhood incident flashed through his mind, he grinned and promptly included it in the group.

In his entire life, he participated in only one other contest, which took place about a year and a half after the first, playing on the latter occasion the second and third movements of the Mendelssohn concerto. When one of the judges, the solemn, bearded Alfred Hertz, stopped Yehudi in the middle of the slow movement, the boy's heart skipped a beat. "Why such a rapid tempo?" asked Hertz.

"I'm afraid there won't be any time left for the third movement," answered Yehudi with disarming candor, "and I must play it, it sparkles so."

Hertz gravely assured the boy that the judges would listen to the very end. Thus encouraged, he finished the slow movement with befitting serenity and gave the third such sparkle that he easily won the prize. For ten successive months he received a check for twenty dollars, the first money Yehudi was to earn with his violin. By that time he was studying with "that man," thanks mainly to the efforts of Cantor Rinder.

Louis Persinger was brought up in a remote village in Colorado but received his musical education in Leipzig, followed by lessons from the great Eugène Ysaye in Brussels. As a young man, Persinger gave concerts all over Europe, played first violin with the Berlin Philharmonic, and later performed as soloist with the orchestras of New York and Philadelphia. In 1915 he became concertmaster and assistant conductor of the San Francisco Symphony Orchestra and subsequently formed the Persinger String Quartet. When Rinder spoke to Persinger about Yehudi, the name naturally meant nothing to him, but when he at last received the boy, the concertmaster was delighted to recognize in him the blond child whom he had noticed listening to the symphony concerts with such absorption. Years later, Persinger described his first meeting with Yehudi:

"Quietly he put the instrument under his chin and began to play. He was halfway through when I stopped him. I shall never forget the fury that lit up his eyes at my interruption. It was an insult to him and his art. But I had heard enough. There was no doubt in my mind that something lay hidden there. His feeling for rhythm was splendid, his ear absolutely true. There was more besides—a potentiality for greatness."

From the workshop of an artisan, the young Menuhin now passed into the studio of an artist. The door to the world of music was thrown wide open for him, and he plunged into it headlong. As work after great work became available to him, serving as an inspiration, a challenge, and a release, Yehudi immersed himself in an inner life of his own. A process had begun which soon prompted his father to say:

"He is just a bright, charming boy who likes to swim and hike and who enjoys the sweet things that tempt all young-sters. But in music there is something uncanny about him. Each year he becomes more of a stranger to us. When he is with his violin, he is a different boy. When he puts it down, he is the child we understand."

Yehudi's eagerness and rapid progress gave his new teacher enormous satisfaction but also precipitated many difficulties, chief among them stabilization of the boy's technical facility, so that it could keep pace with his irrepressible urge to pass on to ever more complicated works. Persinger recalls:

"There was a spontaneous beauty about Yehudi's playing, as if from a deep, mysterious, and miraculous well, and he seemed to absorb everything I taught him the way a sponge absorbs water. His progress both as to the musical and tech-nical side was very rapid. We began our study of a new work, after its general characteristics were made clear to him, by going over it phrase by phrase. I would play the phrase, he would repeat it as exactly as possible, and the manner in which he grasped things as he went along was a constant source of joy and surprise to me. In Yehudi's case there was no danger in this method, for his conception and playing were too fresh and too true to be an imitation of anything.

"It was not only a question of spontaneity. His reasoning powers were extraordinary, quite aside from his musical gifts. To correct a fault you needed only to draw attention to it once or twice. Sometimes, when a point was a trifle elusive, I appealed to his strong sense of humor and got it over to him that way. As I would occasionally turn from the piano while illustrating the musical structure of a new work to him, I would be startled to see the intense look in his eyes. Always beautiful and expressive, they at times seemed to be looking far away and above the earth.

"Yehudi acquired skill so quickly and memorized so rapidly that one of the chief problems was to restrain him. He showed a tendency at times to 'run away' with passage work, to hasten over a slow movement without plumbing its depths, and his fingers occasionally tended to 'kick in' on the vibrato—at first he had a funny little wiggle that passed as such—and for a time his bow was much too long for his arm."

Persinger found it extremely difficult to make Yehudi do routine practice, primarily because the boy mastered with incredible ease the technical tasks set for him and would then press for new compositions. In addition to going over standard technical works, Persinger improvised various exercises, which he set down in his precise, delicate handwriting. On one occasion he wrote out the scales in thirds, which made the notes look like toy trains moving up and down a hill across the musical staves. At first, Yehudi enjoyed practicing these scales, but he soon tired of the game with trains and demanded to be shown a new composition. The difficulty was, in the words of Persinger, that Yehudi "played so magnificently and learned so quickly that I could find no fault with the performance and lost no time in passing on to real music."

Years later, the pupil's impatience and the teacher's liberalism took their toll, but Menuhin has never regretted the course of his studies. Had Persinger been more pedantic, he thinks, he would have felt fettered, robbed of much of the import and élan of his early violin playing. Nor would Persinger himself have been content with the role of a drillmaster. Possibly some happy compromise could have been evolved, but there did not seem at the time any necessity for it. Both teacher and student found highest fulfillment in their quest of music, in the searching for the meaning of a melody, a phrase, or a nuance, and for this Yehudi's technical equipment was more than sufficient. The search was in itself an enormous challenge to the pedagogue, whose charge progressed so rapidly yet remained a child in need of guidance. "One may be born with musical genius," says Persinger, "but never with an interpretative sense or with knowledge of what is good taste and good style in music; there must be direction at the start."

One day, after a particularly gratifying lesson, Persinger declared that he was now going to play a work Yehudi had never heard before—the *Adagio* from Bach's *Sonata in G minor for Violin Alone.* "If I were condemned," said the teacher, "to live for the rest of my life with but one musical composition, to the exclusion of all others, I would select this sonata."

And with great solemnity, he played the *Adagio* for Yehudi and his mother, who, as always, was sitting quietly in her corner. That was the first time the boy had ever heard Bach or a work for the violin alone. He does not recall his exact thoughts and emotions at the time, but he does remember a happy surrender to something bigger and nobler than anything he had imagined man could create. In one heavenly flash, the music opened up unsuspected new vistas for him. If he had thought about the future at all, it had been as a result of overheard adult conversation in which the word "career" figured prominently, but his own attitude had remained undefined. Now, for the first time in his young life, he consciously resolved to dedicate himself to the service of music. Although he had not put it in so many words, he felt as if he had taken a solemn oath. How true he has been to that oath made as a child of eight may be gleaned from reading the critical appraisals of his performances, written by reviewers on five continents over a span of more than thirty years. In many tongues and in varied phrasing the critics have repeatedly emphasized what Olin Downes of the New York *Times* described (in a report of a 1953 concert by Menuhin) as "his selfless musicianship."

Persinger had reason of his own to be thankful for having risked playing the Bach *Adagio* to Yehudi at so early an age. The teacher had long been thinking of introducing the boy to music more complex and subtle than the works of Sarasate and Wieniawski, but he was far from certain that the philosophic and emotional exaltation of Bach would appeal to an eight-year-old. Yehudi's reaction was so intense and so profound that, all doubts dispelled, Persinger readily yielded to the boy's plea for a Bach composition. The work selected was the E-major concerto, the first violin concerto in the great classical tradition that Yehudi was to learn.

The most difficult and rewarding part, he found, was the slow movement, which absorbed all the emotions of which he was capable at the time, absorbed them completely, giving full expression to all he sought to convey. He remembers particularly one afternoon of work on the movement, as he tried to make the music speak and sing, returning to it again and ever again, probing for previously unfathomed meanings. As he played, he did not notice that the noise in the adjoining kitchen had stopped. When he finished, his mother opened the door, and seeing her radiant face he knew that she had been listening. A few minutes later, Aba came home from work, and Marutha, normally restrained in the presence of the children, embraced him and laughed her ringing laugh, and Yehudi was elated, sensing that it was he who had been the cause of her joy and of the demonstration of her affection for Aba.

Having learned this Bach concerto, the boy passed on to the typical "student" concertos by De Bériot, Lipinsky, and Spohr; and from these to the Mendelssohn, Lalo's *Symphonie Espagnole*, the first movement of Paganini's *Concerto in D major*, the Mozart *Concerto in A major*, and the Tchaikovsky. Persinger was astonished by Yehudi's insight into each work as well as by the speed with which he committed them to memory. One time, when he was kept in bed with a cold and could not practice, he read through a Spohr concerto twice and remembered it perfectly.

Of all the works within the year that followed his introduction to Bach, the Mendelssohn made the most immediate impact on Yehudi and has remained a constant companion, growing with him, says Menuhin, in the way a cherished brother or sister grows up with one.

Despite the mounting list of significant works he was mastering, Yehudi was disappointed by his teacher's consistent refusal to grant him his one great wish: the Beethoven concerto. He could not understand Persinger's reluctance and, whenever shown a new composition, he would look at the teacher pleadingly and say: "After this, the Beethoven?" At last, on a memorable Wednesday afternoon, Persinger announced: "We are now going to take up Mozart's A-major and then, once you have learned to play it really well, we shall pass on to the Beethoven." And he proceeded with an analysis of Mozart's work, ignoring Yehudi's uncontainable excitement.

On his way home, the boy asked his mother if he might be excused from going with the rest of the family to the beach that afternoon. Knowing how fond he always was of these outings. Marutha became alarmed and took his temperature. When she discovered that there was nothing more wrong with her son than a desire to get done with the Mozart, she ordered him to come along. He practiced a total of eight hours the next two days, and on Saturday, at his lesson, announced to Persinger that he had the entire concerto committed to memory. The teacher was impressed, but, as Yehudi's performance betrayed greed for the promised Beethoven, Persinger slammed down the score and glowered at Yehudi:

"Go home!" he said in an angry voice. "Use your good mathematical head and figure out for yourself the exact rhythms. I don't want to see you again until you have given thought to every note in each movement!"

Yehudi had never before been spoken to in that manner by anyone except his mother, and he stood silent, his face red and eyes lowered. Marutha rose from her seat and took him home where, without saying a word, she locked him up in his room. When Aba returned from work, she told him in Yehudi's presence that their only son had disgraced them and that he must be punished in a way he would never forget. He was not allowed to have supper with the family that night, and later, when Hephzibah and Yaltah had been put to bed, Moshe and Marutha came into his room. Aba was terribly agitated and avoided his son's questioning gaze, looking instead at Marutha with beseeching eyes, but her face was set.

"Moshe!" she said, and that was the only word spoken.

Miserably, Aba took the belt off his trousers, and Yehudi understood. He remembers bearing no resentment. Indeed, watching the anguish on his father's face, he pitied him and tried to make it easier for him. He went up to the narrow bed and bent over it. Moshe swung the belt with a fierce gesture, but let it fall slowly and there was little pain. He swung again and then once more and rushed out of the room. Marutha followed. Yehudi did not see her face, but, in a groping, childish way, he knew that she, too, was suffering, though hers could not have been the humble misery of Aba; it was her pride which had been hurt, the pride in her first-born, and she retaliated by bringing about his humiliation. Neither he nor his parents ever mentioned the spanking, nor did they ever again subject him to corporal punishment.

Next morning Yehudi began to relearn the A-major concerto. The going was hard at first. The sunny tranquillity of the largo that marks the entry of the solo in the first movement eluded him, and he vainly tried to capture its serenity. When he came to the slow movement, he could make no headway at all; each note was a reminder of the slamming down of the score by his always gentle teacher. In despair, he went on to the final movement before the earlier two had been mastered. It proved a happy impulse, for the graceful, elegant strains of the third movement caught his child's fancy, and the whole grim episode was forgotten in the witty rhythms of the *alla Turca*. He returned to the beginning, and from then on surrendered to Mozart. And Mozart surrendered to him. Throughout the rest of his childhood and adolescence, Yehudi played Mozart with an unequaled purity and perfection which proved more elusive in later years, although at the same time his performance of other composers grew in depth and beauty.

"Even as a young boy," Menuhin said by way of an explanation, "I knew a great deal about Mozart, both from his music and from books, and I worshiped him. The initial carelessness with which I treated the A-major was due largely to my vanity —I was eager to get on to Beethoven, but the moment I surmounted that superficial attitude and immersed myself in the music, I discovered a greater affinity with Mozart than with any other composer. Psychologically, at the time he was the most immediately available composer to me, for his style had crystallized when he was still a child, and remained true to its undefiled simplicity, although it later grew in richness and subtlety. Mozart's appeal to me was as child to child and as innocence to innocence. Guided by the instinctive inspiration and devotion of youth, one can play Beethoven with great beauty and even with a degree of penetration, but, without having first lived, no musician can render him perfectly. A young person, however, can play Mozart with perfection, as if touched by a magic wand. In order to penetrate his music and communicate it to the listener, I did not have to transpose myself—I could play him and remain myself, with no need to feel big, powerful, and grown-up; I did not even have to imagine myself in love.

"Had I been reared on movies, comic strips, and other such crude sophistications of American life, I should probably have been robbed of the spontaneity and innocence without which Mozart cannot truthfully be conveyed. In fact, our entire present-day civilization lacks these qualities, which perhaps, accounts for the decline of the Mozart vogue in the United States. The moderns may be, and are capable of appreciating the heroic tragedy and noble suffering of a Beethoven, but the tender sorrow of Mozart is alien to them. For them, it is difficult to tell the difference between the simple and the affectedly

simple, between the elegant and the sham elegant, even as it is
to distinguish between a sweet girl and a coy one.

"The emancipated modern man is so accustomed to seeing
powerful emotions break the bonds of form in the arts that he
finds it embarrassing to identify himself with such emotions
when they are contained within a traditional framework.
Mozart was able, because of the rigid conventions of his age,
to pour his very genuine feelings into vessels the sheer elegance of which restrained their contents. He thus resolved his
emotions on a level that transformed them into moods uncontaminated by mortal anguish. The child who never ceased to
live within Mozart led him to sublimate his adult emotions into
those he could have experienced had he never grown out of
childhood.

"Thus, from without, in terms of form, he inherited the
elegance and grace of the court; from within, he had the qualities and attitudes of childhood—an age capable of suffering,
but a suffering which does not sear or distort, enabling Mozart
to express the 'angelic anguish' that is so peculiarly his own."

Arriving at Persinger's studio for the first time after he
had been sent away in disgrace, Yehudi made straight for the
piano and, accompanied by Persinger, played through the
Mozart concerto in a way that made that lesson one of the
most memorable they were to have in all their years of work
together. The sympathy and mutual understanding that had
existed between them were restored without a word's being
spoken, with neither of them feeling any need to discuss the
incident of the previous lesson. As he was putting away his
violin, Yehudi saw Marutha take his teacher aside and say
something which caused Persinger to stiffen, then shrug his
shoulders resignedly and whisper something in reply. Marutha
concluded in a loud voice: "We'll come along, but you must do
as I have asked you to."

A horrible suspicion arose in Yehudi's mind. Was his mother
going to reopen the whole incident by forcing Persinger to

apologize to him? It seemed not, for the teacher turned to Yehudi, saying that the great pianist and conductor Ossip Gabrilowitsch was in San Francisco and had invited them to call on him at the Clift Hotel. They took the streetcar on the corner and all three sat down together, but, no sooner had the tramway started than Persinger got up and asked Yehudi to follow him to the empty front platform. There, to a boy whose heart was rapidly sinking into his boots, he apologized for having scolded him the last time. But, Yehudi protested, it was his own fault, and it was for him to say he was sorry. Persinger gratefully silenced him, and a few minutes later they collected Marutha, got off the tram, and went up to the Clift for their rendezvous with Gabrilowitsch. Possibly as a gesture to the boy, Persinger suggested that Yehudi play the slow movement of the A-major Mozart. Gabrilowitsch begged to hear more, and after Yehudi had finished his second piece, the host embraced him without saying a word, looking at him with a kind of disbelief. Gradually the two older musicians became involved in a conversation which in the end drifted to Mark Twain, Yehudi's favorite author and Gabrilowitsch's father-in-law, and the boy felt pleased with a possessive affection that his own teacher revealed an impressive knowledge of Mark Twain's life and work.

The call on Gabrilowitsch marked Yehudi's second visit to a hotel and held for him a significance all its own. A modern hotel with its feverish activity was associated in the boy's mind with the glamor and mystery that surrounded the lives of world-renowned artists. It was to him a symbol of their travels and experiences in strange, faraway places, so different from his own prosaic existence on Steiner Street. The ever changing pattern of travel, with its visions and exotic colors, accounted in his childish mind for the greatness of performances by a Kreisler, a Heifetz, or a Gabrilowitsch. Too young to think of art in terms of experience, suffering, and struggle, his conception of a musician's existence was limited to its external manifestations, and these were embodied in an exalted image of hotels. His first visit had taken place some months earlier, to the St. Francis, where he played for Mischa Elman. The resplendent entourage of the hotel, its vastness, the life seething within its walls, so impressed the boy that he remembers nothing of what the famed violinist said about his playing, nor would he have known at the time that, according to the press, Elman pronounced Yehudi a genius.

Of all the visiting artists Yehudi heard during that period, Georges Enesco impressed him the most, although the two were not to meet until much later. Enesco was then at the zenith of his fame and powers as a violinist, composer, and conductor. Tall, dignified, with flowing raven-black hair that almost reached his shoulders, he so impressed Yehudi that the boy, sitting with his parents in the packed hall, had the feeling that Enesco was playing just for him:

"An awareness overtook me that I wanted to study with no one but Enesco. Not that I was eager to break away from Persinger, but here was someone to whom I responded so completely that I could not envisage my future without some contact with him. I wanted to run backstage and stand close to him. This alone seemed sufficient to complete my happiness that evening, but I knew that my parents would not allow me to 'push myself,' and I said nothing. But I never forgot Enesco."

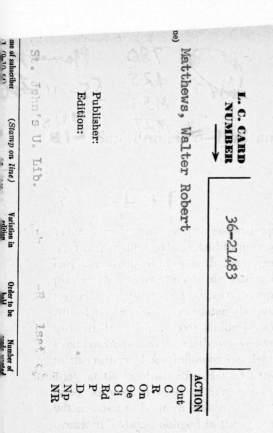

...earance on February ...ss than a year after he ... On this occasion he ...between works per-...ony Orchestra under ...gram was repeated be-...o listened with wide-...r-old and cheered him ...t recital on March 25, ...music critics were on ...co's musicians, one of ...ur pen fly! You cannot ...orning's *Examiner:*

"This is not talent; it is genius!"

The enthusiasm of the audience was no less unrestrained, and big crowds rushed backstage after the performance. The parents, taken by surprise, suddenly found themselves separated from the boy, cut off by admiring ladies who fluttered up to Yehudi, kissing him and insisting that he was a marvel and a genius. Tired and perspiring, he defended himself the best he could, brushing the kisses off his cheeks with the back of both hands and seeking escape, but in vain. One lady was particularly annoying, as she kept repeating that he played like Paganini, nay, better than Paganini. Scornfully, Yehudi stopped her:

"Ah, so, madame, you have heard Paganini!"

Taught by that night's experience, the Menuhins subsequently took the strictest precautions to guard Yehudi against uncontrolled rapture backstage, although they had little to worry about his being spoiled by adulation. If anything, the boy was repelled by these outbursts, arresting them short by such impish remarks as the one about Paganini or, as on a later occasion when an ecstatic lady gushed: "What do you think of when you are alone in the country with your violin, with the beautiful flowers and playful birds flitting about you?" Mimicking her rapturous tone, Yehudi exclaimed: "My mother makes the most wonderful chicken pies!"

One day, a man introduced himself to Yehudi in a most ponderous fashion as Mischa Elman's father. Upon perceiving no reaction, and thinking that the boy had not heard him, the man repeated: "I am Mischa Elman's father!" "Yes, sir," Yehudi replied, still with no sign of happy recognition. The man repeated for the third time: "I am Mischa Elman's father, Yehudi!" Whereupon the boy inquired politely: "What else have you done for him, sir?"

Years have added subtlety but have not dulled the sting of his impatience with indiscriminate praise. After a recent concert, one lady was overheard pressing him: "Please tell me, divine young man, do you still have terrible nerves and tension before a concert?"

"No, madame, now it is the turn of my audience to suffer."

As a matter of fact, Yehudi never suffered unduly before a concert. However, his parents did, and their adherence at such times to the family routine was actually a greater help to them than to Yehudi. As on any ordinary day, the Menuhins had their six o'clock supper in the kitchen. To relieve the strain and make conversation as casual as possible, Marutha would invite their young roomer, Ezra Shapeero, to join them. After supper, Yehudi, still wearing his old sweater and cotton knee pants, would be sent up to his room to do the reading for tomorrow's lesson in history or English, and only at the last minute was he instructed to put on his white silk blouse and velvet pants. This was, however, a very contrived normalcy which tended to

break down every once in a while, as on the dreadful occasion
when Marutha, strained to the breaking point, suddenly cried
within Yehudi's hearing: "I cannot stand it any longer! I shall
not let him play in public any more!"

There was still so much of the child in Yehudi, and such in-
born calm, that even these outbursts and the ovations that
followed the concerts failed to ruffle him, just as they failed
to kill the simple boy in him. Shapeero recalls how, after one
particularly lovely concert he came into Yehudi's bedroom to
kiss him good night. Obviously trying to take advantage of
the occasion, Yehudi wheedled:

"Now do me a big favor?"

Wondering whatever was on the boy's mind, Shapeero consented.

"Then please fix the handle bar on my tricycle the first thing
in the morning."

After Yehudi's debut, San Francisco sat up and took notice
of the child wonder in its midst. The greatest repercussions,
as could well be expected, were among the parents of boys
and girls in the Jewish community. All cheap and medium-
priced violins were sold out overnight, and the beginners
flooded McAllister and adjoining streets with hideous sound.
Attendance in Hebrew schools was cut by half, to be restored
only after several weeks when the grind of practice dulled the
ambition of the would-be Yehudi Menuhins who returned
lamblike to the school bench. But the little boy who had
started it all went on playing the violin.

He knew nothing of the efforts of two friends of his family
to arouse interest in him among the music patrons of the city.
One of those friends, needless to say, was the indefatigable
Cantor Rinder, and the other was Dr. Samuel Langer, director
of the Pacific Hebrew Orphan Asylum, who had met Moshe in
the latter's capacity as educator. Dr. Langer had two children
of his own and occasionally invited the Menuhin family to
Sunday dinner at his home, the finest Yehudi and his sisters

had seen, where they sat for meals in a real dining room, the host at the head of the table, a maid serving everyone in turn.

Among Dr. Langer's duties was the administration of a fund donated by Sidney M. Ehrman, president of the orphanage, to be used for furthering the education of the most talented among the children. Dr. Langer suggested to Ehrman that a scholarship be set up out of this fund for the benefit of a remarkable child musician named Yehudi Menuhin, but the philanthropist declined to divert the money intended for orphans and, instead, offered to contribute five hundred dollars toward Yehudi's needs. This Moshe and Marutha refused to accept. Likewise, nothing came of Cantor Rinder's efforts on Yehudi's behalf.

In the meantime, the Menuhin family was thrown into its first serious quandary since Yehudi had taken up the violin, for one day Persinger announced that he and his quartet were going to New York in the fall for several months. Moshe and Marutha were reluctant to let Yehudi go without instruction for so long a period, and felt that no one in San Francisco could replace Persinger. After long cogitation and not a little heartbreak they came to the conclusion that the only thing to do, since Moshe could not afford to leave his work, was for Marutha to take the three children to New York.

On the day of their departure, Dr. Langer came to the station with a map of the United States for Yehudi, so that he could follow the progress of his journey. Taking the boy out of earshot, he urged him to be kind to Yaltah, for he had noticed a tendency on his part to "gang up" with Hephzibah against their little sister. Moshe, too, had a private talk with his son, impressing upon him that, as the only man with the family, he was now responsible for everyone's welfare. He slipped a small bottle into Yehudi's coat pocket, informing the boy with grave emphasis that it contained smelling salts, to be used at the first sign of a fainting spell his mother might display. As Yehudi had never detected in her the slightest signs of weakness, let alone anything so un-Cherkesslike as fainting, he was puzzled and worried. Throughout the long trip, and for some days thereafter, he stayed as close to his mother as possible, secretly feeling the bottle in his pocket, until she noticed his strange behavior and demanded an explanation. Speaking haltingly, with the feeling that he was betraying his father, the boy explained. For a moment she was furious, but then, as she took the pathetic little bottle from Yehudi and flung it into a wastebasket, she laughed merrily. Not so Yehudi, who felt quite anxious for a time, but the predicted fainting spells never came, and the whole incident was soon crowded out by the onrush of sensations that now assailed him in this big, strange city.

Uppermost among them was his feeling of homesickness. He had been taking his home town for granted, but now, oh how he missed it! Like many another newcomer to New York, he saw its rows of skyscrapers as ominous canyons of cement and steel, the darkness of its clipped winter days frightening him. With time he developed a deep attachment for that great city of challenge and experiment, stimulating in its vigor and yet miraculously pensive at twilight; but during that first visit New York was to the small boy a city of strangers and of darkness, of noise and rush. He missed the sunny ease of San Francisco, and he missed his father, who always thought of such amusing things to do, and whose car was always around to take him to places where green things grew and where people were happy to see him.

Gradually, life became more bearable. Sam Marantz, now a grown young man, came from Elizabeth for occasional weekends with Marutha and her children. He played hide-and-seek with them on their daily walks in Morningside Park, and at home he read to them and played chess with Yehudi, who had learned the game from Persinger. And Marutha, too, in her usual competent way, had lost little time in organizing his studies, so that every Thursday morning, accompanied by his mother, Yehudi went to the Institute of Musical Art (now the Juilliard School of Music), where he attended classes in ear training, sight singing, and harmony. He was the youngest in a class whose twenty-one students were of college age, but he stood out among them in musical knowledge and gift of memory. This was the only classroom instruction he was ever to have, and it was a success all around. Dorothy Crowthers, his teacher in ear training, was especially drawn to the remarkable, disciplined child with the perfect ear and the sweet, unfaltering soprano.

Another reason for which New York was gradually losing its forbidding aspect was the fact that the Persinger String Quartet rehearsed immediately before Yehudi's lessons, and he was allowed to attend those sessions—his first taste of chamber music.

Fully three months passed before Moshe managed to join his family for their last three weeks in New York, and immediately things began to hum. Despite its being the depth of winter, there was more outdoor activity and more concert going and visiting. Moshe looked up some old friends, notably Dr. and Mrs. Garbat (the Rachel Lubarsky of his student days), who had two children the same age as Yehudi's sisters, a boy Julian and a daughter Mania, nicknamed Fifi. Rachel Garbat had become a patroness of talented young musicians and was overjoyed when Marutha casually remarked that "unfortunately, Yehudi is showing some gifts as a fiddler." Yehudi adored Dr. Garbat and spent every free moment in his laboratory, asking innumerable questions about medicine.

As for Moshe, his most important tasks included the purchase of a new violin for Yehudi and preparations for the boy's New York debut. A seven-eighths' size Grancino was bought for five hundred dollars, which Yehudi liked well enough but which was still a far cry from his visions of *the* violin. For several nights following the purchase of the Grancino he dreamed one and the same dream: He was sitting in the front row at a Kreisler recital in Carnegie Hall when the great master, erect and handsome, appeared on the stage to a rousing ovation which subsided quickly as the audience observed something strange about their idol: he was carrying two violins in his hands. Advancing slowly in the amazed silence, Kreisler walked up to the edge of the platform, looked straight at Yehudi, extended one of the violins to him, and said, "This is for you, my boy!"

Yehudi's New York debut was set for January 17, 1926, at the Manhattan Opera House. No established manager wanted to present an unknown violinist of tender age, and, inexperienced as he was at the time, Moshe decided to do it on his own and without much advance publicity. Thus, unheralded, the boy appeared in a great hall not altogether filled, despite the countless hours Moshe and Sam had spent in mailing programs and free tickets to friends, music patrons, and critics. No musician of note attended the concert, but, according to one newspaper, the fathers of three famous virtuosi were sitting in the front row: "Papa Elman, Papa Heifetz, and Papa Max Rosen."

The program, with Louis Persinger at the piano, was formidable, including Handel's *Sonata in E major,* Lalo's *Symphonie Espagnole,* Paganini's *Concerto in D major,* and a number of short display pieces. The audience was so enchanted with Yehudi's performance that it kept recalling him until he exhausted all his encores, and finally let him go only after the management had dimmed the lights. The third-string critics who were sent out to cover the concert gave Yehudi warm but cautious notices, crediting the boy, in the words of *Musical America,* with "a facility and dash almost incredible for one of his years."

The great enthusiasm of the audience, the friendliness of the critics, and the several offers that came from New York concert managers were all promising but did not add up to the results with which a self-propelling career could be launched, nor were they sufficient to induce the Menuhins to change their plan of returning to San Francisco, especially since they all were anxious to get back, particularly Marutha. The burden of those few months which she had shouldered alone was beginning to tell. Although she had challenged Yehudi as being unworthy of a Cherkess when she thought he looked pale and tense on the eve of the Manhattan Opera House concert, he had overheard her a few minutes later cry out to Moshe, "I am going to break that violin!" For days Yehudi kept his Grancino near him at all times, even though he realized that he was powerless to prevent her from doing anything she wished either to the instrument or to him.

It took him several days to get used once more to the bright sunlight of his beloved San Francisco, and months before he could refrain from crossing out the unfriendly words "New York" whenever he saw them in a book or a newspaper.

Persinger and Yehudi lost no time in returning to the sweet old routine of their lessons. There were new works to be studied, and a new recital was in the offing, to take place on March sixth at the scene of the boy's previous triumphs, the Scottish Rite Hall.

It was with great reluctance that Marutha had agreed to the ordeal of another concert. She might not have agreed at all, and most certainly not so soon, had she not been aroused by a challenge to her pride. Armed with some of the more flattering quotations about Yehudi from the New York press, Cantor Rinder had finally succeeded in his self-appointed mission of arousing the interest of some wealthy San Franciscans in this extraordinary boy who was spreading the glory of their city. They decided to give a tea for Yehudi, where he was to play and subsequently receive a purse of five thousand dollars for his education and training. Having completed all the arrangements, the group invited the boy and his parents to the tea, but to the surprise and indignation of the would-be patrons, the Menuhins refused to attend. They were in need of no alms, they said, nor was Yehudi an itinerant musician playing in private homes. As for hearing him play, all those interested were most cordially invited to his forthcoming concert.

Whether the patrons came or not, the critics were on hand on March sixth and were so impressed by the performance that their praises verged on blasphemy. Alexander Fried of the San Francisco *Chronicle*, wrote: "What built the world in six days is what contrived the genuis of Yehudi. He walks on the waves." Following the boy's appearance a few days later with the Symphony Orchestra, Redfern Mason declared that, as he listened to Yehudi, he was thinking "of the boy Samuel in the Scriptures and how the voice of God spoke to him in the night watches." Overcome with emotion at the end of the concert, Alfred Hertz bent down from his enormous height, lifted the boy, and kissed him, and Yehudi still remembers the conductor's beard, prickly and drenched in tears and perspiration, brushing stickily against his hot cheeks.

An incident took place following the Scottish Rite Hall recital which changed the boy's entire life. It began inauspiciously enough as he and his parents were waiting behind the locked door of the artists' room for the clamor outside to die down. Dr. Langer knocked, asking Moshe to come out for a minute. Menuhin soon returned accompanied by a tall, broad-shouldered man, extremely elegant in a dinner jacket.

"Mr. Sidney Ehrman," Moshe introduced him, beaming. "My wife and Yehudi."

Ehrman bowed to Marutha and then put his hand on Yehudi's shoulder. The boy liked him immediately and did not shrink from the caress, and he wondered why his mother suddenly became tense. Ehrman left after a few minutes, saying to Moshe that he would be happy to see him at his convenience. As the boy slowly put on his coat, he was aware of a strain in the silence of his parents, who obviously did not want to speak in his presence. They passed through the now empty hall and, as they reached the main exit, found themselves face to face again with Mr. Ehrman, who introduced them to his companions: his wife, Florence, and his daughter Esther and his son Sidney, both in their late teens. Yehudi was glad to see the wonderful big man once more, but he could not take his eyes off the girl, who seemed to him more beautiful than anyone he had ever seen.

A Rolls-Royce drew up to the curb. As the chauffeur opened the door, Ehrman offered to take the Menuhins home, but Marutha declined, saying they had made other arrangements. The Ehrmans rode off, and only then did Yehudi suddenly become aware of the rain pelting down, his tiredness, and of how pale his mother looked. Several long, silent minutes passed before a chance taxi came along and took them home.

That night, Yehudi, nine-and-a-half years old, was unable to fall asleep for a long time, repeating the name Esther over and over again.

In their bedroom, Moshe and Marutha also were awake. Mr. Ehrman, Moshe was saying, had asked him for permission to underwrite Yehudi's training and education for as long as need be. All Marutha had to say in reply was "No."

It was a confused and unhappy Dr. Langer who called on Ehrman at his law office the next day to tell him that Mrs. Menuhin had vetoed the whole project. Both he and Moshe had tried, to no avail, and only Ehrman himself might succeed in convincing her, if he would agree to make the attempt.

"When I called on Marutha," the lawyer told me, "I found her emotional, sensitive, proud, and stubborn. And logical in what she had to say. She was not sure that she wanted her son to make music his career, for she was afraid that the chaotic and glamorous life of a prodigy might spoil him, distort his vision, and wreck his life. 'I would rather,' she said, 'that he grew up to be a shoemaker, so long as he remained a complete and honest man. I am afraid of too rigid a concentration on his career, for without such concentration I see no way for him to greatness. I am afraid of the disorganization of our family life, the separations, the problems connected with the schooling of the boy and his sisters.'"

Ehrman explained that the offer he made was intended to cover the entire family, so that both parents would be free to devote their entire time to the children; that all necessary trips would include the five of them and that he would take care of the tutors, for he understood that Persinger wanted Yehudi to study in Europe with his former teacher, the great Ysaye, and he, Ehrman, was prepared to cover all their expenses in Europe. He offered his help, Ehrman continued, not as an act of charity but as a duty and a privilege. Of course, there was no question but that the parents alone retained the right of making decisions and exercising control. She might as well accept, he added, for there was no holding the boy back—his talent was too immense.

Slowly, grudgingly, almost with resentment, Marutha at last agreed, and from that point on Moshe took over. He had a long talk with Ehrman, then with Persinger, and the great decision was made. Moshe would ask for a half year's leave of absence from his school duties, rent out the house, and take the family to Europe. Matters having reached this point, Persinger wrote to Ysaye in Brussels, who consented to give Yehudi an audition. The departure was set for the fall, and in the meantime the boy would continue to work with Persinger, while all three children would study French in preparation for life abroad.

The tutor engaged by the Menuhins was Mlle. Rebecca Godchaux, whose home, which she shared with her brother and two sisters, was affectionately known in the city as "San Francisco's little France." At the end of her first lesson with Yehudi, he recollects, Mlle. Godchaux read to him an eight-line poem from his text book, "Les Couleurs," explaining that it was about the names of flowers and how God painted them in many different colors. While walking home with Yehudi, Marutha discovered that he remembered all the French words he was to know by the next day, and she asked if he wouldn't like to know the poem, as well? Of course he would! They started after supper and were making good progress, but the boy soon grew tired and sleepy and wanted to go to bed. "A Cherkess never leaves anything unfinished," she replied, but he was getting drowsier and drowsier, forgetting even the lines he had known by heart only a short while ago. Aba tried to intercede, but the cramming went on until just before midnight. Yehudi does not know whether he had actually memorized the entire poem before his mother let him stagger to bed, but the next afternoon he recited it to Mlle. Rebecca without a slip. Impressed, she never tired of singing the praises of her new pupil's powers of memory and concentration. His progress was rapid indeed, for Marutha worked with him every day, sparing him, however, the rigorousness of her first effort. Hephzibah and Yaltah received less help from Marutha but were able to keep pace with their brother, for they were not yet burdened with a schedule as arduous as his.

In the meantime, a friendship centered around Yehudi was slowly developing between the Ehrmans and the Menuhins. Quite apart from their interest in his remarkable musical talent, the boy's patrons loved him for his sunny disposition, his sense of humor and ability to go straight to the point of any question that intrigued him. Yehudi returned their affection, and to Esther he was attached with a puppylike devotion which Mrs. Ehrman was quick to notice, and she thoughtfully arranged the seating at the table so that Yehudi was placed between her daughter and Mr. Ehrman, or Uncle Sidney, as the Menuhin children soon learned to call him. It was Uncle Sidney who thought of giving Yehudi a bicycle. He had long grown out of the tricycle stage, but his parents refused to buy for him a machine on two wheels lest he fall and damage an arm or hand. As luck would have it, Alfred Hertz was visiting the Menuhins when Uncle Sidney's gift arrived. Taking one horrified look at the bicycle, the conductor warned Yehudi that riding on the dangerous streets and hills of San Francisco might be the end of violin playing for him. The boy reluctantly gave up his machine, for how could he argue with Hertz, speaking in the name of music?

Mr. Ehrman did not share the fears that led Yehudi's parents to keep him from many of a boy's normal sports and games, and he succeeded in coaxing Moshe into permitting his son at least to take swimming lessons and play catch, using a tennis ball. Moshe would miserably watch the two, exclaiming from time to time: "Please, Mr. Ehrman, don't throw the ball so hard!" But Yehudi loved it, as he loved swimming and the few other sports available to him. He was a sturdily built youngster with a ready response to challenge, a quick grasp of detail, and a determination rare in one so young.

Despite his persuasiveness, Ehrman failed to break down Moshe's objections to the one sport which fascinated Yehudi even more than bicycling—horseback riding. One of the first things Yehudi did after he became master of his fate was to climb on the back of a horse and indulge in the luxury of a few good falls. He is still not altogether at home in the saddle, but it takes a very determined horse to unseat him.

A few days before the Menuhins were leaving for Europe, the Ehrmans gave them a farewell dinner in their lovely house, from the back windows of which one looked on to the Golden Gate, Alcatraz looming in the distance. As always, Yehudi sat next to Esther. He had long since noticed her wearing a beautiful Chinese-puzzle ring, made in gold with three small turquoise stones. Knowing that he was to leave in a few days, he now made bold to ask her to let him see it. She took it off, dropped it into his hand, and, to his surprise, he found himself holding four small intertwined rings. He tried to put them together again, but failed, as he did also in his request that she show him the trick. But on the day of their departure, Esther called unexpectedly with a going-away present for Yehudi, a replica of her ring, and showed him how the puzzle worked. Tucked in his violin case, the ring has been traveling with him ever since.

Many other farewell gifts were waiting for Yehudi on the train, among them a photograph of Persinger with the following inscription:

"To dear Yehudi, hoping that he will one day develop into a great artist—one who will prove to be not only the *master* but also the worthy *servant* of the Beautiful. With the love and admiration of his friend and teacher, Louis Persinger."

As he read the message, Menuhin recalls, his thoughts carried him to Enesco, the man in whom he saw his ideal of one who is both master and servant of the Beautiful. And it seemed to him that the train was speeding him to his idol rather than to Ysaye or to anyone else in the world. He read

Persinger's inscription once more, and in a burst of tenderness and affection for his faithful teacher, he sat down and wrote:

Sweet Master:

As the train is going eastward, within me are growing sentiments. For as soon as we parted last night I felt that lonely sensation, that one which I had a year ago for my father. Indeed, Mr. Persinger, you are my father of music. I have never felt you so near to me as I do now. Wherever life brings me, whether east, west, north or south, I will always hear your sweet voice. That voice which ofttimes corrected me, and if I would be without it, only God would know the kind of life I would lead.

Your loving pupil,
Yehudi Menuhin.

FIVE

Paris and Georges Enesco

Yehudi had set his heart on approaching Enesco immediately upon arrival in Paris, but Marutha would not hear of it. They had left Persinger with the understanding that they would go to his old teacher Ysaye, she argued, and they were in duty bound to keep the promise, especially since Persinger had gone to the trouble of securing the consent of the grand old man of the violin to give Yehudi an audition. She was going with him to Brussels, where the crucial decision would be made.

One morning, several days later, they rang the bell at the door of Ysaye's house on an elegant tree-lined avenue and were led up two flights to a large room filled with furniture, books, and music scattered in disorder, the whole permeated by the strong, stale atmosphere of neglect. Slumped in a large armchair near the window was Ysaye—massive, pale, and motionless. Yehudi remembers a powerful arm rising in a sweeping gesture of welcome, only to collapse in mid-air. Marutha helped the boy to take off his coat, and he slowly approached Ysaye, violin case in hand. On the desk near the armchair, he noticed, lay the master's Guarnerius, one of the most exquisite instruments in existence, of which he had heard a great deal from Persinger.

"Can you play Lalo's *Symphonie Espagnole?*"

Yehudi nodded, and the sick man motioned him to play. Within a minute or two, a cautious smile appeared on Ysaye's face, a smile of approval and recognition: here was *his* pupil's pupil, shades of himself, transmitted through Persinger to this boy out of distant America.

As Yehudi played on, Ysaye reached for his Guarnerius and began to pluck an accompaniment with an unfaltering hand and with a richness of sound Yehudi had never heard anyone produce from a violin by pizzicato. Occasionally, to the boy's mystification, Ysaye paused for a fleeting moment to watch his fingering and bowing. Despite the old man's exquisite accompaniment, Yehudi remembers finishing with a sense of relief, hoping that his mother would feel the same as he— that he had done his duty and could now go back to Paris, to Enesco.

"You have made me happy, little boy," said Ysaye. "Very happy! And now," he added unexpectedly, "play an arpeggio, just an ordinary arpeggio in three octaves."

Yehudi was puzzled but obediently began playing as requested. To his surprise and humiliation, he who had just rendered faultlessly the intricate Lalo, barely struggled through the simple exercise.

"I thought so," Ysaye muttered. "You will do well, Yehudi, to work on your scales and arpeggios."

The boy tried to say yes, he would, but could not bring the words out of his mouth. The staleness of the air in the room, the disorder and dilapidation, became oppressive, and he violently wanted to escape. As if sharing his wish, Marutha started to pack the violin and then helped him on with his coat. Ysaye did not stir and seemed to have forgotten his visitors, seemed not to hear Marutha's words of gratitude nor her explanation that she would have to consult her husband in Paris. As soon as they were alone in the street, Yehudi turned to his mother, pleading: "Take me to Enesco, please, Imma!"

The same day they returned to Paris.

Years later, Menuhin regretted that he had not remained to study with Ysaye, for however brief a period. The regret stems not only from the thought that, had he followed Ysaye's admonition to work on scales and arpeggios, he might have spared himself much hardship in the future, but also from the realization that he had deprived himself of an opportunity for communion with a great artist and man. In the preface which Menuhin wrote to a biography of Ysaye, published in 1947, he said in part:

> *Eugène Ysaye was indeed a giant. Not only for those who saw and heard him, but even for such as I who know him only through the spell he cast on others, his commanding figure still stands unchallenged, the last of the romantic race of mighty men who were violin virtuosi.*
>
> *I feel I can claim a deep spiritual heritage which I absorbed partly during my first years' study with Louis Persinger, a pupil of Ysaye, partly through the compelling imprint Ysaye left upon the great masters I came to love and revere, namely Enesco and Thibaud, and lastly through my own unbounded admiration for Eugène Ysaye, the artist, violinist and man as my imagination pictured him, fed by the many musicians and beloved friends who knew him.*
>
> *. . . The task of the interpreter is to strike a balance between the work of the composer and his own conscience. He is ever trying to fill to the utmost with his own essence another man's form. In no circumstances may he distort the form, yet in order that it may re-live, it must contain the reality of his own conviction and his own emotions. Eugène Ysaye had the wherewithal to fill every vessel.*
>
> *Though I regret that my name does not figure among those who knew and loved Eugène Ysaye from day to day, it is a great compensation that as a young man I may now lay before his memory the full extent of my tribute, my allegiance to all that he represented, and my gratitude to the tradition he developed and upheld.*[1]

[1]Antoine Ysaye and Bertram Ratcliffe, *Ysaye: His Life, Work and Influence* (London: William Heinemann, Ltd., 1947), pp. ix–xi.

The artists' room was crowded following Enesco's recital a few days after Yehudi's return to Paris, filled with friends, admirers, and autograph seekers. The tired violinist was grateful for the quiet efficiency with which his friend, the cellist Gerard Hekking, handled the crowd, gradually emptying the room.

With his parents' permission, Yehudi went backstage by himself and stood quietly in a corner, not taking his eyes off Enesco. When Hekking spotted him, the boy insisted with such gravity on speaking to Enesco that the cellist introduced him.

"I want to study with you," he declared.

"There must be some mistake; I do not give private lessons."

"But I must study with you! Please give me an audition!"

"It's impossible! I am going away on tour, taking the six-thirty train tomorrow morning."

"I can come an hour earlier and play while you pack, may I?"

Enesco was tired, but there was something endlessly appealing in the boy's manner, direct and purposeful and at the same time defenselessly childish, and he put his hand on Yehudi's shoulder.

"You have won, little boy," laughed Hekking. "Come at five-thirty to 26 Rue de Clichy. I'll be there, too."

When, at a few minutes before six the next morning, Yehudi finished playing, Enesco agreed to start working with him after the end of his tour, in about two months. As to payment, he told the amazed Moshe, he had no right to accept anything: "Yehudi has as much to offer me as I have to give him."

Despite all his exhilaration over Enesco's consent, the next few weeks proved to be extremely trying for the boy. The family had settled in an old, depressing apartment house on the Rue de Sèvres, the bedrooms looked out on a somber, narrow courtyard which, as in so many French houses, allowed little light or air to penetrate. In contrast to the dark stillness of the yard, the street was deafening with din and clatter as peddlers shouted their wares, trams and horse-drawn delivery wagons shook the windows when they thundered by, and the then fashionable bulb horns in automobiles exploded their raucous sounds with Latin fervor.

The general mood in the Menuhin family did little to brighten the existence of the boy who was impatient with waiting for Enesco and beset by homesickness for California. Mr. Ehrman relieved Moshe and Marutha of financial problems, but his very generosity burdened them with a sense of obligation, which compelled them to budget expenses as if they still had only their small income to depend on. Their coming to Paris loomed increasingly in their eyes as a gamble rather than the glorious adventure and opportunity it had seemed only a short while ago. Moshe had to decide within a few brief months whether to return from his leave of absence or lose the job which by that time was bringing in a comforting $100 a week.

The Menuhins succeeded in keeping their problems from the seven-year-old Hephzibah and five-year-old Yaltah, but Yehudi was older and could not help overhearing remarks and noting sudden silences. Thus he easily gathered that the fortunes of the entire family rested upon the Paris sojourn, that he was the cause of so crucial a gamble and he alone was responsible for the outcome. What if he failed?

Overcome by worry and by a feeling of confinement in what was to him a grim old city, Yehudi began to have nightmares. They were started off by a violent incident not unusual in a metropolis. One early dawn Yehudi was awakened by a shot fired in the courtyard below, followed by a scream and shouts. In the morning he learned that a man had been murdered in their courtyard, where all efforts to wash away the blood stains had failed. That night Yehudi dreamed of someone monstrous pursuing him until, just in the nick of time, he woke up and blindly reached out for the wall but, unable to find it in his horror-stricken confusion, screamed for help. His parents came and calmed him down, but he was so ashamed of himself that he never again called for them although the nightmares continued for months on end.

Thus it came about that, on looking back, Yehudi remembers his early life in Paris as one of weariness and depression. Uncomforted by the friendly and the familiar, the little family lived in dejected isolation, weighed down by the waiting and by Moshe's agonizing indecision as to the next step, hardly noticing how life, asserting its rights, gradually lifted the pall of gloom. Yehudi continued to wake every morning, listless and heavy, but the little apartment was somehow losing its forbidding darkness, and the streets of Paris were beginning to seem less painfully noisy and unfamiliar. Likewise, Marutha's insistence on daily walks no longer appeared arbitrary, as they acquired a fascination all their own, gradually uncovering for the boy the ancient and everlasting charms of the Paris that lay just outside his own ugly Rue de Sèvres. Yehudi usually walked in front of his parents, Hephzibah and Yaltah holding him by the hand, all of them rejoicing at each new discovery in a city that was so much unlike San Francisco. He clearly remembers his enchantment with the unfamiliar indentations in the cornerstone of most of the buildings, which endowed each with an individuality, evoking in him a complaint:

"Why do American skyscrapers have only those long straight lines? Why are they all made to look alike?"

In good weather, the children were allowed to run along the boulevards, rolling their large, slender hoops, the pleasure of those hours marred only by the French coats which Marutha had bought for them, the smart-looking hood of which, attached to the coat by a villainous rubber substance, so irritated their wretched necks that the young Menuhins, used to the free and easy clothes of California, hardly dared to turn their heads in any direction.

With the facility of childhood, Yehudi and his sisters were rapidly picking up French, and before long used it in daily conversation with each other and with Marutha, who suggested at this point that they call her "Petite Mère," instead of "Imma." Later, when they began to learn German, this was changed for "Mütterchen," and to "Mammina" when Marutha launched them on the study of Italian. She is "Mammina" to this day, but Moshe has always remained "Aba."

Gradually, the Menuhins acquired friends, although Marutha's pride and the family's self-sufficiency tended to make this a slow and difficult process. The most fruitful and lasting friendship made at that time was with the Jan Hambourgs.

A former student of Ysaye, Jan Hambourg was an amateur violinist who owned a priceless Amati and a Peter Guarnerius, lived in an ultra-modern apartment, and boasted membership in the exclusive Société Gastronomique. A *bon vivant* and an unquenchable enthusiast, Hambourg was forever excited about one thing or another, his enthusiasms as momentarily unyielding as they were quickly passing. But he never wavered in his passion for fine food, his admiration for Yehudi's talent, and his worship of Bach's six works for the unaccompanied violin. Attired in a resplendent wine-colored jacket, Hambourg played these sonatas weekly, starting with the first on Monday and ending with the last on Saturday. Sunday was a day of rest, following which the ritual started all over again. Grateful to anyone who shared his adoration of Bach, Hambourg was particularly touched by the way Yehudi cherished these hours of listening to "Uncle Jan," who thus introduced him to the complete cycle.

Shortly before Enesco's return, Yehudi became the proud owner of a full-size Grancino made in 1690, bought for $3,000 which Ehrman sent them. Moshe also bought for his son three gold-mounted bows made by the great Sartory.

In the meantime, the cellist Gerard Hekking was not forgetting Yehudi. Undismayed by several rebuffs, he finally persuaded the famous Paul Paray to give an audition to the ten-year-old violinist. The conductor, immediately convinced, engaged him to appear with the Lamoureux Orchestra on February 6, 1927, playing Lalo's *Symphonie Espagnole* and, a week later, Tchaikovsky's violin concerto. Writing to Dr. Langer, Yehudi said:

Yesterday I played the Tchaikovsky's concerto with the Lamoureux Symphony. The funniest thing happened on the third page, the E string broke. Lukily the violinist next to the Concertmaster happened to have the string with him and it was changed quikly. But for the rest of the movement I had to play on an 'out-of-tune' violin. However, I did my best. At the end of the Concert, Monsieur Paray the conductor of the Symphony, in the name of the whole orchestra, presented me with a magnificent copper plate, all carved out so it assumed the shape of a beautiful woman, sitting on a rock and playing the flute and on the side is a flower wreath of flowers. It is the most exquisite piece of art I have ever seen. This copper plate is framed in a beautiful square frame of wood on the back of which is a rectangular piece of gold on which is engraved:

à

Yehudi Menuhin
en-souvenir de son
premier concert à Paris
Février 6ème, 1927
L'orchestre Lamoureux

Of course it is prettier handwriting than this. This last concert that I heard was exceptionally beautiful. It played the Mozart's Symphony exquisitely. Of course, each one (of the musicians) is an artist, but what can a hungry artist do? The highest salary of a musician in Paris is $320.00 a year! Others get $100.00 a year. It is terrible! Their are fine violinists, and probably if they would be in America they would be better than any of our orchestras. 1926 was considered a fine year for the orchestra, it had 100 francs in the treasury, $3.30, which they gave to Mr. Paray, the conductor. He is a wonderful man. He won the highest honor of Europe, the medal of Rome. With one rehearsal he knew every little point that I did in the Tchaikovsky. He is an amiable man, a dear fellow, adorned with the qualities of youth.

The "dear fellow" presented his soloist with a photograph of himself, on which he inscribed:

Pour Yehudi Menuhin à qui je dois une des plus pures émotions de ma vie [to whom I owe one of the purest emotions of my life], *Paris, Février, 1927.*

The reaction of the audience and the magnificent press made Yehudi a celebrity overnight, showered with offers for appearances. But all offers were declined, as Yehudi was soon to devote his entire time to studies with Georges Enesco.

Grandson of a Greek Orthodox priest and son of a small landowner, Georges Enesco manifested his musical gifts at an unusually early age. "I am five in one in the world of music," he enjoyed saying in jest, "composer, conductor, violinist, pianist, and teacher. I value the gift of writing music most, and no mortal can possess a higher blessing. Every composer, it seems to me, experiences upon the completion of each new work an exaltation akin to Haydn's, who, upon attending the first performance of his *Creation,* fell to his knees with a cry of joy: 'God did it, not I!'"

In his childhood, Enesco absorbed the oriental strains of Rumanian music and Gypsy songs. As a boy of seven, he was enrolled at the Vienna Conservatory, from which he graduated at eleven with the highest honors. At the age of fourteen he was the youngest violinist of the Vienna Philharmonic at the great Opera House, then under the majestic leadership of Gustav Mahler, who had raised the symphonic and operatic life of the city to heights hitherto unknown. Enesco's most unforgettable experience during that period was a performance of a Brahms symphony conducted by the composer himself.

All through his formative years as a musician he remained in the Austrian capital, which had already drawn to itself Haydn, Mozart, Beethoven, Brahms, Schubert, and a host of lesser composers. Vienna's greatness lay in the fusion it had achieved of the disciplined yet restless and soul-searching

North with the impulsive, melodic South. To Enesco, the city represented also the fusion of East and West. He had brought with him the untamed, almost barbaric Eastern music, which, in Vienna, he learned to mold into the traditions and forms of Western art.

From the Austrian capital, Enesco moved on to Paris, which became his second home, then the center of a school all its own, represented by the music of such illustrious exponents as Martin Marsick, Eugène Ysaye, Henri Vieuxtemps, César Franck, Gabriel Fauré, André Gédalge, and Jules Massenet, with the last three of whom Enesco studied composition. He achieved world fame with his *Rumanian Rhapsodies*, which, followed by other compositions, gained him recognition as founder of the first Rumanian school of music as well as its leading exponent.

When still a young man, Enesco came under the spell of the beautiful wife of Prince Cantacuzene. The whole of Rumania, including the Prince himself, followed the turbulent course of their romance with touching benevolence. This lovers' tangle was untied with the passing away of the Prince many years later, and in fulfillment of their destinies, Enesco and the Princess were married.

This was the man whom Yehudi had chosen as his teacher, and who became, in Menuhin's own words, "the greatest single factor in my musical growth and development. The radiance he emanated, his deep humanity, integrity and tolerance—it all came out in the music he made, and in his teaching. I loved to watch his face, the most beautiful and expressive I have ever known, reflecting the mood of the music we were playing, quietly lyrical or alive with ecstasy and suffering, and always retaining its characteristic gentle manliness."

The lessons, begun late February, 1927, took place in Enesco's apartment on the Rue de Clichy. Busy with her two girls and with keeping house on the Rue de Sèvres, Marutha now let Moshe take over the full responsibility for Yehudi's musical activities. During the lessons, Moshe sat in a corner, ostensibly puzzling out his own problems in a small, thick

notebook, but in reality faithfully recording the remarks made
by the master. The session over, father and son would go to
a nearby *bistro* where Moshe would order coffee for himself
and mineral water for Yehudi, then go over with him the nota-
tions he had made, directing the boy to copy them into his
score. Yehudi always complied, although he had no difficulty
in remembering the essence of his teacher's remarks during
those days or, indeed, for many years to come.

Every now and then, on Enesco's suggestion, the lessons
took place at his country place in Bellevue. Yehudi cherishes
the memory of those rides on the suburban train, the view of
the Seine, the fields and woods beyond it, the sun, the fragrance, the green and brown of the damp earth. His study of
César Franck's sonata dedicated to Ysaye happened to coincide
with two or three consecutive visits to Bellevue, and to this
day the visions and smells of that countryside come back
whenever Menuhin plays the piece.

There was nothing formal about his lessons with Enesco,
nor was there any homework or exercises. Enesco repeatedly
stated that there was nothing he could teach Yehudi about
violin playing as a craft, that he could only play music with
him and talk to him as musician to musician rather than as
teacher to student. "Real art comes from the inside, not the
outside," he would say. The one idea Enesco never tired of
impressing upon Yehudi was that the performer was at all
times the servant of music; that no great composition was ever
written merely as a vehicle for the virtuoso; that greatness lay
in giving true expression to the intent and purposes of the
composer. Enesco helped the boy to make a new and enrich-
ing friend of each composition they studied, seeking with him
the right approach to the particular style of each work.

"At home in all schools, Enesco was sensitive to the need of
an appropriate style for each composition," relates Menuhin.
"He rarely indulged in theorizing about music, directing my
attention instead to the passage or phrase at hand. He invariably found the right word, image, or symbol to help me
understand. In driving a point home, he frequently referred to

the life of the composer, urging me to read books about him and his works. In criticizing me and correcting my faults, Enesco never caused pain or humiliation, remaining at all times urbane and friendly, however harsh the import of his criticism. He united in his person the primeval forces of nature along with a most exquisite sense of style, the melodic single-mindedness of folk songs, and the most refined traditions of the great masters. No matter how rarefied the music he played, it became in his hands earthy, full of vitality and vigor. This quality in Enesco seemed to answer my inner needs, and bound me to him."

Teacher and pupil enjoyed playing sonatas and concertos, with Enesco playing the piano accompaniment. A concerto, Enesco impressed upon the boy, is a *symphonic* composition wherein the orchestra and the solo instrument are intertwined as an organic unit. Enesco's first words as he began working with Yehudi on the Beethoven concerto were: "This is a great symphony. The violin has a leading voice, but it is merely one of the many orchestral voices which make up the whole."

To the boy's delight, his teacher had a way of bringing the orchestration to life by imitating the various instruments on the piano and with his own voice. He sang, groaned, thundered, whistled, and trilled, always in perfect pitch and rhythm. Yehudi thus learned to immerse himself in the progress of a concerto from the moment the first strains sounded. Many years later he came across a passage in the autobiography of the late Albert Spalding describing the thoughts that passed through his mind as he was listening to the long orchestral introduction of the Beethoven concerto. At first Spalding contemplated the strings sagging in the heat of the crowded hall. "You think, too, of many less relevant things: a neglected telegram, a needed haircut; a pair of tickets you forgot to leave at the box office for a friend; the man in the third row staring at you fiercely as though you were about to do him a personal injury; and the woman next to him, whose hair is as tautly stretched as fiddle strings; students in front rows who, taking their Beethoven seriously, are armed with pocket scores."

Having read this passage, Menuhin remarked in a tone almost conveying regret: "Even if I tried, I could not think of so many different things while listening to a *tutti*. I begin playing the work from the moment the conductor raises his baton."

Menuhin's absorption in the *tutti* has caused some reviewers to suspect him of striving for effect, but nothing could be further from the truth. On one occasion when he was playing the Beethoven with the Boston Symphony Orchestra under Serge Koussevitzky, his concentration on the music brought him perilously close to missing his cue. The second *tutti* was rendered so exquisitely that he became lost in the music, hypnotized by it to the point of a trance as though he had no part in the performance. Only his lifelong conditioning as a concert artist enabled him to wake up at the last possible moment and make his entrance.

Under Enesco's guidance, Yehudi discovered new musical worlds, proceeding apace from Bach to Beethoven, to Brahms, Mozart, Schumann, Franck, and Chausson. Carried away by his journey among titans, Yehudi felt little inclination and found no time to follow Ysaye's injunction regarding scales and arpeggios, although the thought did come to him from time to time. Enesco did not altogether neglect technical problems, arousing among other things Yehudi's interest in Paganini's intricate Caprices, particularly the second, fourth, and sixth. He also imparted on the wing, as it were, certain technical information and various devices of the complex skill of violin playing. A born violinist, if ever there was one, Enesco played the instrument as a bird would sing, with the facility and instinct of a true son of the land of Gypsy fiddlers. He was, therefore, able to impart to Yehudi a natural way of handling the instrument, of producing multicolored sound effects, and of imitating the human voice in its breathing, its vibrato, and its portamento (the connecting of the notes by raising or lowering the pitch between them, as in a human voice, in contrast to a mechanical instrument). In his impressionable boyish enthusiasm, Yehudi tended to be more of a gypsy than Enesco

thought advisable, provoking sharp comment on the improvisational quality of his fingerings and bowings, which the boy
varied with practically each rendering of a work. A performing artist, Enesco repeatedly stressed, must adhere, after
sufficient search and experimentation, to one definite way, at
least for the purposes of the concert stage.

Trills were a frequent subject of discussion. "You must have
noticed," Enesco would say, "that whole-tone violin trills often
sound out of tune: they sound too low, even though in testing
the notes you will actually find them in tune. The reason for
this striking discrepancy is that the faster the trill, the less is
the finger able to press the string all the way down at each
strike; the less the string is shortened, the lower the upper note
sounds. Therefore, the faster the trill at which one aims, the
higher one must hit the upper note."

The vibrato depended on the mood of the performer no less
than on the style of the work being performed, he stressed,
comparing the vibrato with the human voice. Like the voice,
the vibrato must vary in width and speed in order to express
the full range of moods and emotions. "There is, Yehudi, the
vibrato of amiable conversation, the vibrato of passion, the
vibrato of exasperation—you must master them all, for you will
need them all."

Once the lesson was interrupted by Maurice Ravel, who
dashed into the room in a state of great excitement. Barely
waiting to get through the formalities of introduction to Moshe
and Yehudi, the composer presented his problem: he had just
finished a sonata for piano and violin which had to be played
that same evening for his publishers. Would Enesco do it
with him? He knew of no other violinist who could master
the complicated score on so short a notice.

Apologizing to Moshe and Yehudi for the interruption,
Enesco played through the sonata with Ravel, stopping here
and there to clear up a difficult passage. As they were about
to go over it for the second time, Enesco set the score aside
and did the entire complex work from memory, without stopping once. Ravel could not contain his astonishment, but

Yehudi was not at all surprised. He had known about his teacher's phenomenal memory and had written about it to Dr. Langer in San Francisco on April 14, 1927:

This week Mr. Enesco gave me four lessons and to-morrow he will give me another. He is a wonderful man. He is a beautiful violinist and a fine pianist, as well as a great composer. I love him, and I hope to have him for a long time. He plays everything by heart, even my accompaniments. When he was fifteen years old, Queen Marie of Rumania gave him a present of the Urtext edition of Bach. The complete set has sixty volumes but Enesco counted only fifty-eight in his, but he did not say anything about it to the Queen. He knows all fifty-eight volumes by heart. He is the pride of Rumania. When he was about seventeen years old and was in need of a good violin, there was a national subscription which paid for half the price of the violin, and he paid the rest by installments. Rumania has good reasons to be proud of him.

While Yehudi thus reveled in his work with Enesco, his little sisters were not neglected. Moshe one day descended upon Marcel Ciampi, one of France's outstanding concert pianists and a professor at the Paris Conservatory, leading a child by each hand. Both girls were bursting with charm, despite their plumpness and odd clothes, but Ciampi was irritated by this invasion of his privacy and was not in the least mollified by Moshe's proud announcement that his boy was studying with Enesco and that his eldest daughter—seven—was already a veteran of three years' standing with San Francisco's Judith Blockley and Lev Shorr. Saying that he did not instruct little children, Ciampi suggested that one of his pupils might undertake the task. Meanwhile, nothing daunted, Moshe had plumped Hephzibah down upon the piano stool, and she, not a whit disturbed by the ungracious welcome, plunged into Weber's *Rondo Brilliante*. Ciampi stopped in midsentence. Those firm, confident sounds, the amazing precision, and the grand style of the Hephzibah to come were already apparent, and there was nothing to do but capitulate. But, no sooner was the battle won, than Moshe launched a new attack, saying, as he pointed at Yaltah:

"You'll have to take her on, too."

"But she is a mere infant!" Ciampi protested in horror.

The said infant, all of five years old, was already at the piano, thumping her way determinedly through Schumann's *Kinderszenen,* which she had picked up by watching Hephzibah practice.

Routed, Ciampi muttered to himself:

"Mrs. Menuhin's womb is a veritable *conservatoire.*"

From that day on, Marutha established a schedule which subjected all three children, more or less, to the same routine. They rose at 7:30, were finished with their breakfast by 8:30, studied and practiced until lunch, which was served at twelve sharp, took walks or played out of doors for three hours. From half past three on, the children studied or read for two hours, Yehudi doing some practice as well, then played about for an hour or so, and had supper. The girls were put to bed at 7:30, Yehudi a half hour later.

With the problem of their children's musical studies successfully resolved and the sense of not belonging on the wane, Moshe and Marutha now found it easier to decide that he should resign from his job in San Francisco and remain with his family in Europe. Thus began a new phase in the life of the Menuhins, so that their California friends who on occasion arrived on visits to Paris found them well settled, contented, and hard at work. These visits provided a welcome change in the daily routine which the children embraced with a spontaneous eagerness. One visit particularly is remembered by them with great affection, that of Mrs. Koshland, a well-known patroness of artists and musicians in San Francisco. She introduced them to George Dennison and Frank Ingerson, distinguished Californian artists and master craftsmen who had been commissioned by her to construct and decorate an ark for San Francisco's Temple Emmanu-El in perpetuation of her late husband's memory.

It was hard for the children to follow the artists as they were telling about research into the religious Hebrew symbols which were to ornament the ark, but they were fascinated by the stories that followed about "Cathedral Oaks," the estate and workshop of "the boys," as the two artists were affectionately known to their friends, in the Santa Cruz Mountains near San Francisco. Deer came down every evening, they said, the unspoiled mountains were full of wildlife, and in the spring the valley was one sweep of fruit blossom. Yehudi had explored the region during the family excursions to Holy City and Santa Cruz, and he exclaimed with boyish impetuousness that he'd give anything to live in those mountains. "The boys" gravely assured him that they'd be on the lookout for just the right spot for him, at which everyone laughed, little suspecting how important a part this chance conversation was to play in the life of the Menuhins.

The Sunday following, the whole party went to the Louvre at the invitation of the artists. George's diary records that the boy asked to be shown the Mona Lisa, about which he had heard so much. "Yehudi was very serious, almost grave, as he looked at the painting from all angles. He took a step or two back, to look at it from a distance, and asked me to stand on his right, and Frank on his left.

" 'Does she look at you, Mr. Ingerson?' he asked.

" 'Yes, she does.'

" 'Does she look at you, Mr. Dennison?'

" 'Yes, she does.'

" 'She looks at me, too, and she is beautiful and mystifying. If we could only understand how Leonardo da Vinci did what we see there, we would know the secret of creation.' "

During the rest of the artists' stay in Paris, the children saw a great deal of "Uncle Frank and Uncle George" and felt quite sad when their work eventually took them to England. Soon thereafter, the Menuhins themselves were preparing to leave Paris, as Enesco persuaded Moshe and Marutha to join him with their children in Sinaia where he was planning to spend the summer at Villa Luminish.

The Orient Express was passing through Munich, Salzburg, Vienna, and Budapest, but the Menuhin children got no closer view of those unique cities than the one seen by pressing their noses against the window panes. Looking out of the train, Yehudi did at least perceive a gradual change in climate, architecture, and the clothes the people wore. He watched the sun grow brighter and hotter with every day, the blackness of earth richer, the colors of vegetation and dress more intense. Yehudi recalls a strange sense of familiarity, almost as though he were revisiting the East, which in reality he knew only from books and the music he had absorbed from Enesco.

Marutha did not permit the two-day train ride to interfere with the measured routine of her family. While Yehudi practiced in one *wagon-lit* compartment, Marutha gave French lessons to Hephzibah and Yaltah in another and Moshe was attending to his mail and reading newspapers in still a third. The violin practice over, Yehudi studied languages with his mother while Aba taught arithmetic to the little girls and told them stories; then, as Marutha and the girls rested, he discussed history and foreign affairs with Yehudi. Twice during the day, the children were told to run up and down the corridor of their car until they had exercised roughly to the extent of their daily walks. During the infrequent train stops, Moshe paraded them on the platform, urging them to breathe in deeply, to lose not a single precious moment of being in the fresh air. As the small Menuhins trotted up and down the platform, the other passengers watched with curiosity and delight the blue-eyed, yellow-haired trio: a protective Yehudi leading on either hand a small, self-conscious sister clad in awkward peasant dress and long homespun stockings.

From the very day of their arrival, the whole family felt at home in Sinaia, Rumania's summer capital and fashionable resort in the shadow of the Carpathian Alps. Practically every villa had its own fruit orchard and a garden, while all around the small town lay a world of rich black soil, primitive woods, and wild mountains, of countless sheep on high pastures, and of shepherds who played on their plaintive flutes the airs

Yehudi had heard from Enesco, the ancient tunes of the
Rumanian peasants.

The exploration of Sinaia and the countryside was an adventure to which the children looked forward every day. There
was the market place, an almost oriental bazaar, where peasants sold meat, vegetables, fruits, and berries while vendors
peddled crude tools, toys, and embroidery which followed the
patterns of age-old folk designs. There was the monastery of
Sinaia with its sweeping colonnades, masses of flowers, and the
somber, black-hatted, black-bearded monks. Most exciting of
all, tucked away in the hillside above the monastery was the
royal castle of Peles. Yehudi well remembers the first time he
was taken to the castle, on a visitors' day. He walked with his
family past the monastery until they came upon a well-tended
park carved out of medieval forests. In the distance, as if it
had just stepped out of a fairy tale, loomed the castle, its
countless gables rising against the backdrop of high summer
pastures, craggy peaks, and wild woodlands. Inside, Yehudi
knew, lived the beautiful, generous Queen Marie, who had befriended Enesco, and with her lived her grandson, the boy
king Michael, whose portrait was displayed everywhere in the
town below. As the Menuhins walked through the grounds
they were overtaken by a boy riding in a small carriage drawn
by two white ponies. To their excitement, they recognized the
boy king passing them at a rapid pace, supremely confident
that he would be given the right of way. Yehudi watched
Michael disappear beyond a bend in the road and was seized
by a sudden impulse to pick up a stone and throw it in the
wake of the carriage.

"I don't remember clearly," he said, "what had awakened
the impulse in me. It may have been a resentment at the
unconscious haughtiness of the boy. It may have been a childish envy that he had the run of the palace, a stableful of
ponies, toys, and servants. Just before he had trotted by, I was
immersed in a dream world in which everything was possible,
and I must have hated the boy king for bringing me down to
earth. Later on we were shown the throne room where he

alone had the right to be seated. I ran up to the throne and planted myself on it. An outraged guard ordered me to climb down, and Aba was rushing up to get me, his face pale with fright. I stepped off the throne and we continued our tour. I was ashamed of my resentment and envy and spoke about it only to Hephzibah, with whom I was then beginning to share my thoughts."

A few days later a letter came from Queen Marie, inviting Yehudi to play at the royal castle. The parents' refusal was polite but firm. A performance at the court, the Menuhins wrote, would give the boy too much notice and tend to make him self-conscious. But they raised no objections when a few days later Enesco informed them that Queen Marie had accepted his invitation to sit in Princess Cantacuzene's room at Villa Luminish while Yehudi was having his lesson on the floor above, the door of the studio left ajar. The session over, Enesco presented the boy and his father to the Queen. Yehudi knew that the right thing to do was to kiss her hand, but he would not any more than did his father. Instead, he put out his hand, which the Queen shook in the forthright way in which it was offered. Enesco said with a smile:

"This is probably the first time, Yehudi, that you have met a real queen."

"Oh, no," Yehudi protested, "in America every woman is a queen."

"Yes, I know," said Queen Marie laughingly, "I've recently returned from a visit to your country." And she proceeded to speak to Yehudi about the sights she had seen in the United States, speaking in a way so natural and simple that the boy was completely disarmed. On leaving the villa, she gave him a copy of her book, *Queen Marie's Fairytales,* in which she wrote: "To Yehudi from Marie."

During that faraway summer in Sinaia, the Menuhins lived at a pension famed for its diversified cuisine, but for some strange reason Marutha decided that no meat was safe in

Rumania except chicken. Orders were given accordingly, affording Yehudi an opportunity to learn the anatomy of a chicken so thoroughly that by the end of the summer he was able to carve one with his eyes closed and for months there-after could not bear the sight of a chicken, alive or dead. Apart from this dietary misfortune, the stay in Sinaia was marked by a happiness and a contentment he had not known since the time of his visits to the Kavin farm at Petaluma.

In Sinaia the Menuhins met Konrad Bercovici, well-known to the readers of popular magazines in the U.S.A. for his tales of Gypsy life. One night, in response to Yehudi's pleas, the writer took him and his parents to an open-air tavern where a Gypsy fiddler and his companions were entertaining the pa-trons under the huge stars of a clear summer night. Yehudi was amazed that the Gypsies could play at all on their crude homemade instruments, especially the fiddlers, whose bows were but ordinary bent sticks strung with unbleached horse-hair. Yet the music they produced held a poignant, searching quality, and the boy could hardly believe his ears as he lis-tened to the full-throated melodies and the incredible, almost lifelike imitations of animal and bird calls. Before leaving, Yehudi persuaded his father to arrange with the Gypsies that they come to the pension, where they played until they had exhausted their entire repertoire. Then he played, choosing the *Devil's Trill Sonata* by Tartini, which, of all the pieces he knew, seemed nearest to the mood the Gypsy music had evoked in him. Now it was their turn to listen in fascination and delight. In an impulsive farewell gesture, Yehudi pre-sented one of his Sartory bows to the leader of the group, who responded by supplying the boy with baskets of wild straw-berries for the remainder of his stay in Sinaia.

This happy stay was soon nearing its end, all the Menuhins healthier, filled with the exhilaration born of the sharp tang of mountain air and the long walks in the pinewoods. The boy was probably the happiest of all, for his nightmares had dis-appeared and he slept well. He had also lost his fear of the dark, feeling nothing but peace and contentment as, lying in

his bed at night, he watched through the window the stars of
the vast Rumanian sky. Like his sisters, he had made great
strides in music and in French, a language in which every
evening the trio acted Yehudi's own condensed versions of one
or another of Molière's plays. Little Yaltah held her ground
with the two older children even if her efforts were somewhat
unorthodox; what she lacked in accuracy she more than made
up for with histrionic improvisations which both exasperated
and delighted Yehudi and Hephzibah.

No concerts had been contemplated for him in the near
future despite the continued pressure on the part of French
impresarios, but when an invitation came for Yehudi to appear
in Carnegie Hall with the New York Symphony Orchestra and
the famous German conductor Fritz Busch, Moshe wavered.
Reassured by Enesco that the boy was ready, he accepted the
invitation, suggesting on Yehudi's insistence that the program
include the Beethoven concerto instead of the Mozart, as
planned by Busch.

Yehudi was ready, indeed. In addition to the works mastered under Persinger's tutelage, he was now prepared to perform the Beethoven and the Brahms, as well as Mozart's
Seventh Concerto in D major, César Franck's and Tartini's
sonatas, Chausson's *Poème,* and Corelli's *La Folia.* He also
learned the *Chaconne* from the Bach *Partita in D minor.*

During those last days at Sinaia, Yehudi's concentration on
the *Chaconne* turned the gentle, affectionate boy into a
stranger to his own family and at the same time forged an
insoluble bond between him and his master, Georges Enesco.

SIX

Carnegie Hall

The clouds had completely cleared by the time Yehudi and Moshe were driving back to Sinaia after the farewell lesson with Enesco, when the boy had played the *Chaconne* to the accompaniment of the thunderstorm. A blanket of newly fallen snow was glistening on the mountain ridges, making them seem strange and distant, not unlike a familiar friend appearing in unaccustomed attire. The cleared sky also looked new, as the setting sun flooded the horizon with hues of rose and crimson while the clop-clop of horses' hoofs resounded in the still air.

Moshe was the first to speak. "Do you realize, Yehudi, that tomorrow we are off to New York?"

"Yes, Aba, and without the master," Yehudi said quietly. A moment later his face lit up and he jumped in his seat:

"Aba, I'd almost forgotten! I am going to play the Beethoven at last!"

Trying to sound casual, Moshe said:

"Are you sure you'd rather play the Beethoven? Everybody in New York insists on Mozart."

"But I've been waiting for the Beethoven so long! I feel I can do it, and Mr. Enesco says I can, too. I'll play the Mozart as an encore, but I must do the Beethoven first. Please make them let me! Aba, please!"

Still under the spell of the afternoon at Villa Luminish, Moshe replied, "I'll do my best, Yehudi. Today I can refuse you nothing."

"Why today? I've been working on the Beethoven for so long."

Moshe appeared not to have heard. In his pocket were two cables which he kept from Yehudi. One, signed by George Engels, manager of the New York Symphony Orchestra, stated that Fritz Busch refused even to consider the Beethoven, insisting on the original suggestion of the A-major Mozart. The conductor's one reply to all arguments was: *"Man lässt ja auch Jackie Coogan nicht den Hamlet spielen!* [One does not allow Jackie Coogan to play Hamlet!]." The second cable, from Mrs. Garbat, was no less discouraging, warning Menuhin that the New York music critics were extremely antagonistic towards Yehudi, regarding his intention to play Beethoven as nothing short of sacrilege.

After having put the children to bed that night, Moshe and Marutha considered the grave problem which the two cables had created. Marutha said little, but Moshe, torn between his promise to Yehudi and a very real fear of pitting his own instinct against the New York current, held forth at great length. Marutha stopped him at last and spoke for them both when she said that Yehudi would play the Beethoven, come what may.

The next day the Menuhins were speeding on the Orient Express bound for Paris. The same strict routine of study and exercise that was observed on the train to Sinaia was also maintained now, and again on the *Rochambeau,* which carried them to New York. Soon after arrival, Yehudi's managers, Evans and Salter, arranged a meeting between him and Fritz Busch in the presence of the elder Menuhin, George Engels, and Walter Damrosch, permanent conductor of the New York Symphony Orchestra. The room was crowded with photographers, and Yehudi, whose first taste this was of the commercial side of concert giving, was somewhat taken aback by their noisy and good-natured lack of ceremony. "Smile, Yehudi!" they shouted. "Wonderful! Hold it, kid!!" "Now, one shot in playing position!" "Mr. Busch, please, your arm on the boy's shoulder!" "Smile at each other!" "Hold it! Hold it!"

Yehudi quickly adapted himself to the situation, posing

without any show of excitement or self-consciousness, but the tall, dignified Busch, who hardly spoke any English, was impatient, betraying by his whole bearing that he found the scene lacking in taste and irreverent toward the art he served. He displayed also a studied coldness toward his young soloist, provoked by Yehudi's blasphemous insistence on playing the Beethoven concerto. True, he liked the looks of the boy: "A healthy, sturdy lad," he wrote later in his autobiography, "with a fine sense of humor and with beautiful eyes, very calm and measured in his movements." But he happened to dislike all prodigies, even when they had personal charm. Busch and his brother Adolph, the violinist and composer, had been prodigies themselves and had sweated away their childhood, so that ever since the conductor actually shuddered at the sight of a *Wunderkind* in his inevitable kneepants. Moreover, at that concert Busch was giving the world *première* of a new work by his brother, and he would never forgive himself if this small boy ruined the evening. Only out of respect for Damrosch, who had heard Yehudi play at the Manhattan Opera House, did Busch agree to give Yehudi an audition, so that when the boy asked if he would please let him play the Beethoven the conductor replied sternly:

"Come to my hotel and play it for me; then we will see," and, nodding curtly, took his leave of the company. In the embarrassed silence that followed, Damrosch led the boy aside:

"Tell me, Yehudi, have you ever heard of Jackie Coogan?"

"I've seen him in *The Kid.*"

"Do you think that he could play Hamlet?"

"No, I can't imagine Jackie Coogan as Hamlet."

"Now, Yehudi, you probably realize that Beethoven is to music what Shakespeare is to the stage. What is it, then, that makes you think you can play his concerto?"

"I don't know, I've never thought about it. I just play. Maybe to speak on the stage one needs more than instinct."

Damrosch looked long and thoughtfully at Yehudi.

"It might interest you to know," he said slowly, "that the poet Robert Browning sees it the same way. He wrote: 'The

others may reason and welcome, 'tis we musicians know.'"
And, after a pause: "One thing more, Yehudi. I've heard you
play, and I really do not object to your trying the Beethoven,
but it is a very difficult work, and a great many people in the
audience are well acquainted with it. If you don't do it justice
it will hurt you in your career."

"But I don't care about a career. I just want to have some
fun playing with the orchestra."

Two days later Yehudi called on Busch at the Gotham Hotel
in the company of his father and Persinger, who had come to
New York to resume lessons with his pupil. Yehudi was wearing a thick, light brown overcoat that made him look shorter
and fatter than he actually was, and Busch looked on mockingly as the boy disengaged himself from the coat, emerging in
flannel pants that ended well above the knee. Persinger made
a start towards the piano, but Busch sat down at the instrument himself. Calm and purposeful, Yehudi lifted the lid of
his brown case, laid back the green velvet shield, and handed
the violin to his teacher to be tuned. Busch smiled sarcastically
and was about to say something but, instead, plunged into the
final part of the orchestral introduction. The moment had
arrived at last. Yehudi adjusted his instrument, raised the bow,
and released the first measures with their broken octaves so
feared by violinists.

"Yehudi played so gloriously and with such complete mastery that by the second *tutti* I was already won over," wrote
Busch in his memoirs. "That was perfection."

As the boy played on, the conductor signaled to Persinger
to replace him at the piano and retired to a corner, his whole
bearing betraying excitement and unbelief. Suddenly, no
longer able to restrain himself, he interrupted the music and
threw his huge arms around Yehudi.

"You can play anything with me, anytime, anywhere!" he
cried.

To Moshe's consternation, Yehudi impatiently disentangled
himself from Busch and continued to play. When, in the slow
movement, he made a somewhat hasty entrance, Busch stopped

him, saying in his awkward English, further crippled by excitement:

"*Ach, nicht so, mein lieber Knabe!* You must count the eighths like this, *nicht?* One, two, five, four, three, *nicht?*"

Yehudi laughed delightedly and cried in his boyish soprano:

"*Nicht, nicht!* You must count like this: one, two, three, four, five, *nicht?*" and resumed the music.

Busch kept him for more than an hour, going over a passage here and there and pointing out the pauses, which are so significant in Beethoven, the phrases which should be played in the same tempo as the preceding ones, and those which should be accelerated or retarded. Later, at Yehudi's first rehearsal with the orchestra, even the completely conquered Busch was amazed to find that the boy had not overlooked a single point.

The audition over, Yehudi carefully wiped his violin and was about to place it in the case when he suddenly announced:

"I can play the Brahms concerto, too."

"Impossible!" Busch's voice was incredulous. "How can your small hand stretch the tenths?"

"You mean this?"

And Yehudi executed with ease the bars to which the conductor referred, precipitating another outburst of affectionate amazement. Moshe, whose emotions during the session had gone from anxiety through relief to happy confidence, now left his corner. Directing Yehudi to pack the violin, so as to get him out of earshot, he lectured Busch in a whisper:

"You will spoil him with your praise."

"No one can spoil *him!*" roared Busch.

"That's exactly what you are doing! And if you insist on keeping it up, I shan't let him perform with you!"

Astounded, the conductor looked over the head of the disturbed parent at Persinger, and the two exchanged an understanding smile.

"Never again," promised Busch, "I swear!"

When, at the end of the first rehearsal, the orchestra musicians accorded Yehudi a standing ovation, the conductor watched Moshe with a malicious twinkle in his eye. There and then he made a decision which ran contrary to the general usage at the time: he shifted the soloist and the concerto to the concluding half of the program, frankly admitting in his autobiography: "No orchestra and no conductor could compete with the overpowering effect of this, Yehudi's first appearance. Not a creature in Carnegie Hall would have had ears for any music whatever, after Yehudi had played the last bar of the rondo."

Carnegie Hall was packed to the roof and charged with expectation on the evening of November 25, 1927. Yehudi arrived in the company of his father and Persinger, having deposited Marutha in the Garbat box. On his way from the stage entrance to the artists' room, Yehudi asked the guard, pointing to a large fireman's hatchet hanging on the wall:

"What's that for?"

"To chop the heads off the soloists who don't play well," was the ready answer.

"And how many heads have you already cut off?"

"Oh, quite a few," and he gave Yehudi a friendly wink.

This little dialogue came back to Menuhin when the same guard greeted him upon arrival for a recital commemorating the twenty-fifth anniversary of his first performance in Carnegie Hall. As the two shook hands, the guard pointed to the hatchet: "Quite a few heads have rolled since then."

Fritz Busch was greeted warmly when he appeared on the stage after the intermission, but all eyes were turned to the canvas door on the left as the people waited for the boy whom few had heard but whose name and story had excited their imagination. There was an outburst of applause when he came out, appealingly chubby and awkward in a white silk blouse and black velvet knee pants. Showing no trace of self-consciousness, Yehudi took his place near Busch towering on the podium, acknowledged the applause with a jerky nod of the head and, businesslike, handed his Grancino to be tuned by Mr. Gusikoff, the concertmaster.

There was a breathless silence in the hall when the kettledrum announced the opening of the concerto, followed by the clear, lyrical voice of the woodwinds. Yehudi stood so un-ruffled, so absorbed in the music, seemingly oblivious of his part in the performance, that tension mounted as people began to fear that he would miss his entrance. But with only seconds to spare, he adjusted a thick, black pad which dangled from his violin, placed the instrument under his chin, and raised his bow. The great singing tone that filled the hall caught the audience by surprise. There was a gasp, an exchange of amazed glances, a slight stirring, and then—the hush of com-plete absorption. Forgotten were the curiosity, the unbelief, that had brought so many to the concert, and lost was the awareness of the incongruous difference between the size of the conductor and the soloist. Yehudi seemed to grow in stat-ure along with the serene progress of the concerto until he dwarfed everyone on the stage, simultaneously remaining so reverential to Beethoven that the listeners felt the very soul of the music had been revealed to them.

It was only during the Joachim cadenza, when the soloist remained alone to face its exacting technical and intellectual challenge, that the audience once more became aware of the absurd size of the violinist, and was able to reflect on his pure intonation and sense of rhythm, or marvel at the fingering, the trills, the perfect co-ordination between spirit and muscle. Unable to contain their gratitude and excitement, the listeners burst into applause at the end of the cadenza, threatening to stop the performance, but, supported by Busch and the orches-tra, Yehudi returned them to Beethoven with all the authority and presence of mind of a veteran performer. The pent-up enthusiasm in the hall found release at the end of the move-ment, while the young soloist took advantage of the pause to hand over his instrument for tuning, as indeed he had to do at the end of the second movement as well, for the violin strings kept sagging in the hot, overcrowded hall, and the boy's small hands were still too weak to twist the pegs while holding the instrument in position beneath the chin. The

audience delighted in the natural way in which he handled his
problem, its existence alone betraying the child in him.

There was poetry in Yehudi's slow movement as it flowed,
tender and benign, devoid of all sentimentality, and it remained for the grace and the unforced humor with which
Yehudi executed the finale to complete a performance that
was followed by an unforgettable ovation. Stirred by the
strangeness and wonder of it all, people applauded, shouted,
many with tears in their eyes, while the men in the orchestra
were moved to rise and join in the ovation, without first waiting for a signal from the conductor. Busch generously retired
from the stage, but Yehudi brought him back to share the
acclaim with him. The conductor, nonetheless, disappeared
after two bows, and the boy pointed at the orchestra, inviting
the audience to pay tribute to the musicians, but they sat
down, applauding him and shouting *"Bravo."* With a gesture
he had observed conductors use to bring an orchestra to its
feet, Yehudi directed the musicians to rise, but they resolutely
remained in their seats, cheering him louder still. At this point
Yehudi's extraordinary detachment and aplomb left him and
he suddenly looked like the bewildered small boy he was, in
search of help to still the torrent. Catching sight of Persinger
in the wings, he rushed towards him and, before the teacher
realized what was happening, dragged him to the center of the
stage, laughing, pointing at him and applauding. The audience, still cheering and pressing towards the footlights, decided that the man was the boy's father and shouted: "Bravo,
Papa Menuhin!" Persinger finally managed to disengage himself, and vanished, but still the applause went on, and Yehudi
had to appear on the stage in his overcoat, cap in hand, before
the audience let him go with a final outburst of cheers.

Even the music critics stayed on to applaud the young violinist, completely forgetful of deadlines. Olin Downes, of the
New York *Times,* told me that, loathing the very idea of hearing a mere child play the Beethoven, he had resolved "in my
indignation at the boy's effrontery to stay just for the first
movement, but I simply couldn't tear myself away. I had come

to the hall convinced that a child could play the violin no more effectively than a trained seal, and I left with the conviction that there is no such thing as an infant prodigy, but there is such a thing as a great artist who begins at an early age. I knew, as I sat down to write my review, that I had just listened to such an artist, and yet, when I read the finished story, I tore it up—it was too rhapsodical. I rewrote the article and tore it up again: I had held myself in check all too well; the words were too cold, giving no voice to my reaction, and doing no justice to the extraordinary boy. I then rewrote the review once more and sent it off to the paper, without taking another glance at it."

Reading his own review next morning, Downes came across passage after rhapsodic passage, such as this:

> *Menuhin has a technique that is not only brilliant but finely tempered. It is not a technique of tricks, but one much more solidly established, and governed by innate sensitiveness and taste. It seems ridiculous to say that he showed a mature conception of Beethoven's concerto, but that is the fact. . . . A boy of eleven proved conclusively his right to be ranked with the outstanding interpreters of this music.*

"I was convinced, as I read on," Downes remarked, "that after this I would be the laughingstock of my colleagues, but one glance at what the other critics wrote proved me wrong."

If anything, they were even more lavish with their praise. Lawrence Gilman wrote in the New York *Herald Tribune:*

> *Young Menuhin played yesterday Beethoven's violin concerto with a ripeness and dignity of style, a sensitive beauty of conception, an easeful brilliance of technique, which brought great names involuntarily to the tip of the listener's tongue.*
> *. . . What you hear . . . takes away the breath and leaves you groping helplessly among the mysteries of the human spirit.*

Writing in the New York *Journal,* Irving Weil echoed Mr. Gilman's wonderment:

> *If you had closed your eyes you would immediately have lost the picture of the rather fat little youngster in blouse and knickers and bare knees, with his fiddle to his chin, staunchly bowing away in front of the orchestra. You would have forgotten that those were tiny fingers flying up and down the keyboard. Instead, you would have imagined another ten years and a couple of feet added to what was actually before you. The reality was, in a way, a kind of miracle.*

Samuel Chotzinoff proclaimed in the *World:*

> *It was at once apparent that Yehudi Menuhin was an authentic violinistic genius. . . . From the fingers of this child of eleven the Beethoven concerto flowed in all its nobility, its unbounded repose, its thoughtful, subjective beauty.*

On November 27, Yehudi repeated the Beethoven concerto and the triumph. The only person not elated over this second performance was young Menuhin himself; he wanted to play the Brahms, because to repeat the same program within the brief space of two days was to him merely "a piece of business and no fun at all." But there was "fun" galore on December 12, when he gave his first Carnegie Hall recital, with Persinger at the piano. That night Yehudi played the Bach *Chaconne,* Mozart's *Concerto No. 7 in D major,* Chausson's *Poème,* Tartini's *Devil's Trill* and Wieniawski's *Souvenir de Moscou,* in addition to a number of small virtuoso pieces.

The hall was more tightly packed than ever before in its history, the audience overflowing onto the great stage in numbers sufficient to fill an ordinary-sized auditorium and hardly leaving any room for the two performers. It was an unusual audience, highly informed and critical, including many musicians, chiefly players of string instruments. Skeptical of child prodigies, most of them had ignored the first concert and were unable to get tickets for the second, but now they came to hear Yehudi for themselves. The performance not only dispelled all doubt but moved them to voice their tribute with an abandon the like of which Carnegie Hall had rarely witnessed. The audience rushed to the platform, while those who had seats on the stage mobbed the boy, clapping and shouting, climbing over chairs to touch and hug him. The large bouquet of flowers which Yehudi had received in a pretty box during the intermission was now torn to bits for souvenirs, and energetic efforts had to be made to save him from being stampeded by his ecstatic admirers.

The next morning's papers ran long columns filled with superlatives and dominated by amazement. Edward Cushing, of the Brooklyn *Eagle*, even went so far as to state that "one is inclined to doubt Yehudi's mortality," while Richard Stokes, writing in the New York *Evening World*, found the boy's musical ability "well-nigh supernatural, plunging the hearer into metaphysical speculations as to the theory of reincarnation." This theory, incidentally, was soon to be worked to death in newspaper articles and editorials throughout the country.

Swamped by the deluge of praise was a brief paragraph in the Stokes review sounding a warning, not unlike the one voiced by Ysaye. Observing that Yehudi possessed "the technical armament of a virtuoso," the critic remarked:

> *The method appears to me faulty, in that the violin is permitted to slope down from the shoulder, instead of being flung aloft as in the American system; while the tone is dependent wholly on strength of bowing, instead of partly on the pressure of the fingers of the left hand.*

Unfortunately, as Yehudi was to learn years later, the criticism went unnoticed or ignored. At the moment, certainly, there was not a cloud on the horizon, as recognition seemed universal while impresarios showered upon the Menuhins enticing proposals, offering unprecedented fees and guarantees for more concerts than there were days in the year. All offers, however, were turned down, the jubilant Moshe informed the press, declaring that he had no intention of exploiting the boy's fame and talent, and would return with him and the rest of the family to their own San Francisco. "We are now convinced," he said, speaking for himself and Marutha, "that Yehudi's job in life is to be a musician. If he has a touch of genius—and I am compelled to believe that he has—our task is to surround him with such a sane, helpful atmosphere that his capacities will unfold as plants unfold in a healthy environment."

SEVEN

Fame and Discipline

The Menuhins were now masters of their own fate. Yehudi's triumph in Carnegie Hall and the subsequent deluge of offers relieved the family of financial worry, giving Moshe the awaited opportunity to inform the Ehrmans with gratitude that he no longer required their help. While this financial independence was not yet based on solid security, the proceeds of the three Carnegie Hall performances and of the homecoming recital in San Francisco were more than sufficient to take care of the family until Yehudi's tour of fourteen cities, scheduled to begin early December. Moshe spoke at length to newspapermen about his and Marutha's decision to limit their boy's public appearances to a mere ten or twelve annually, leaving him free to practice, study, and amuse himself as other boys would. Therefore, Moshe announced, he had rejected offers totaling two hundred thousand dollars in 1928 and at least as much for the following year.

The pressures of public attention which usually accompany sudden fame were now plaguing the family in bewildering variety. The Menuhins now had to cope with invitations, gifts, advice, requests, and offers, some incredibly naïve, others brazenly impudent. In a class all to themselves were the parents of would-be Yehudi Menuhins and various species of music-stricken eccentrics, ruthless in their invasion of the family's privacy, yet somehow pathetic. Soon after the concert, the Menuhins were faced one day by a determined lady who insisted that Yehudi play for the little girl she had brought along, so as to inspire her to practice her music the more diligently. On another occasion, a man forced his way into the Menuhin suite, planted himself in a chair, and demanded with staggering aplomb that Yehudi play the *Chaconne* for him there and then. Observing only indignant faces around him, he became so abusive that the frightened Menuhins summoned the help of two husky hotel attendants. This incident taught the innocent Moshe not to allow anyone into the Menuhin rooms without first being announced.

Even the daily walk in the park with the children was no longer the simple exercise it had once been for Moshe, stopped as he frequently was by effusive women eager to express their admiration for Yehudi. On one such outing, a particularly exalted lady insisted upon kissing the father of so phenomenal a boy, provoking, as can be imagined, angry lectures from Moshe on manners and privacy. However, when this romantic episode repeated itself on an occasion when Persinger happened to be with them, Moshe appeared to concede, graciously identifying the horrified teacher as Yehudi's lucky father.

Similar attention and annoyances awaited the family also in San Francisco, where, in addition, many people went out of their way to go past the Menuhin home on Steiner Street in the hope of getting a glimpse of the boy and his sisters. Answering the doorbell one morning, Marutha was informed by a society matron who had come with her little girl and the governess in a chauffeur-driven limousine that she had brought over her child to play with Hephzibah and Yaltah. Coldly telling the lady that the girls were busy practicing, Marutha closed the door.

Newspapers and magazines were constantly pressing for stories and interviews, with reporters finding Marutha and Yehudi inaccessible, though Moshe proved quite alive to the virtues of publicity besides relishing his role as spokesman. He would, as a rule, give the journalists a brief glimpse of Yehudi, then whisk him away, placing himself at their disposal, eager to talk about his son and to air his views on the care and edu-

cation of children. Despite the confidence with which he
oracled, he stated on at least one occasion:

> *. . . the responsibility of bringing up a child is very
> often more than a parent can perfectly fulfill. In the case of
> Yehudi, I believe that I am speaking the truth when I say
> that if I found anyone who could bring him up better than
> I, I would tell that person: 'Take Yehudi and do your best
> for him.'*

As no such person was ever found, Menuhin continued to
shoulder the responsibility, mystified by Yehudi's gift no less
than were the music critics and the general public. On rare
occasions, an outsider managed to speak to Yehudi, always of
course in Moshe's presence, emerging with a portrait of a
simple, healthy boy, dignified and straightforward and endowed with a fine sense of humor. His robustness was the first
thing that drew attention.

> *He stood there on his two muscular legs, a healthy-
> looking boy, more like a young bull than a consumptive
> prodigy!*
> *When one day in London, I asked Georges Enesco, the
> great violinist and composer, what it was like to teach a
> boy like Menuhin, he replied: 'Oh, it is very nice and easy;
> he is so healthy!' I understood exactly what he meant, and
> concluded that that was one of the first principles to work
> on in connection with teaching the violin.[1]*

Similarly noting Yehudi's sturdy physique and good health,
Diana Rice proceded with a pen portrait of the boy:

> [He] *meets a stranger with reserve. He is not embar-
> rassed, just inquiring. He has amazing dignity for one so
> young. He answers questions promptly and laconically. . . .
> His English is formal and slightly old-fashioned, and he
> never slurs the last syllable of a word. . . . Challenged the
> other day about his singing talents, he clasped one hand*

[1]André Mangeot, *Violin Technique*, (London: Dennis Dobson,
Ltd.).

*over his heart and, throwing out the other in a Carusorian
gesture, warbled a short musical ditty. . . . On this afternoon Yehudi was not pleased with his violin trills. He called
them 'nervous' trills, in contrast to 'healthy' trills. He showed
the visitor what he meant by that, playing one measure over
several times to make it come out right.[2]*

Yehudi's onetime teacher at the New York Institute of
Musical Art, Dorothy Crowthers, wrote in *Musical America* in
1928:

> 'Have you heard the story of Vieuxtemps and mood?'
> asked the little violinist. 'He used to smoke a big cigar and
> hold it near the F holes of his violin so that when he played
> the Bach Chaconne he would smell the smoke and think of
> a cathedral.'
> Yehudi's conversation is refreshingly devoid of the per-
> sonal pronoun, I. He does not speak of his art or his concerts
> unless questioned, preferring to discuss such dissimilar
> topics as Wagner and his operas, of which he is eager to
> hear more performances, dogs which he adores, some of the
> new scientific inventions which interest him, and anything
> with an element of humor in it. If one were to present a list
> of the things Yehudi likes best, it would be a delightfully
> heterogeneous mixture such as this: Beethoven, Bach and
> of course Handel, Haydn and Mozart; St. Bernard dogs; icy
> weather; the new Cadillac cars; French pastry; the meas-
> ured tread of knights in Parsifal; San Francisco; ice cream;
> playing ball and climbing rocks!

The elder Menuhins had no experience to fall back upon in
trying to cope with the problems and pressures which Yehudi's
sudden fame had created for them. The big problem was how
to manage his life and career without making him cognizant
of the fact that he was an unusual child. All friends and
would-be friends were scrutinized from this point of view.
Would they be tactful and casual enough? Were they attracted

[2]New York *Times*, January 8, 1928.

by a genuine friendship or by fame? Were they equipped to
make a positive contribution to the development of the children? Marutha assumed the burden of making the decisions.
She had the iron will that enabled her to carry them out, and
the fact remains that, despite her youth and inexperience, she
instinctively chose people of integrity and genuine value. In
spite of the kaleidoscopic developments and changes in Yehudi
Menuhin's life, some of his friends today are men and women
who knew Moshe and Marutha in their early New York and
San Francisco days. And yet, instead of lightening her burden
by sharing her problems with teachers or older friends, she
simply discouraged contacts of any depth or intimacy. Not
even the Ehrmans were permitted to overstep certain undefined but unmistakable bounds. In this way she drew a circle
around the family, knitting it into an ever tighter unit.

With strangers she was alternately haughty and sweet, but
reserved at all times, exerting a restraining influence on her
exuberant husband. Eventually, he too grew to resent the intrusion of the outside world on the privacy of his family. "Our
hardest job is to keep the world out!" became an ever recur-
ring complaint of his in interviews, private conversations, and
letters to friends. The determined battle of the elder Menuhins
against outside intrusion tended to crystallize a process that
had begun much earlier: the parents were becoming more
completely wrapped up in the sheltering and education of
their children within the four walls of the home, while the
children were increasingly cut off from the opportunity of discovering reality outside the family unit. Discussing this dominant aspect of his life, Yehudi said:

"I would compare the modern child with a boiler that has
many outlets, all of them wide open. There is the school with
its many-sided activities and athletic games; there is the rough-
and-tumble of boyhood friendships, rivalries, and fights; there
is the radio, the cinema, the corner drugstore, the naïve and
sacred secrets, the gradual awareness of life. My sisters and I
had none of this. The fire burning under my 'boiler' had no
outlet except for music, and even this within the shell of the

family, for my mother had converted our self-sufficiency into self-isolation. This state of exclusion from the rest of the world was so complete that for many years my sisters and I were not even aware of the possibility of a different mode of existence for us. We knew from books that other people managed their lives in ways that were radically unlike ours, but there was nothing in our experience to provide a basis for self-identification with what was taking place in those books.

"I do not recall consciously resenting our self-isolation, just as I did not resent the discipline in which we were brought up. The reasons for this went beyond my ignorance of other ways of life, or my obedience and passivity. Even as a small boy I had somehow sensed that there was a wide door waiting for me at the end, a passage to the whole world, toward which my parents were leading me in the only way they knew, so that discipline assumed an aspect of self-discipline, precluding any strong desire to rebel. This was true also of Hephzibah, for whom, as for myself, the rigid routine was evolving gradually. But our younger sister, Yaltah, more temperamental and spontaneous than either of us, was immersed in the chilly waters of our routine scarcely before she had emerged from babyhood and, therefore, had a much tougher time of it in her childhood and adolescence."

Having imposed upon their children a routine which controlled every minute of their waking hours, governing their studies and behavior, Moshe and Marutha found themselves its captives as well. Everything was done in the name of the care and education of the children, including the very act of exacting their unquestioning obedience. The parents felt they had a right to it, since they themselves religiously adhered to the principle laid down by Marutha that not a fraction of the children's time nor an iota of their efforts be directed toward performing services for her or for Aba. And this, no matter how small the services nor how eagerly their performance might have been sought by Yehudi or his sisters in a subconscious effort to establish a more normal relationship with their parents on a humbler and more human level. Marutha pushed this principle to such an extreme that she made it impossible for her husband or herself to ask their children even so natural a request as to turn on a light, bring a glass of water, or fetch a book or a newspaper from another room.

She was most demanding toward herself. The youngsters were required to rise at 6:30 every morning, but she was up earlier still. She was on her feet and still working when they were having their afternoon nap, and she went on with her chores long after the children had been put to bed at night. Neither Yehudi nor his sisters remember ever having seen their mother idle or untidy, her iron self-discipline reflected in her proud, unyielding bearing. Small and slender as she was, she had worn a heavily boned corset since early girlhood, and she compelled Hephzibah, as well as Yaltah, to wear one when they reached their early teens.

Moshe had complete charge of Yehudi's career, signed contracts, traveled with him, and was his official spokesman, but it was Marutha who made the decisions upon which her husband acted. Even when away on tour with Yehudi, he reported to her daily and awaited further instructions. She was the single authority, the disciplinarian, the perfectionist who laid down the rules and set the standards. In establishing the principles for the schooling, behavior, and the very *Weltanschauung* of her children, Marutha borrowed from the education she had received, an education limited in the main to the study of languages and classical Russian literature while she was with her mother. To fill what gaps remained, she leaned heavily on the lofty traditions which she claimed for her family. For the rest, she relied on intuition, will power, and fierce pride. In speaking of her family tradition, to outsiders and to her own children as well, Mrs. Menuhin is both eloquent and vague. She might refer to "generations of scholars, writers, and musicians" in her family, or to a long tradition of comfortable living, travel, and creative effort, but when asked for details she withdraws into a silence that hints at mystery and secret knowledge. Even her son's legendary career pales in comparison with her family's past, she has said, because

his is the career of a "traveling fiddler." "I always told
Yehudi," she once wrote, "that he could enjoy his music just as
much at home as on the concert stage. I have told him that in
my tradition our people did not go about the world performing, they stayed in their homes, among their books, with their
music. Yehudi is always a little apologetic to me because of his
career."

Of her father she said: "He was a scholar, a dreamer. A
strange wisdom and innocence were his; he was both wild and
civilized."[3] She has never been more specific even with her
own children—so that to this day they know little of their
mother's background and have been therefore unable to con-
firm or deny the information gathered from newspaper clip-
pings and from old friends of the Menuhins that her father,
originally a well-to-do merchant in the Crimea, emigrated
without his family to the States, where he filled a lowly clerical
position in a Midwestern orthodox Jewish synagogue. In contrast to her reticence in talking about her father, Marutha
often spoke to the children about her mother, describing her
as a paragon of virtue and a fountainhead of wisdom, and as
a rule sanctified her own decisions and actions by quoting her
mother's sayings and maxims and by invoking her name in a
manner suggesting awe and finality. The children learned very
early that, once Marutha announced "my mother did it this
way" or "my mother told me that," a law was being laid down
for them. It was their grandmother's axiomatic wisdom, as
interpreted and formulated by Marutha, that started Yehudi
and his sisters on the study of one language after another,
determined the choice of books they were allowed to read,
allocated three hours a day to outdoor activity, established
the importance of music as a career for men but not for women,
singled out mustard plasters and hot baths as a cure-all, and
caused periodic changes in the family diet, which included
at various times goat milk, kumiss (fermented mare's milk,
for which Marutha substituted cow's milk), and kvass (fermented black-bread cider).

[3]*Woman's Home Companion,* March 1938.

Shortly after Yehudi had reached his tenth birthday, Marutha had a premonition of disaster and cabled her mother only to learn that the old lady had passed away on the very day on which the cable was sent. Marutha was visibly shaken by the news but displayed a degree of self-control which made an indelible impression on her children. She was pale and unsmiling for days, and yet went about her chores as if nothing had happened.

His grandmother's death had a special sad significance for Yehudi. Although she was just an oracle unseen, she represented the only contact of his immediate family with the rest of the world, and now that his grandmother had died he felt forlorn, alone in the big wide world, living in "a family without a family." The little boy mourned the passing away of his grandmother for yet another reason, for he remembered the gift of his first violin. His childish mind rebelled against the thought that his benefactress was no more or that his mother could irretrievably lose someone she revered so deeply, and he was possessed by the idea that one night he would step out of the house and soon return, triumphantly leading his grandmother by the hand. He would recognize her, he was sure, the instant he saw her in the street, for he knew her broad, forceful face from the photograph that hung on a wall in the hallway. He used to stand there, staring at the photograph until he could swear he saw her eyes come to life and give him a wink.

Yehudi's refusal to accept the reality of his grandmother's death was part and parcel of a general protest then awakening in him against all death, unhappiness, and evil. Through his reading and studies with Moshe, who belonged to the old liberal school that admired Eugene Debs and was soon to be heartbroken over the execution of Sacco and Vanzetti, Yehudi was becoming aware of the ills of the world and was suffering its woes. He had dreams of getting up on a soapbox and talking to the people, saying things that could not but blaze a way to universal happiness and goodness. He was certain he could find words big and powerful enough if he could only get away

from home so he could learn to know the world and his fellow
men better. This thought and the rare but fierce fits of resentment against his regimented life actually crystallized at times
into an impulse to run away. He remembers several occasions,
both before and after his first trip to Europe, when he would
rise in the middle of the night, dress, walk all the way to the
front door, the violin case in his hands, only to run back to his
room and lie down in misery and despair.

Throughout that entire period, lasting roughly from his tenth
to his thirteenth year, Yehudi was particularly attached to
Tchaikovsky's *Sérénade Mélancolique,* which he had learned
from a Heifetz record, as he did a few other short pieces
recorded by that great violinist and by Fritz Kreisler, who
was greater still in the eyes of the young Yehudi. Unsurpassed
elegance was the one thing he found the two virtuosi had in
common, possessing it on different levels as it were: Heifetz's
was the elegance of technical perfection which the boy found
easy to emulate, at least to his own satisfaction, while it took
a little growing up before he felt he had captured also the
tenderness and the throb that gave Kreisler's elegance its
sublimely human touch. As Yehudi's mastery grew, the violin
became increasingly part of himself, as only a violin can, for
it alone among the leading concert instruments is capable of
becoming an integral part of the musician in the most literal
sense, growing into an extension of his arms, throat and his
very voice. With the atmosphere inside the family lacking
inducement for uninhibited self-expression, and with all other
outlets shut off, Yehudi's inner life turned to music for release
until it had become more natural for him to make music than
to talk.

"My playing," he recalls, "whether in public or within the
confines of my room, absorbed me so completely that only
after I had grown up did I come to see in music a profession
and a technique as distinct from its being a means of expression. Music was my existence, the means and the end-all. It
still is, to a very large degree."

Yehudi's identification with the music he played probably

accounts for the absence of stage fright in him. Instead, he was in the grip of an emotional tension in anticipation of the effort to rise to the heights demanded by the music. Appearing completely self-possessed, he was, nevertheless, so worked up toward the end of a concert that he was often unable to cease giving encores to his insatiable audiences even after his chubby legs wobbled with exhaustion. In his absorption, he would sometimes fail to recognize people he knew well when they came backstage to congratulate him after a concert.

Moshe and Marutha did everything in their power to prevent Yehudi from becoming conscious of the import of his concerts and of the unique quality of his appeal to an audience and, above all, from equating the meaning of his work with public approval. There was never any talk at home about the number of tickets sold, the acclaim of the crowds, or the praise of the critics. All reviews were withheld from him until his twentieth birthday, although passages containing constructive criticism were read aloud at the breakfast table or at lunch. Moshe was careful not to leave the boy with a whole newspaper in his hands, clipping for him, instead, articles of a political or scientific nature which Yehudi could read in his spare time.

Unlike so many prodigies spoiled by exaggerated attention and leniency because of their talent and earning capacity, Yehudi received no special consideration within the daily life of his family because of his miraculous gift for the violin. Any concert, no matter how decisive in the shaping of his career, was not allowed to be seen by him as a major goal reached but as merely one more step in his work and study. An after-concert presentation to Yehudi of a giant portion of his favorite sweet, ice cream, was the one great concession granted him. The many feature articles written about Menuhin as a boy invariably contain stories describing his addiction to ice cream and ice cream sodas. Among them is the story of Walter Damrosch entering the artists' room to congratulate Yehudi on his performance of the Beethoven concerto. On the heels of the maestro came a friend of the Menuhins, Samuel Cohn, carrying a dish of ice cream which he had promised Yehudi provided the boy played well. Circumventing Damrosch, Yehudi ran up to Cohn, shouting: "So I did play well!"

Menuhin's present manager, Kurt Weinhold, relates a conversation between Yehudi, thirteen, and the celebrated Metropolitan Opera prima donna Elizabeth Rethberg:

"Someone asked her how much she was getting for singing a concert. 'Well, it depends on the size of the hall and the audience,' she replied, then turned to Yehudi: 'And how much do you get for playing to one of your large audiences?' 'An ice cream,' he answered, adding: 'Confidentially, strawberry is my favorite.'"

Yehudi's addiction to ice cream was variously ascribed to a child's normal love of sweets or as an idiosyncrasy of youthful genius, but he himself thinks of it differently:

"An ice cream meant to me something infinitely more than applause—not only because I loved ice cream, which I did, but because an offer of ice cream was to me a symbol of my parents' joint approval. I lived within the bosom of my family, not in the world, and I was acutely conscious of differences between my parents, so that everything they did jointly gladdened me as no ovation ever could. If the performance brought happiness to my mother, the entire family basked in it, especially Aba, who was then in seventh heaven. This gave my ice cream a flavor no manufacturer in the world could imitate."

The Menuhins returned to Steiner Street in January 1928. No longer in need of roomers, they now had the entire house to themselves, converting it into a home, school, and conservatory where the daily routine, conceived and implemented in Paris, now crystallized in its final form. Seven teachers were engaged—including tutors in English, French, and German; Professor Arnold Perstein, of the University of California, to read literature with Yehudi; an instructor of harmony, John Paterson; and two piano teachers for the girls. In addition,

Louis Persinger continued to guide the boy's musical training and to rehearse with him for the forthcoming tour. Marutha was the "principal" and the dietitian of this unique educational establishment, while Moshe was business manager and teacher of history and mathematics.

Yehudi's studies included the reading and critical analysis of nineteenth century and contemporary fiction, exercises in vocabulary building, the writing of compositions, and reading aloud. A list of books for him to read when on tour was compiled by Professor Perstein and discussed by the family at meal hours. Among the books Yehudi read in English during that period were *Huckleberry Finn, Ivanhoe,* the *Odyssey,* H. G. Wells's *Outline of History,* and a collection of Greek mythology. Of his reading in French, Mlle. Godchaux told Dorothy Crowthers: "Yehudi speaks the language with fluency and a pure accent. We have read Molière's *Les Femmes Savantes, Le Misanthrope, Le Malade Imaginaire.* He knows the *Précieuses* thoroughly and can quote lines of some of this great author's comedies. Racine followed, then Corneille, La Bruyère, La Fontaine, and various poems. Also Rostand's *Chantecler* and *Cyrano,* which he adores."[4] Remaining a child at heart, Yehudi preferred *Paul et Virginie,* by Bernardin de Saint-Pierre, a sentimental story of a French boy and his playmate, with whom Yehudi identified himself and Hephzibah.

In 1928 he began to study algebra and geometry and to read with his father newspaper reports on the contemporary scene. He also read the liberal weekly the *Nation,* which had placed him on its 1927 honor roll "for proving that musical genius of the highest quality still lives in this mechanistic age." Among the others similarly honored that year were Edna St. Vincent Millay, Will Rogers, Carl Sandburg, and Deems Taylor.

Rebecca Godchaux often spoke about Yehudi's "deep sympathy with the oppressed and his abhorrence of injustice. We once read a story of the Middle Ages about the cruelty of

---

[4]*Musical America,* Dec. 22, 1928, p. 9.

overlords toward their vassals. 'Happily,' I said to him, 'such things exist no more.' 'Oh, yes, they do!' exclaimed Yehudi. 'They still exist in some parts of Europe.' On another occasion, the boy was sought out by a very great lady but he was averse to meeting her because, said he, 'I heard that she is not kind to people who are dependent upon her.' "[5]

The major part of Yehudi's time and energy continued to be devoted to musical studies and to the expansion of his repertoire. The new works he was prepared to perform by the end of 1928 included two concertos by Vivaldi, two by Mozart, and one each by Vieuxtemps, Wieniawski, Paganini, Joachim, Sinding, Boccherini, Goldmark, Bruch, Glazunov; as well as sonatas by Beethoven (the "Kreutzer") and Brahms (the A and the D-minor), and shorter works by thirty-two other composers.[6]

In addition, Yehudi advanced rapidly in his studies of harmony with John Paterson, who, today a kindly eighty-year-old man, still vividly remembers the violinist as a boy: "He was a wonderful pupil to work with, but sometimes he seemed to be miles away, daydreaming. Irritated, I would stop in mid-sentence and demand: 'Am I talking to you or to the furniture?' He'd look at me earnestly and say: 'But I am listening.' And he'd repeat the idea I was explaining to him, cite the examples I had given and improvise two or three of his own. By the time he was twelve he made his acquaintance with counterpoint and studied accompaniments. The latter had a particular fascination for him ever since his first appearance with the San Francisco Symphony Orchestra, and he knew every instrument, at first by ear and later also by name. In 1928, I remember, Yehudi mastered the *raison d'être* of what we call the transposing instruments, such as the clarinets, trumpets, horns, and their various clefs. He found harmonic analysis unusually easy, so that he was able to catalogue in his mind for future reference any new chord combination he would

[5]*Inquirer-Sun*, Columbus, Ga., October 20, 1929.
[6]For full list see article by Dorothy Crowthers in *Musical America*, December 22, 1928, p. 9.

come across. He likewise knew whether a given theme was harmonized according to church modes or according to stand-ard major or minor modes."

For recreation, Yehudi and his sisters devoted three hours every afternoon and most of Sunday to outdoor activities which now included tennis for the boy. The entire family attended all the afternoon symphony concerts and recitals, while Yehudi was also taken to the major musical events held in the evening. Phonograph records were played at breakfast and during supper, with the luncheon period reserved for table talk, in which eight-year-old Hephzibah excelled, emerging as the family's leading conversationalist. The least respect-ful listener was her younger sister, Yaltah, who rarely missed a chance for an impish remark. On one such occasion, as Hephzibah was at her dramatic best in the midst of unfolding the misfortunes of a poverty-stricken family she had read about, Yaltah chimed in: "I know why they were poor—they spent all their money on concert tickets, and there was no money left for food."

Every now and then, Yaltah would launch a story of her own, improvising as she went on, often getting bogged down under the weight of contradictory details or tripping over the flow of her own words. It was usually Marutha who dammed the flood by a devastating remark or by an impatient glare, but on one occasion, at least, Yehudi remembers interrupting his little sister with a severe admonition: "Yaltah, you don't know the meaning of the word you've just used!"

"But must I never, never use a word, unless I know what it means?"

"Never!" replied Yehudi with all the conviction of a twelve-year-old, and, turning to his parents and Hephzibah, he quoted La Bruyère to the effect that one must never be satis-fied with a word unless it expresses one's thought precisely. "The most wonderful thing La Bruyère discovered was that the right word is usually also the simplest. It's just like fin-gering for the violin—the simpler it is, the more effective. Oh, what fine, easy fingering Enesco used to show me!"

Yehudi missed his Paris teacher with a longing so strong that it eventually produced a crisis in his relationship with Persinger, forcing the boy to take measure of his devotion and loyalty to the two men. Enesco, in his conception, towered above all mortals, but, for as long as they were separated, Yehudi was happy to work with Persinger. This, however, did not prevent the boy from subjecting the latter's patience and understanding to a severe test. With the innocent tactlessness of a child, he sometimes underscored the gap that had come between him and his first teacher under the impact of an influence rooted in a soil different from that which had sustained Persinger's own world of music. Increasingly, teacher and pupil failed to see eye to eye as to emphasis and interpretation.

"But Enesco thought the passage ought to be played this way!" Yehudi would exclaim, oblivious of the pained expression in Persinger's eyes. One day the teacher exploded: "I don't want to hear that name any more!" It was only then that Yehudi understood how unfair he had been. He also became aware of having made his choice. It had to be Enesco—this he felt with his entire being—but in the meantime he resolved never again to hurt Persinger, to whom he owed so much, and with a consistency rare in a boy of his age, avoided every mention of Enesco in his presence. Marutha had witnessed the outburst but kept her silence. As soon as Persinger left, she removed the photographs of Enesco from the walls of the living room, where the studies took place, and transferred them to Yehudi's bedroom.

With the passing of years, Menuhin grew to understand more deeply the difficult, unfair position in which Persinger had been placed. He had begun working with Yehudi when the boy was too young to absorb much of what he had to give him. No sooner, however, did Persinger succeed in widening Yehudi's musical horizon and imparting to him considerable violinistic skills than the boy was transferred to Enesco, ready to receive and to grow.

Upon their return to Steiner Street, the Menuhins had found a brand-new Buick waiting for them in their garage, a gift from the Ehrmans. The weekend trips into the countryside were resumed amid much rejoicing and, anxious to renew their acquaintance with "the boys," the two artists with whom the children had got on so well in Paris, the Menuhins decided to take them at their word and to visit Cathedral Oaks. The delighted artists guided them through their estate and workshop, and afterwards Yehudi and his sisters ran ahead to the highest hill, from which they could see to their delight the entire narrow valley hemmed in by the low, shaggy Santa Cruz Mountains, which blocked the path of fog from the ocean, keeping the valley sunlit most of the year. When Yehudi rejoined the adults, he discovered that his father had asked "the boys" to be on the lookout for land near by which they might purchase.

From time to time the Menuhins saw the few friends they had made before the trip to Europe, but the only contact that continued to grow and strengthen proved to be the one with the Ehrmans. Begun as a relationship between patron and recipient, the tie soon deepened into a friendship for the sake of which Marutha made an exception to her rule of not permitting Yehudi to perform privately, so that, every now and then, after an early dinner at the Ehrmans', Yehudi would play for both families. Sometimes there was a special occasion, such as the memorable evening when Mr. Ehrman, an amateur violinist in his younger days, presented Yehudi with his cherished Guadagnini. There was also the farewell party given for Sidney junior on the eve of his departure for study at Cambridge University. And one night Hephzibah was allowed to play, having prepared a short piece at Uncle Sidney's request.

No one had thought of asking little Yaltah to perform, nor did she have any music with her, but as soon as the applause for Hephzibah had died down, she announced that she, too, was going to play and, pretending not to hear Marutha's protest, boldly launched her piece. At first everything went smoothly enough, but soon she paused in hesitation, then started all over again. At the same place, there came the same pause, the same agonizing moment of uncertainty, and once more Yaltah defiantly returned to the beginning. When she stopped at the fateful place for the third time, Uncle Sidney saved the day by embracing the child and telling her that she didn't really have to finish, and that she played beautifully just the same. It was the same touching desire for equal recognition that prompted Yaltah, on seeing Hephzibah's two wobbly front teeth fall out, to pull at her own perfectly firm milk teeth with such success that, although Marutha caught her in the desperate act, thus balking the grisly operation, Yaltah did lose them prematurely.

Like their parents, Esther and Sidney junior were very fond of the Menuhin children and always managed to be at home when they came for a visit. Yehudi was becoming conscious of the difference in years between him and Esther, but this in no way prevented him from being more love-smitten than ever, and he failed dismally in his efforts to conceal it. By a feat of tact and devotion, Esther succeeded in keeping their relationship on a plane that was both tangible and mysteriously romantic, neither killing his childish attachment by sarcasm nor vulgarizing it by treating him as an equal. She was the only girl he knew well, and it was but natural that she became to him an image of perfection despite—or possibly because of —the unbridgeable barrier of age between them.

The reunion with Esther upon his return from Europe coincided with Yehudi's homecoming concert in San Francisco, to which, after an early dinner at the Ehrmans', he was driven with his parents and Esther in Uncle Sidney's Rolls-Royce. Yehudi held Esther's hand all the way to the concert hall and discovered, after she had left him in the artists' room, that his hand smelled of perfume. The Civic Auditorium was bulging with twelve and a half thousand people, but neither the size of the house nor the wild ovation he was given made Yehudi as happy as the smell of the perfume on his hand. There were many handshakes that night, but he shrewdly managed not to wash his hands until bedtime and, at that, only after he had made certain that the fragrance had evaporated.

One day, Esther casually remarked to Yehudi that she had recently heard Heifetz play the Schubert *Ave Maria* with a perfection which she did not think any living violinist could match. Without saying a word to her or anyone else, he accepted the challenge implied in the remark and began working on the piece. He was then also rehearsing the Tchaikovsky violin concerto with Persinger, which he performed in San Francisco on the eve of his first American tour. At that concert, the hall was again packed, causing Yehudi to perspire profusely, but when he looked for a handkerchief while the audience applauded after the first movement he found his pocket empty. Bewildered, he looked at his mother, who sat with the Ehrmans in the front row. Esther reached for her handbag, caught Marutha's approving glance, got up and handed her handkerchief to Yehudi. The concerto over, he gave three encores, the last of which was the *Ave Maria*. Esther applauded along with everyone else and later congratulated Yehudi on his performance, but he was miserable for he knew there was no magic in his *Ave Maria,* at least not the kind of magic that could match Heifetz's. Moreover, he sensed that Esther, too, knew it. His only consolation was her handkerchief, which, soiled and spotty, now joined the Chinese-puzzle ring in his violin case.

Among Yehudi's overwhelming recollections of that period remains his preoccupation with scientific and mechanical inventions. He spent every spare moment tinkering with whatever tools and materials he had at hand, "improving" on the gadgets in his mother's kitchen, designing new inventions, and reading technical and scientific magazines. Half-seriously, half in fun, he entertained his sisters with wondrous stories of the inventions he would make one day: an ice cream soda the flavor of which would change in the mouth through the simple expedient of pressing a button, a sky bicycle that could be pedaled hundreds of feet above the ground, a "grasshopper car" that could raise itself above all other cars in a traffic jam and jump clear of impeding vehicles.

The boy's attention was directed primarily toward the automobile and the airplane. Under the guidance of Ehrman's chauffeur, Barney, Yehudi learned what makes cars run, knew thoroughly the engines of the Buick and the Rolls-Royce, and learned to drive a car before he was thirteen. The driving lessons were, of course, kept secret from the cautious Moshe, who learned about them only a year later, when Yehudi received his driver's license and was made an honorary police officer of the city of San Francisco, with golden badge, certificate, and all. Trying to improve the automobile, Yehudi evolved a brake based on the hydraulic principle long before he had heard about it. He also had an idea for reducing vibration and shock to a minimum by eliminating the standard axles, replacing them with axles through the center of the car, on which the body was to rest. For the airplane he devised a glider with a propeller, the only motive power of which were pedals, and designed a wing so adjustable to wind resistance that it could slide into the plane's body and alter the angles. He mailed the design to the Douglas Aircraft Corporation, along with a twenty-page explanatory letter, the reply to which—alas, a rejection—was couched in terms so polite that, with renewed inspiration, he proceeded to invent a Diesel-engined seaplane that was large enough to serve as an airborne airplane carrier.

Nor did his interest in inventions fade away with the passing of time. When, as a young man of nineteen, Menuhin visited a South African gold mine, he was so shocked by the underground darkness, heat, and dangers, that he worked out an automotive system of gold-mining, a machine designed to follow the vein (checked by samples of the ore) drilling, dynamiting, and bringing the ore to the surface. This time there was not even a rejection slip, for mine owners found African labor cheaper than any machine.

Years later, in 1940, he was discussing in Melbourne,

Australia, a bomb range with Air Vice-Marshal Williams, and outlined a principle he had worked out only to learn from the astonished vice-marshal that a secret bomb range based on that principle was already in operation.

To this day, when he visits a shop or somebody's house, Menuhin enjoys playing with the many gadgets and devices of modern living in search of possible improvements. Busy with his career, Menuhin is looking forward to the time when he slows up his concert activities, free to tinker to his heart's content in the workshop he hopes one day to set up on his California estate.

Noting Yehudi's interest in science and inventions, Marutha presented him with the four-volume edition of Professor Thomson's *Outline of Science,* not the least rewarding feature of which was a full-page dedication which she had written, bespeaking her pride in him. Yehudi immediately sought out Hephzibah, who by now had mastered the great feminine art of listening with admiration, even if half-comprehending. As he was showing her the books, Yaltah barged in. At first he tolerated the intrusion, but when, tired of his explanations, she began to interrupt with her own, he lured her into a closet and locked the door, careful to take out the key so as to give her air to breathe. In response to the child's desperate screams, Marutha came rushing in, liberated Yaltah, and led her out of the room, but she also took away with her the four volumes, saying she had made a mistake; her son did not deserve them.

Both little girls were becoming very attractive, with their deep blue eyes and long fair curls. Although their mother dressed them alike in dark blue reefer coats and saucy sailors' caps, each had a distinct personality. While Yaltah was exuberant in her moods, eagerly clinging to anyone who showed any interest in her, Hephzibah was self-contained and distant. Treating everyone, even Marutha, with a composure that had a strange, clear-eyed maturity about it, she obediently followed the routine at home, yet somehow imparting the impression that this routine merely happened to coincide with her own preference. While Yaltah, reluctant to hurt people's feelings, tended to gloss over those adult shortcomings which children rarely fail to notice, Hephzibah found these niceties superfluous. A friend of the family discovered this one day when she ventured at the end of a piece Hephzibah was practicing: "How beautifully you play, and what a lovely sonata!" Measuring the lady with cool, unsmiling eyes, the little girl said: "That was not a sonata; it was a concerto."

Hephzibah's progress was so remarkable that, at the urging of the Ehrmans, the Menuhins arranged a recital for her on October 25, 1928, by way of "an educational and cultural experience," to cite the printed program. Hephzibah's teacher, Lev Shorr, was confident that she would do beautifully at the recital, but, fearing that even this composed child might get flustered on the stage, he warned her against getting too excited. "What does it mean, 'excited'?" she asked. When someone inquired after the performance how she enjoyed it, Hephzibah frowned: "I don't like to practice in front of so many people."

The "practice" included the following: Beethoven, *Sonata, Opus 26;* Bach, *Concerto in the Italian Style;* Weber, *Rondo Brilliante;* Chopin, *Fantaisie-Impromptu;* Weber, *Perpetual Motion.* The task of memorizing the program was in itself a formidable feat for an eight-year-old, but she did more, as her chubby fingers ranged over the keyboard with a confidence and a brilliance that prompted Curran D. Swint to exclaim in the San Francisco *News* the next morning: "Yehudi had better look out or his little sister will some day be a greater pianist than he will be a fiddler! And that means among the greatest!"

For the time being at least, Yehudi had little to fear. No further public appearances were being planned for Hephzibah, and he was about to launch his first concert tour.

EIGHT

The "Prince Khevenhüller"

The boy's first concert tour started under the most auspicious circumstances. The demand for Yehudi was so great that Moshe had the choice of any city in the United States—and in the rest of the world, for that matter—and could practically name the price. The Soviet Government apologized in its communication to Yehudi's managers that it was unable to offer more than six thousand dollars per concert. Rejected along with many others, that offer nevertheless added grist to the publicity mill, as did also the refusal of Boston authorities to grant Yehudi the right of a professional appearance on the grounds that he was under age.

The tour and the subsequent concerts in Europe presented a tremendous challenge to the boy, for he had to live up to the Yehudi Menuhin legend that had arisen out of his Carnegie Hall performance. On this tour he was playing, among other works, the Tchaikovsky concerto, which had already won him acclaim in San Francisco and Paris, and the majestic Brahms, to the first performance of which he was looking forward with a kind of boyish excitement and pride, as he also was to the presentation of the first two works dedicated to him. One was Sam Franko's arrangement of Vivaldi's *Concerto in G minor,* Opus 4. Originally written for the violin and subsequently arranged for the piano by Bach, the Vivaldi score was later lost, and it was Franko who returned the concerto to the violinists.

The other work dedicated to Yehudi was Ernest Bloch's

Abodah.[1] A resident of San Francisco, the composer had long resisted suggestions to meet the boy who was to him "a mere prodigy." However, several days before Yehudi's San Francisco concert on December 5, 1928, at which he was to perform Bloch's *Nigun,* the composer did accept an invitation to the Menuhins' house, where he played the work with Yehudi. The next day Bloch wrote to the elder Menuhin: "I am preparing a surprise for Yehudi; don't tell him. For years I have wanted to arrange the beautiful *Abodah,* but always I have waited. Now I know why—it will be done for him." The *Abodah* was completed in time for the composer to play it through with Yehudi before the boy's departure for his tour. Twenty-one years later, in a letter dated December 9, 1949, Bloch wrote to the violinist: "I haven't forgotten anything of the past. I can remember as if it were yesterday the day you played the *Abodah* with me in San Francisco, and above all I remember your *divination* of certain bars marked in the music by rests only—in the violin part! (You have perhaps forgotten that, but not I!)" Yehudi had actually forgotten it, but he remembers clearly how impressed he was by Bloch's vitality and restlessness, by his curious high-pitched voice, as he told stories of his life in the Old and New Worlds, ornamenting them with details and digressions more fascinating than the stories themselves.

The San Francisco concert, the first of the tour, was followed by a recital in Los Angeles, where a meeting with Charlie Chaplin easily overshadowed all else. Like millions of other American children, the young Menuhin idolized Chaplin and eagerly responded to his offer of a personally conducted tour of his studio, where he performed for the boy a solo scene from *City Lights,* on which he was just then working, and posed with him for photographers.

From Los Angeles, Moshe took Yehudi straight to New York for a performance of the Tchaikovsky concerto with the distinguished Dutch conductor Willem Mengelberg and the New York Philharmonic Symphony Orchestra. Engrossed in prepa-

[1] *Abodah*—God's Worship, a sacred Hebraic theme.

rations for the world *première* of Alexander Tansman's suite from *La Nuit Kurde* billed on the same program, Mengelberg rushed through the rehearsal with Yehudi in exactly twenty-five minutes, with the result that, having successfully completed the first two movements at the performance, soloist and conductor suddenly found themselves playing the third in different tempi. Yehudi quickly adjusted his pace and, he recalls smilingly, "we finished together." The momentary lack of synchronization between the soloist and the orchestra did not detract from the critics' admiration of the young violinist even if, in Olin Downes's words, they preferred, "on grounds of conception and interpretation, Menuhin with Beethoven to Menuhin with Tchaikovsky." That this was also the boy's own preference became apparent from the only interview he was allowed to give during that stay in New York. Replying to questions on what he thought of some of his older colleagues, Yehudi referred respectfully to Mischa Elman, but of Kreisler he spoke with adoration, defining the difference between the two in the following manner:

"Mischa Elman has a warm tone; Kreisler also has a warm tone, but a cold-warm tone. That's funny but that's what I mean. Beethoven is my favorite composer, and Kreisler is like Beethoven to me. Elman is like Tchaikovsky."[2]

Had Yehudi looked up toward Dr. Garbat's box in Carnegie Hall as he played his solo recital on January 6, 1929, he would have noticed that his old friends were sharing their box with a meticulously dressed man in dark glasses, and a handsome, stately lady. They were the banker Henry Goldman and his wife, people of great wealth and patrons of artists and musicians, whose interest in the violinist had originally been aroused by Fritz Busch. When, after Yehudi's performance of the Beethoven concerto, Goldman spoke glowingly of the boy to the Garbats, the doctor remarked that Yehudi was sorely lacking a violin worthy of his talent. The banker checked with Fritz Busch, who replied in his characteristically

[2] New York *Telegraph,* January 6, 1929.

impetuous way: "It is true, but it does not matter. He can play divinely even on a broomstick!"

There the matter rested for the time being, the real reason for Goldman's indecision being rooted in his belief that most prodigies were destined to deteriorate into ineffectual mediocrity. Yehudi's recital must have dispelled all doubts in Goldman's mind, for several days later he was receiving the boy and his father in his drawing room, on the walls of which hung paintings by Titian, Giorgione, Fra Angelico, Van Dyck, Rubens, Holbein, and Rembrandt. Afflicted by an eye ailment, Mr. Goldman was almost totally blind, but he sensed the boy's wide-eyed curiosity and led him from masterpiece to masterpiece, pointing out a patch of light, a depth of perspective, an unusual boldness of color as though he could see them clearly, giving Yehudi his first sense of intimate contact with the great world of painting.

Having returned to his seat, the host asked Yehudi what violin he would select for himself, if he had his choice. The answer was instantaneous: "A Stradivarius!"

"Not one of mine!" returned the banker, explaining to the startled boy that when he first came to the States from Germany, he earned a living as a door-to-door salesman of cheap fiddles bearing the proud trademark "Stradivarius." Then, turning to Moshe, he asked for permission to present Yehudi with a violin of the boy's own choice.

The days that followed are remembered by the Menuhins as "the Strad fiddle week." Practically all the Stradivari in the hands of dealers were sent up to Yehudi, who, together with Persinger, was trying them out in a kind of delirious rejoicing. Among the dealers was one Emil Herrmann, who brought the famed "Prince Khevenhüller," for which he asked sixty thousand dollars, and it was this instrument that Yehudi finally chose.

Wanting to make certain that the choice was right, Goldman turned for advice to Efrem Zimbalist, the famous violinist and owner of a priceless collection of violins which included Stradivarius's last instrument, the "Swan." Convalescing from a recent operation, Zimbalist received Mrs. Goldman, Persinger, and the Menuhins at his home and listened to Yehudi playing piece after piece on the "Prince." Reporting the scene, the *Musical Courier* cited Zimbalist: "Yehudi is right in his choice. This is one of the most marvellous Strads on earth, but Yehudi is the most marvellous violinist of his age."[3]

The instrument, which thus became Menuhin's constant companion, was made by Stradivarius in 1733, when the immortal craftsman was in his ninetieth year. Many of the great violinists prefer this period of Stradivarius's creative life: Heifetz's Strad was made in 1731; Ysaye's and Adolf Busch's in 1732; Bronislaw Huberman's in 1733, the same year as Menuhin's; Fritz Kreisler's in 1734; and, finally, Efrem Zimbalist's in 1735. Stradivarius was indeed so proud of the blossoming of his genius so late in his life that, before closing the violin which Goldman bought for Yehudi, he wrote inside its body: "*d'anni 90* [at the age of ninety]." Originally made for Prince and Princess Khevenhüller of Vienna, this superbly preserved, full-bellied violin of grand proportions, covered with a deep red varnish, passed on in the 1820s to the famed Josef Böhm, teacher of Joachim and Ernst (the two greatest German violinists of the nineteenth century), and eventually into the possession of a Russian professor of music, Popov, from whom Emil Herrmann purchased it after the Revolution of 1917.

Young as he was, Yehudi knew that violins, if constantly used, develop "fatigue," as do all objects subjected to vibration, eventually losing immediacy of response and the bell-like quality of the sound. Moreover, violins are sensitive to excessive heat, cold, humidity, and dryness, which affect the tensions in the wood, sometimes causing a separation at the joints. Yehudi solved his problem by doing most of his practicing on his Grancino and by ordering an exact replica of the "Prince Khevenhüller" from the eminent French violin maker, Emile Français. This proved such a good instrument that when Menuhin uses it at times in the concert hall not even critics are aware of any difference in quality.

[3]February 7, 1929.

In 1939, to continue with the story of Menuhin's violins, he came into possession of a Guarnieri del Gesù of 1742. The dealer again was Emil Herrmann, to whom Menuhin wrote at the time: "You can well imagine how happy I am with the Guarnieri. It is useless to describe to *you* the glory of this instrument. It is fitting that I should again find another lifelong friend through you." In the Guarnieri, Menuhin found a companion to the "Khevenhüller" rather than a rival for his affections. The latter has a tone of greater warmth and loveliness, while the Guarnieri possesses the earthy beauty of an untutored peasant voice. Finally, in 1951, the violinist purchased from the same Herrmann the Stradivarius "Soil," made in 1714 and subsequently named for M. Soil, a nineteenth-century Belgian collector of violins. This violin is generally recognized as one of the ten greatest Stradivari, in a class with the "Messiah," the "Betts," the "Dolphin," and the "Alard." Apart from its magnificent appearance, the "Soil" has tremendous carrying power and incision, particularly striking when it majestically overrides the heaviest orchestral accompaniment.

With the "Prince Khevenhüller" carefully put to bed in a brand-new, antelope-lined, pigskin violin case, Yehudi resumed his concert tour, which the audiences and critics converted into a triumphal procession. The schedule was so arranged that, with only one concert in each city, he stayed there for about a week, to have ample time for rest, practice, concerts, and sightseeing, as well as to maintain his required reading in English and American literature.

During the tour Aba was fussing around Yehudi like a bee around a rare desert flower, checking and double checking train schedules, hotel reservations, menus on the railway diners; keeping Yehudi bathed, fed according to Marutha's instructions, and away from irrepressible admirers. All the packing was, of course, done much ahead of time. One night, after a concert, he undressed Yehudi, gave him a shower, and put him to bed. Then he packed the bags and sent them down with instructions that they be delivered to his morning train as early as possible. On that morning, Yehudi found that all his clothes had been packed except the overcoat, and the bags had already been dispatched. The flustered father was in despair, but the boy calmly put the overcoat over his pajamas and walked the several blocks to the station with princely unconcern.

Most memorable was the stay in Minneapolis, where Yehudi played with Henri Verbrugghen, the distinguished conductor of the Minneapolis Symphony Orchestra, a former star pupil of Ysaye whose fierce, waxed mustaches and collection of old musical instruments impressed the boy no less than his musicianship. It was under Verbrugghen's baton that Yehudi gave his first performance of the Brahms concerto, which will forever be engraved in his mind, for in the course of it he experienced the only lapse of memory he has had in his thirty years of active professional life. At first everything had gone beautifully. The rehearsal with the orchestra on March 6, 1929, was a triumph all by itself:

> *Sixty blasé musicians forgot their dignity and took part in a mad demonstration. Tears trickled from the grizzled chins and splashed into the bass horns. Music stands were upset as the musicians leaped to their feet at the conclusion of the rehearsal and shook the rafters with a chorus of 'bravos'—which is a few steps further than a dyed-in-the-wool musician usually allows himself to go.*
>
> *Yehudi grinned happily and boyishly, and offered to try it again if they liked. And after it was all over the enraptured musicians shook their heads and muttered that there never has been anything like it.*[4]

Both times the boy played faultlessly and without using the score. At the concert, however, he suddenly lost the thread of the music at the end of the fifth bar of the second movement's violin solo. He hesitated for a fleeting second, gracefully slipped back to the beginning—and lost the thread again after the fateful fifth bar. At this point the conductor stopped him,

[4]Minneapolis *Evening Tribune*, March 6, 1929.

turned to the audience and explained that Yehudi had never before played the complex Brahms in public. A contemporary account[5] said that the audience reacted with "ejaculations of unfeigned amazement and wonder" while the boy glanced at the music on the conductor's stand "and brought the movement to a splendid fruition." He was rewarded with "unstinted homage," while the reviews spoke of the "nobility and dignity of his interpretation" and the "beauty and fullness of his tone." Yehudi alone was unable to forgive himself. He ran up to Persinger after the end of the concerto, shouting: "This will never happen to me again!" It never has, in fact, causing music critics to speak of "the miracle of Menuhin's memory." Asked about the "miracle," he responded with what is in effect an extemporaneous essay on musical memory:

"Yes, my memory has served me quite well, but it is in no way remarkable, if measured by the standards of such giants of retentiveness as Georges Enesco, Arturo Toscanini, Dimitri Mitropoulos, Antal Dorati, George Szell, or Louis Kentner, any one of whom can indelibly imprint upon his memory a complete symphony at a single reading.

"Musical memory consists of several distinct kinds of retentiveness, not one of which is in itself miraculous but does become so when strongly reinforced by the other kinds. They are the memory of the mind, the eye, the ear, and the fingers.

"I am particularly fascinated by the workings of the memory of the mind. It is complex and subtle, one part conscious of itself—it knows, and knows that it knows; while another part is latent memory—it exists but is inactive and has to be prodded along. When it is awakened, which usually happens during an emergency, it can be a veritable lifesaver. During a visit to London in 1953, I had to play Saint-Saëns' B-minor violin concerto from memory with only four days in which to prepare it, and with many other obligations crowding my schedule. I had not heard, read, or played the concerto for about twenty-eight years, and was convinced that it had completely escaped my

[5]Minneapolis *Star,* March 9, 1929.

memory, but it actually came back to me with the greatest of ease.

"The conscious memory, on the other hand, has nothing automatic about it, and is most vital to the musician because it is analytical, helping to juxtapose and correlate themes, to illumine the path among the mosaics of notes—in a word, to fathom and interpret musical compositions.

"The three other types of memory are more obvious, especially the aural, which is automatic, as all our senses are.

"Visual or photographic memory has nothing whatsoever to do with music, but is amazingly helpful, especially to me, as I have discovered that I am able to find without difficulty a desired passage or even a single note, for I see clearly before me the page on which to look for it in practically all the compositions I have ever played. I became aware of my photographic memory early in life and have learned to take advantage of it, but I have trained myself to think of it as an adjunct rather than an essential, preferring to rely on my aural memory. My ear, I have discovered, records and recollects more quickly and faithfully than does my eye not only the music which I play, but also an orchestral *tutti* and accompaniment, as well as the piano parts of sonatas.

"The tactile or finger memory is purely and simply the result of long training; it belongs to the craftsman, the professional. Because it cannot be depended upon to carry the weight of a complete piece, its one great service is confined to bridging a momentary gap. Tactile memory functions as does a splice to a break on the 'tape' of the other types of retentiveness. When one forgets, or is tired or distracted to the point of complete inability to summon the other types of memory, the thing to do is to close the eyes and shut off the mind, leaving the field to the fingers. More often than not, they will come to the rescue. They failed me miserably during my first performance of the Brahms, but I was not as yet a professional. In addition, my mental and physical reserves were under a particularly heavy strain on that occasion, for I was keyed up to the performance, seeking to recapture the overpowering virility of Brahms.

When, a few months later, after a restful sea voyage, I played the Beethoven and Brahms concertos in one evening, I found the Brahms the easier of the two, although still a formidable task. Granted the necessary physical strength, the Beethoven presents a much greater intellectual and artistic challenge."

Marutha and the girls rejoined Moshe and Yehudi in New York some two weeks before the departure of the Menuhins for Germany, where a concert was scheduled with the Berlin Philharmonic Orchestra. They had all missed each other terribly, the female half of the family having been by far the more miserable. "What the men did on their frequent journeys away from home," Hephzibah subsequently wrote in a letter, "was a mystery to me, because we had always been inseparable and always in support of each other, in terror of losing that link which represented full happiness and security. It was beastly sad and lonesome for us when Yehudi and Aba were away." Yehudi, too, was happy with the reunion. Awkward and inarticulate, he was completely free only with his adoring sisters, and talked a great deal to them, especially the serene and all-understanding Hephzibah. There was so much he had to tell them now: about the cities he had visited, the new inventions he had dreamed up; the time he cut his finger while tinkering in Dr. Garbat's laboratory, how he told no one about it until the finger had begun to fester, compelling him to seek the doctor's help.

The happiness of the children was somewhat marred by the differences between the parents, which the elder Menuhins could not altogether conceal from the youngsters, however hard they tried. Marutha objected, among other things, to the style in which her husband gave interviews as Yehudi's spokesman, finding them undignified and boastful. She was also worried by the magnificent gift her husband had accepted from the Goldmans. True, he had kept her informed by telephone and letter, reassuring her as to the banker's character and motives until she finally gave her halfhearted approval. Likewise reluctantly she came with her family to a luncheon at the Goldmans'. After the meal, the two little girls lay down to rest in one of the guest rooms while Yehudi was sent to the library for his usual nap. Fascinated by the many silver, copper, and pewter ash trays in the room, Yehudi, instead of sleeping, arranged them on the floor in the shape of an armor breast-plate, and then proceeded to tie the trays together with a string he always carried in his pocket along with other equipment found on most boys: a penknife, a few small nails and screws, paper and pencil to jot down ideas for his inventions. It was quite a chore to tie those ash trays together so that they re-tained the shape of a breastplate, but Yehudi finally succeeded, struggled into it and strutted about the room, clanking loudly, imagining himself a medieval knight. Suddenly his parents came in, accompanied by the Goldmans and the famous lieder singer, Elena Gerhardt, their house guest. Seeing the anger in his mother's eyes, Yehudi hastily began to take off his shining armor, but Mrs. Goldman exclaimed: "Don Quixote!" and led her half-blind husband to the boy to feel the ingenious knots Yehudi had devised to keep the ash trays together. The two immediately got involved in a discussion of medieval armor and sailor's knots, both displaying a surprising knowledge in two odd and unrelated fields.

Despite the graciousness of her hosts, Marutha remained cool and distant, and when, on the eve of the Menuhins' de-parture, Mrs. Goldman suggested a ladies' tea in her honor, Marutha refused.

Her relations with the Garbats were also somewhat strained following a few disagreements on the upbringing of children. For one, their eight-year-old Fifi had generously presented two of her dolls to Hephzibah and Yaltah, only to have Marutha order them to return the gifts because "my mother believed that to play with dolls is a waste of time." The little girls were tearful but did as they were told. A more serious incident took place at a Garbat dinner, the day before the Menuhins sailed for Europe. Yehudi had been taken by his father that afternoon to see the house in which he had spent the first nine months of his life. Moshe also showed him the grocery where once Marutha had been refused credit, and the long viaduct where the two young parents used to sing during their walks. Excited and hungry after the trip, Yehudi exclaimed upon seeing the huge turkey on the dining-room table: "Oh, what a turkey! Everybody can eat all they want!" Marutha reprimanded him for being greedy, and sent him out of the room. Observing her disapproving hosts, Marutha said:

"Don't you believe in discipline?"

"There is such a thing as too much discipline," rejoined Dr. Garbat.

The Menuhins sailed next day on the S/S *Deutschland*, where, on his bed in the cabin, Yehudi found the four volumes of Professor Thomson's *Outline of Science* which Marutha had taken away from him. With joy he picked up the first volume, but he was shocked to discover that the page containing his mother's inscription had been torn out. He was so deeply hurt that for a moment he thought of returning the gift, but the temptation was too great. He opened a volume and soon became lost in the marvels abounding on every page. To his surprise, Marutha, who had previously shown little interest in his preoccupation with science and invention, now listened for hours to his reading from the *Outline* and to his tales of the inventions that still awaited realization. He was so touched that, knowing what pleased her most, he learned by heart several short poems in English and in French, which he recited to her with great feeling and expression. During that trip, mother and son found a new intimacy, precipitating what Menuhin calls "the golden period in our relationship."

With the entire family reunited, Marutha mellowed, treating with easy good nature the few transgressions her children made during the trip. She even unbent to the point where she allowed her family to form a friendship with two fellow passengers, Mr. and Mrs. Fritz Peisach of New York. They had heard Yehudi and admired his extraordinary talents. Now their admiration multiplied as they took advantage of the opportunity to spend much time with him.

One day Mr. Peisach was allowed to sit in Yehudi's bedroom while the boy practiced, still in his sleeping pajamas. Catching the visitor's eye on the heavy woolen underwear lying on a chair, Yehudi explained:

"Imma makes me wear it all through the spring, even if I perspire and am terribly uncomfortable."

"Then why not wear regular underwear?"

"Imma thinks this way is better." He paused. "I shall be making my own decisions after I am twenty-one."

NINE

Berlin and Adolf Busch

The Menuhins were happy to learn upon arrival in Germany that Mr. Ehrman, who had been visiting Paris, was planning to come to Berlin for Yehudi's concert on April 12, 1929. Moreover, he would stay on for another four days to celebrate the boy's thirteenth birthday with the family. To add to their pleasure, Yehudi's second benefactor, Henry Goldman, was to attend the concert, having come to Berlin with his wife to undergo an eye operation in the hope of restoring his sight. Among the other American friends present were the violinist-composer Sam Franko, Samuel Cohn's daughter Eda, and the Peisachs, who generously offered to baby-sit with Hephzibah and Yaltah on the night of Yehudi's concert so that Marutha could attend.

On Fritz Busch's recommendation, the performance was arranged by the Herman Wolff agency, the largest and most distinguished in Germany, headed by Frau Louise Wolff. The position she occupied in the concert world was so dominant that entrepreneurs and artists alike spoke of her as "Königin Louise" (Queen Louise). The echo of Yehudi's successful appearances in Paris with Paul Paray and with Fritz Busch in Carnegie Hall had already made his name familiar among the music lovers of Berlin, yet the population of the then musical capital of the world was reluctant in its response. The main objection was the difficult, unprecedented program which a mere boy dared to undertake—three of the greatest concertos in the violin repertoire; by Bach, Beethoven, and Brahms.

Some papers mockingly described Yehudi as "the latest American freak" and his program "the latest American trick." As a last resort, the enterprising Queen Louise published in the form of an article the glowing letter Busch had written to her about Yehudi. Its concluding words: "America has acclaimed him but Germany will love him," winged their way among the Berliners, with the result that the tickets were all sold out as Yehudi, Busch, and the orchestra were about to begin their rehearsals. At this point, Fritz Busch received the news of his father's death and arranged for the celebrated Bruno Walter to replace him.

"This happened a quarter of a century ago," Bruno Walter recalls, "but to this day I can remember Yehudi's playing. He was a child and yet he was a man, a man and a great artist. The astonishing thing was not that he had mastered the music technically, but that there was a spiritual mastery, a maturity. Therein lay the miracle. I felt as one with him. I could have made a suggestion here and there during the rehearsals, of course, but it was not necessary, and I did not do it: the mutual understanding was complete. Yehudi's musicianship was particularly striking in the slow movement of the Bach; it is sublime music, which requires complete technical authority and cannot be played without the deepest insight."

Probably no musical audience anywhere is more knowledgeable and critical than the German, but when it surrenders to an artist, it does so with a total completeness. Such was their surrender on the night of Yehudi's "Three B's" (Bach, Beethoven, Brahms) concert. Somewhat cold and distrustful at first, the people in the hall soon yielded to the towheaded boy who was producing those unbelievable sounds, and when he approached the end of the cadenza in the Beethoven concerto they made the unprecedented gesture of rising to pay their tribute to a great artist. When the concert was over there was such a rush to the platform that the police had to be called in to restore a semblance of order and to enable the audience to leave the hall. Among those trapped by the milling crowds were the American Ambassador Schurman, Max Reinhardt,

Ossip Gabrilowitsch, and Albert Einstein. The latter was sitting in the front row, so that Bruno Walter, absorbed though he was in conducting the orchestra and listening to Yehudi, noticed the amazement and joy in the large expressive eyes of the scientist.[1] Einstein was imprisoned for thirty minutes, his hands high above the head where he had placed them to clap his approval, but he finally fought his way to the artists' room, embraced Yehudi, and exclaimed: "Now I know there is a God in heaven!" To the *Musical Courier* he said:

> *The talent of the boy is the greatest I have ever observed. The spiritual conception of everything he plays, whether by Bach or Brahms, plus the technical perfection with which he masters a large violin with his little, plump fingers, reminds me of my sensations forty years ago when I heard the great Joachim play for the first time.*[2]

The German music critics wrote in a similar vein and at great length, embellishing their accounts of the performance with sentimental outpourings, metaphysical digressions into the why and wherefore of Man and Genius, and speculations on the sources of Yehudi's gifts and the probable course of his future. Yehudi was, as usual, unaware of the full extent of the furor he had created, but he had his share of the excitement: Uncle Sidney presented him with a pocket watch, the boy's first, on which was engraved: "To Yehudi from his old chum Sidney M. Ehrman." Moreover, Goldman permitted the boy to examine *his* watch, which, at the pressure of a latch, chimed in three distinct sounds the hour, the quarter hour and the minute.

The "Three B's" concert was soon repeated, this time with Fritz Busch in his own Dresden, where he was *Generalmusikdirektor* of the State Opera and Orchestra. Those were happy days at Dresden, in the company of the Menuhins' American friends—the Goldmans, Uncle Sidney, the Peisachs, and Eda

[1]Bruno Walter, *Theme and Variations* (New York: Alfred A. Knopf, 1946), p. 233.
[2]November 30, 1929.

Cohn. For once, Yehudi had a companion of his own age—Busch's son Hans, who shared with Yehudi the delights of operating an electric train. The elder Busch was overjoyed that his soloist displayed the same enthusiasm in playing with the train as he did in making music. But neither he nor Yehudi's parents knew that, in the process of inspecting the enormous bathroom in the Menuhin suite at the Bellevue Hotel, the boys had discovered that the many shining hooks on the bathroom walls had been screwed on in a way that gave them absolutely no symmetry, and were inspired to design a wonderful pattern of their own. Now they were only waiting for the necessary privacy to execute the change but, as usual, Yehudi was kept busy practicing, rehearsing, reading, with one of the parents always keeping an eye on him. The longed-for opportunity arrived at last during the after-concert dinner at the Bellevue, at which Fritz Busch made a solemn speech on the grave responsibility which befalls the parents and teachers of a prodigy like Yehudi. Although the boy's knowledge of German at the time did not go beyond two or three children's poems, he sensed the solemnity with which the conductor spoke and whispered to Mrs. Goldman: "I knew that Mr. Busch was a good conductor but now I think he could also make a wonderful rabbi." At this point Moshe told him to go to bed, to which Yehudi agreed with alacrity, only asking that his friend Hans accompany him to the suite. Moshe refused and himself escorted the boy, returning thereafter to the dining room. When the party was over, he and Marutha caught Yehudi, nothing daunted, laboriously arranging on the bathroom floor the shining hooks which he had removed from the walls, to conform to the pattern he and Hans had designed. Now, alas, under his parents' outraged guard, he toiled through half the night, returning the screws to their original spots.

When Eda Cohn called on the Menuhins late next afternoon she found Marutha bathing the girls. It was Yehudi's turn for a bath afterwards, and Marutha asked the young woman if she would not mind taking the boy for a twenty-minute walk, as Moshe was away on a business call. Finding herself alone with Yehudi, Miss Cohn protested that he was being treated like a baby and why did he not "stand up for his rights"? After all, he was fully thirteen, and was doing a man's work! Yehudi made no answer, but the young woman insisted on knowing whether or not he was going to do anything about it. Whereupon he said:

"Is it not sufficient to know in one's mind that one is right?"

To this she had no reply. Besides, the twenty minutes were about up, and they hastened to retrace their steps.

The Menuhins returned to Berlin for Yehudi's second concert and, what was of greater importance, for his meeting with Adolf Busch, with whom Enesco advised Yehudi to study so as to get acquainted with the German school of music. Adolf Busch had made it a rule not to teach child prodigies, mainly because the parents of most of them were money-mad, and he had agreed to interview Yehudi only to please his brother Fritz, who assured him that the Menuhins were determined not to exploit the boy. After a brief conversation, and hearing him play for a few minutes, Adolf Busch agreed to accept Yehudi as a pupil and also invited him to the Busch Quartet concert at the Singakademie, where the unsurpassed musicianship of the ensemble and the reverence and earnestness of the occasion left an indelible impression on the boy.

The Menuhins, it was decided, would settle down in Basel, where Busch resided, after a brief trip to Paris, where the boy was to repeat his "Three B's" concert, followed by a two-week vacation at Baden-Baden.

The visit to Paris was marred for Yehudi by the absence from the city of Georges Enesco, then touring the Continent, but there was compensation in a reunion with Uncle Sidney, Aunt Florence, and Esther. Elegant, and with an aura of romance about her, the girl found a free evening to join her parents and the Menuhins for dinner at the Maisonnette Russe, one of those typical White Russian restaurants resounding with songs of the steppes to the accompaniment of an accor-

dion and a balalaika. As always, Yehudi sat next to Esther,
sensing from her appearance and the few stories she told of her
activities the pulse of a life of glamor, so very different from
the dedicated one he was leading, crowded with hard work
and harder study.

He appreciated all the more his first taste of leisure at
Baden-Baden. There the Menuhins were the guests of Mr.
and Mrs. Goldman, who had planned to put them up at the
luxurious hotel where they themselves were staying, but on
Marutha's insistence a small apartment was reserved for her
family in a modest pension near by. This automatically limited
the contact with the Goldmans to afternoon tea every day and
to Elena Gerhardt's two lieder concerts. Neither the naturalness of their hosts nor Yehudi's growing attachment to them
were able to overcome Marutha's reserve. Herself extremely
gracious to those admitted as friends, she preferred, and still
does, extending hospitality to accepting it. Yehudi noticed
nothing of the strain. He was too enchanted with the novelty
of a life free from practice and studies and too excited over the
Zeiss binoculars which his parents had given him. Large and
magnificent, the binoculars represented the best of Germany's
unrivaled optical industry, and he carried them with him
wherever he went, producing them out of their rich leather
case at the slightest provocation, and at no provocation at all.
Needless to say, the binoculars went with him on the noon-
time walks to the Promenade, where a band played every day,
giving him the fascinating opportunity of studying the faces
of the men blowing the wind instruments and of regaling his
sisters with imitations of the players. For years thereafter,
Yehudi treasured the binoculars as a memento of those happy
days, parting with them only during World War II, when the
U.S. government appealed for donations of optical instruments.

The holiday over, the Menuhins left for Basel, where they
rented a three-story stucco house at 12 Gartenstrasse. Indeed,
the trees and flowers that surrounded the good burghers' villas
made the street look like a veritable garden. The ground floor
of the new Menuhin home comprised the dining room and

kitchen and a huge hall extending to the entire height of the three stories. A staircase which narrowed as it spiraled its way upward led to the second floor, consisting of the living room and Yehudi's studio. On the third floor were three bedrooms, and in the attic two or three maids' rooms. Marutha did the living room in the Crimean Tartar style, with Oriental rugs on the walls and sofas and small pillows scattered everywhere. The house settled, Moshe bought an enormous secondhand Packard touring car, in which the family made frequent out-of-town excursions, sometimes for days on end, so that soon they became acquainted with the whole of Switzerland.

Very little time, if any, was lost for the children to slip into harness once more. For the present, French was relegated to the background, supplanted by English as the family language (as a result of their recent sojourn in San Francisco), while the main effort was directed toward mastering German with the help of daily instruction by a gentleman of the resounding name of Justin Gehrig-Geisst.

On Busch's recommendation, a young pianist, Hubert Giesen, was brought over from Germany to join the Menuhin household as Yehudi's accompanist. In addition to the two sessions a week with Adolf Busch, Yehudi worked three hours every morning by himself and two hours in the afternoon with Giesen, whom Yehudi found "as mad as a hatter but an excellent musician, of whom we became very fond and whom we nicknamed Hoopsie." Giesen was surprised and indignant when Moshe insisted as a condition of employment that he work at the piano each morning while Yehudi was practicing by himself, but soon had to admit that this was the only way he could keep pace with the boy, whose intuitive drive for perfection was being reinforced by the precision and discipline of the German school, into which Adolf Busch was now initiating his young pupil.

At that time, Busch had reached the height of his power and popularity and was universally regarded as the greatest exponent of the classical German tradition among instrumentalists. Indeed, in appearance, performance, attitudes, and

musical tastes, he was the very embodiment of that great tradition. Like his brother Fritz, he was tall and blond, somewhat
heavy, with a ruddy, boyish face and a friendly yet uncompromising look in his blue eyes that arrested one's attention
and commanded respect. Very little existed for him outside the
exalted world of music, but that "little" he approached with
fearless integrity. When, with the coming of Hitler, he was
asked not to play with the pianist Rudolf Serkin, a Jew, whom
he had discovered and befriended, Busch responded by refusing to return to Germany for as long as the Nazis were in
power.

The period Yehudi spent with Busch was one of rapid
growth and much learning, and yet also of incomplete harmony
and only partial fulfillment. The incompleteness stemmed from
several sources. There was, to begin with, the discord between
Busch and Moshe. The former seemed to have expected Yehudi to come to him as a disciple and apprentice living in his
master's house and sharing with him the rich world of music
for its own sake, while Moshe, although careful not to push his
son too hard, was thinking of him as a performing artist to
whom it was imperative to give concerts, however few. Apart
from the mere necessity of meeting bills, Moshe was genuinely
concerned over the grave results that might arise from keeping
the boy from his audiences, a concern which Yehudi and
Enesco also shared with him. Fritz Busch, too, sympathized
with this problem and offered to introduce Yehudi to yet another country, England. Adolf, however, refused to recognize
the very existence of the problem; if his work with Yehudi
served to enlarge the boy's repertoire, it came about only as an
incidental by-product.

Yehudi himself did not give much thought to the question
of repertoire. As a matter of fact, he was at his happiest in the
realm of pure music, in which he was now immersed, constantly in search of original editions, the *Ur*-texts, with which
Busch preferred to work, instilling in his young pupil a venera-
tion for the composer's intent and original idea and giving
them precedence over the changes made by subsequent ar-

rangers. By a happy coincidence, Moshe was able at precisely that time to buy for Yehudi the complete *Ur*-text edition of Bach which had belonged to the composer Max Bruch, thus laying a solid foundation for his son's present invaluable collection of first editions.

Busch's most characteristic attributes as a teacher combined an unflinching sincerity and devotion, tempered by precision, with a most painstaking attention to detail and a scrupulous exactitude of interpretation, all in all an approach so scholarly that it bordered on the scholastic. Under such guidance, the young violinist disciplined and enriched his enormous talent to the point where even the uncompromising Busch said: "His individual preparation and interpretation of the greatest compositions are classical, perfect, reaching the finest and subtlest *bel canto*, needing no reproach, no criticisms. What the boy does is noble, his intonation exact, his interpretation divine. He is his own most rigid critic."[3]

But Yehudi himself was dissatisfied. Certain deep needs within him remained unfulfilled. The boy who was weaned on the abandon of his father's Chassidic songs and grew up on Enesco's creative flights missed the spontaneity he had known and was not now free to indulge in. Speaking of this period many years later, Menuhin said:

"Adolf Busch was warm and generous in giving me the best he had in him, he was one of the most sincere musicians I know, with an integrity beyond reproach. He was fundamentally a pure classicist. He was all purpose, all devotion and service, but without the exalted atmosphere Enesco always created. Busch was deliberate, slow, sans wings; Enesco was all wings. I felt I had switched from poetry to prose. It was fine prose, clean and honorable, but it lacked the ecstasy of poetry. Enesco was blessed by the Muses, and being blessed he could do no wrong.

"Busch contributed enormously toward my musical knowledge and growth, towards an achievement of a pure classical style. My studies with him helped me to escape the danger of

[3]Montreal *Gazette*, February 12, 1931.

becoming too improvisational, possibly even undisciplined. Not that Enesco had no discipline, but he wanted me to evolve a discipline of my own, leaving it to me to take from him as much as I felt like, and I am not certain that my instinct would have proved infallible. Enesco always faithfully adhered to the basic patterns of a musical composition, warning me to leave nothing undone in studying a work, to acquaint myself with all the pertinent biographical and historical data, but he left the details of bowing and fingering to my own inclinations and moods. Busch, on the other hand, tended to emphasize and supervise the execution of the minutest details, although, of course, he did not neglect general characteristics, the spirit and the inspiration of a piece.

"While Busch developed in me a sense of discipline, precision, and authority, particularly in the playing of Bach, it was Enesco who fired my imagination, imparting to me the mystic quality that has always been his, and thus awakening an insight into the sweep and grandeur of Bach."

Symbolic of the difference between Busch and Enesco was the use of the metronome: the latter never expected Yehudi to employ it during practice; with Busch, the metronome came as a matter of course.

However kind Busch was in his relationships with people, he was unbending in following the letter of the composer's intent, and he impressed upon Yehudi that one can give a satisfying performance of a classical composition only within a strict rhythmic framework. Yehudi sensed, and today the mature Menuhin is convinced, that one might achieve more rewarding results by adhering to a continuous rhythmic pattern, the actual subdivisions of which may be somewhat distorted by calculated, though never arbitrary, irregularities. Such a performance is vibrating, living, ever creative, and never mechanically predictable. To Menuhin, the progress of a musical work is not unlike the flow of a stream which adapts itself to variations of grade, caprices of nature, and yet always remains itself—a living stream.

In his studies at Basel, Yehudi missed the feeling of oneness

The Menuhin family in
San Francisco about 1923.

In Paris, 1927.

With Persinger, in his
studio, 1925.

At Ville d'Avray. *Front row:* Yaltah Hephzibah, and Yves Ciampi. *Second row:* Enesco, Yehudi, Alfred Cortot. *Third row:* Mme. Ciampi the conductor Nicolai Sokoloff Jacques Thibaud, Jan Hambourg *Fourth row:* Marcel Ciampi and Sam Franko.

Mr. and Mrs. Henry Goldman, Yehudi, and the Khevenhüller Strad. 1929.

ALBAN, PARIS

Jacques Thibaud and Yehudi at Ville d'Avray, Enesco looking on.

With Willa Cather
in Pasadena, 1931.

Yaltah, Yehudi, and Hephzibah
at Ville d'Avray, about 1933.

Yehudi, Enesco, Ciampi, and Hephzibah
in Paris, 1935.

With Emil Ludwig and Bruno Walter
at St. Moritz, 1934.

A picnic in Switzerland, 1934. *Left to right:*
Marutha, Yaltah, unidentified, Eda Cohn,
Hephzibah, Wanda Toscanini, Horowitz,
Yehudi, Marietji Van Rossen, Piatigorsky,
Lozinsky, Moshe.

The three Menuhins in the Botanical Gardens in Sydney, 1935.

The family in the artists' room, Carnegie Hall, 1933.

With Adolph Busch
in Basel, 1929.

With Bruno Walter and Dr. Wilhelm Brockhaus,
in Leipzig, 1932.

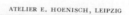

With Sir Edward Elgar and Sir Thomas Beecham,
London, 1932.

With Pierre Monteux
at Ville d'Avray, 1933.

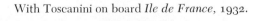

With Toscanini on board *Ile de France*, 1932.

With Nola, 1938.

With Zamira and Krov, at Alma, 1944.

ANNEMARIE HEINRICH,
BUENOS AIRES

HAROLD STEIN, N.Y.

he had known when working with Enesco, but he had such enormous respect for Busch's human qualities and scholarship that he never challenged the judgment of his new master beyond making mental reservations for the future. Once, as they were discussing the Bach fugue, Busch ruled that the initial theme must always be *forte*. But when Yehudi began the fugue of the A-minor sonata, he followed his intuitive tendency to play it softly, whereupon Busch stopped him and Yehudi dutifully changed to *forte*. A year or so later, while playing a Bach sonata with Enesco, Yehudi energetically announced the theme, only to be interrupted by an impatient:

"Softer, please! Do you not sense that the character of the theme is not aggressive? It is in minor, it's evocative, not affirmative."

"But shouldn't all fugue themes begin *forte?*"

Guessing the source of this conception, Enesco refrained from criticizing Busch. Yet, unable to compromise, he said: "If you feel this way, I must not stop you from doing it, but I believe that you will change as you grow older."

Yehudi "grew older" overnight, to play the introduction *piano,* feeling as he had originally that the enunciation of the theme in a fugue must be clear, pregnant, authoritative, but not necessarily aggressive.

It would seem that the only thing which Busch had in common with Enesco was his acceptance of Yehudi as a musician of overwhelming talent and in possession of a technique so stabilized that it seemed to require no particular attention. His first assignment was the Bach solo *Sonata in C major,* which calls for a special technique of three- and four-part chord playing, requiring tremendous strength in the bow arm and in the left-hand fingers. This technique, new to Yehudi, had to be mastered methodically in order not to jeopardize elasticity and lightness. The boy plunged headlong into the piece in characteristic fashion and, to Busch's amazement, played it superbly after three months of arduous work, with no one suspecting that this and similar extravagances were to impose their penalty years later.

Yehudi's daily two-hour sessions with his new accompanist, Hubert Giesen, were devoted to the assimilation of the vast repertoire the boy had built up with Persinger. "Hoopsie" and the young Menuhin were now preparing for a late-fall tour of Germany, to be followed by concerts in the U.S. scheduled between January and April 1930, at fees which incidentally made Yehudi the world's highest-paid concert artist. Adolf Busch was disappointed with the interruption in Yehudi's studies, but his joy in working with the youngster was so great that he agreed to take him on again when he returned from the United States.

"Hoopsie" was a most accomplished pianist, temperamental, with a flair for the dramatic, whom Yehudi occasionally had to stop with a plea to play softer "so that I can accompany you more effectively." Each time this happened, "Hoopsie" would cast a sheepish look at Moshe, then roar with laughter, bang Yehudi on the back, and resume playing.

With Yehudi away so much of the time, and busy practicing and rehearsing when at home, Marutha inevitably concentrated her energies on her two little girls, filling up their time with study, piano practice, and long walks. As always, the schedule was regular and exacting, with Yaltah occasionally bursting out in protest and Hephzibah adhering to the routine with a seemingly happy compliance. But even she, amenable though she was, cried out to Yaltah one day: "Imma is simply horrid sometimes!" Considering that this probably was Hephzibah's first and only transgression, it was unfortunate for the child that Marutha happened to be outside the door. The unhappy remark would have been irksome enough but not altogether unexpected had it emanated from the rebellious Yaltah, but, falling as it did from Hephzibah's lips, it cut to the quick. Marutha opened the door and accused her elder daughter of disloyalty. Hephzibah apologized with a cool dignity which only served to enhance the offense, and for the first time the children saw their mother helpless before any of them. They doubt even now whether she ever overcame her disappointment and shock that the only one who had seemed to respond ideally to her system of child upbringing had let her down. There was no formal punishment, as there had been no transgression of any established rule. Instead, an icy gloom spread over the little household, lasting for days until Marutha took sufficient hold of herself to take note of Hephzibah's presence once more. Stung by this experience, mother and daughter took great care in the future to avoid a test of will.

TEN

Ville d'Avray

Fritz Busch introduced Yehudi to England on November 10, 1929, in a performance of the Brahms concerto with the London Symphony Orchestra followed by a recital with Giesen at the Royal Albert Hall. The overwhelming success was sensationalized by the press with headlines that had an American touch to them: "Yehudi Menuhin's Genius"; "Greatest Prodigy of Our Time"; "Boy Violinist Mobbed on Platform"; etc., etc. He was indeed mobbed in the most literal sense, so that firemen had to be called in to reinforce the attendants unable to control the admiring crowds. The critics exhausted their stocks of superlatives, vying with each other in the lavishness of their praise. As usual, Yehudi accepted the adulation of the crowds in his calm, matter-of-fact way, far more excited over the number and variety of the automobiles he saw en route to the concert hall than over facing a new, not yet won audience. When his taxi was jammed in the traffic a few blocks before the Royal Albert Hall, he wistfully exclaimed: "What fun it would be to run from roof top to roof top of the cars ahead of us!" and looked up at Moshe as if expecting permission to do precisely that.

In addition to the concerts, there were two special events during that sojourn in the British capital. One was Yehudi's first recording with orchestra: the Max Bruch concerto, conducted by Sir Landon Ronald. The other was his meeting with Aunt Edie, his mother's cousin, of whom he had vaguely heard and who now relieved the sad thought that his was "a family without a family." The wife of a prosperous businessman, Aunt Edie lived in a comfortable house in Regent's Park North, where she entertained her many friends in London's musical world and, an excellent amateur pianist, took part in frequent sessions of chamber music at her home. She was gentle and warmhearted and grew to love Yehudi no less than her own Sonia and Jon, his seniors by a few years, with whom he played in the garden adjoining the house.

While Yehudi's first impressions of London, colored by the exceptionally dismal weather that autumn, were somewhat relieved by the cheerful kindness of Aunt Edie and her family, there was nothing to brighten the atmosphere for him, once he started out on a tour of England's manufacturing towns. Little did he guess as he lay in the cold, whitewashed, high-ceilinged hotel room in Birmingham or Liverpool, how much he would grow to cherish the people of England, so undemonstrative in personal contact, and yet so sensitive and faithful, their warmth and humor capable of overcoming the effect of the chilliest rain and of banishing the desperate feeling of aloneness which plagued him, as it does every concert artist.

The tour of the Continent that followed his concerts in England took him back to Germany, where, in the meantime, Hitler's brown shirts were becoming an increasingly dominant force. Aware of the Nazi anti-Semitism, Yehudi insisted on the inclusion of Bloch's *Abodah* in every concert, including that in Munich, where the Nazi party was strongest. Moshe hesitated, fearing harm to the boy, but with Adolf Busch's encouragement Yehudi carried out his intention without, fortunately, precipitating any untoward incidents. There followed recitals in Zurich and in Amsterdam, where the Dutch astonished him by rising to applaud after each piece, and on December 21 he left with Moshe and Giesen for a tour of the United States.

By that time, Yehudi Menuhin's name had become a household word in millions of American homes. Supplementing the news items about the boy's conquests of faraway European music centers there were countless up-to-date photographs, feature articles, editorials, and reprints of rapturous reviews.

Yehudi's name appeared in such widely syndicated features as "This Curious World," "Strange As It May Seem," and "Do You Know That?", with the latter proclaiming him an astonishing musical phenomenon and "one of the world's intellectual prodigies" to boot. He was invested with such supercolossal titles as "The Miracle Boy," "Genius," "America's Pride," "Uncle Sam's King David of the Violin," "Caruso of the Violin," "The Boy Wonder," "Goliath of the Violin," "Orpheus of the Violin," "The Violinist of the Century," "Menuhin the Great," and "The Einstein of the World's Virtuoso Violinists."

Reviews of his concerts in the music centers of America voiced amazement at his growth as a musician, noting that the deeper and more profound the work he played, the more perfect his performance. Especially memorable for Yehudi was his New York concert on the afternoon of February 22, 1930. He had developed a sore throat, and Moshe was all for canceling the performance, but when Yehudi learned that Arturo Toscanini had bought his own ticket for the concert, he insisted upon playing, and was rewarded by a backstage visit from the conductor who embraced him, shouting in a high-pitched voice: *"Bravissimo, Yehudi caro! Bravissimo!"*

Had the boy been allowed to read the reviews of his concerts during that U.S. tour he would have been grateful to the several critics who declared that it was no longer necessary to preface their comments by a mention of Yehudi's tender years. His claim to the full dignity and recognition of an artist was now undeniable. Nearing his fourteenth birthday, taller, slimmer, he was irritated by being treated and spoken of as a child prodigy. In fact, chancing soon after his arrival in the States to notice a poster announcing him as "the world's most famous prodigy," he had alternately begged and demanded of his manager that the word "prodigy" be deleted from all advertising material about him.

"A person is either an artist or he is not, and age has little to do with it! There is only one standard by which music must be judged—it is either good or bad." Thus he argued with the few friends and the still fewer reporters whom Moshe per-

mitted to see him, unwittingly adding fuel to the fires of publicity. Commentators devoted full columns to his protest,
analyzing the mystery of young genius, its evanescence,
sources, characteristics, trials, and the ways and means of pre-
venting it from deteriorating with the passing of time. Some
insisted that Yehudi would soon fall by the wayside, while
others made optimistic forecasts, citing an astonishing number
of prodigies who actually fulfilled the promise of their childhood and adolescence. It goes without saying that the classical
example of Mozart was cited, and of Felix Mendelssohn, as
well as the little-known fact that Camille Saint-Saëns composed waltzes at five and led an orchestra at ten, conducting
Beethoven and Mozart by heart. Josef Hofmann, it was recalled, launched regular concert tours at the age of five, while
Paderewski began to play the piano at three and Leopold
Godowsky was touring Russia at twelve. The names of Ján
Kubelik, Mischa Elman, and Jascha Heifetz adorned many a
dissertation which also pointed out that, although Fritz Kreisler gained fame in the U.S. long after he had passed adolescence, he won the first prize at the Vienna Conservatoire at
ten and the Prix de Rome at twelve.

Yehudi was still inaccessible to the press, but his father gave
interview after interview. Siding with those who did not believe in the evanescence of youthful talent, Moshe Menuhin
insisted that Yehudi's genius was primarily a result of the perfect harmony reigning in his immediate surroundings. The
wish being father to the thought, he declared in a wistful outburst: "Show me a perfect union and I will show you a perfect
child! A child who is the product of a fully harmonious union,
however humble his parents may be in native endowment, has
a greater 'genius capacity' than a child of a brilliant heredity,
blocked by the inharmonious union of his parents. I believe
ability or genuis is but the absence of friction in the human
organism. There is nothing for Yehudi to overcome in the
mastery of his violin."

This utterance moved the doctors and psychologists who

wrote daily or weekly columns to enter the lists and argue the pros and cons of the elder Menuhin's theory.

Thus Yehudi's name was bandied about in the American press as he traveled from city to city, absorbed in his work and reading, and in writing letters to his mother and sisters. His first act upon entering his hotel room was to take out their photographs, just as Moshe in the adjoining room was placing on his desk a photograph of his wife, on which she had written: "Bring him back as he was before he left."

The most memorable events for Yehudi during that American tour were his reunion with the Ehrmans, in San Francisco, and several meetings with Georges Enesco, who happened to be lecturing on music at Harvard University. The boy wanted to return to his old master, but Enesco's schedule would not permit it. Besides, he thought that additional work with Busch would consolidate the boy's gains. "You may later reject much of the German school," he said, "as you probably will, but you must know it, and no one can bring its great traditions to you as closely as Adolf Busch." And so Yehudi returned to Busch and to his own family in Basel, where he spent a rewarding though uneventful summer of hard work on his violin, studies, reading, games, and long weekend trips that took the family once more to many an unexplored nook and corner of Switzerland. The summer over, the Menuhins decided to go back to Paris, where Jan Hambourg had found them a lovely house in the wooded and pleasant suburb of Ville d'Avray, where Moshe and Yehudi would join the rest of the family after a new tour of Europe and the United States.

The parting with Adolf Busch was warm, but there was no heartbreak about it. Busch, and now also his brother Fritz, regretted, as the latter wrote in his memoirs, that "in spite of all warnings to the contrary, Yehudi began prematurely to develop into a virtuoso. He began a nomadic life that disinterested friends would have wished to spare the child." Moshe and Marutha, on the other hand, felt that the twenty or so concerts a year which Yehudi was now giving left ample time for him to develop and grow, simultaneously affording the financial security without which neither he nor his sisters would have the necessary opportunities for travel and education. The boy himself unquestioningly accepted his parents' decision, and not only out of sheer passivity: he enjoyed giving concerts and everything that went with them—travel by train and ship, new sights, reunions with friends, and the relaxation of discipline, a delightful consequence of being away from Marutha's unyielding supervision.

While staying with the Ehrmans during his American tour early in 1931, Yehudi learned from Esther that she was engaged to Claude Lazard, of the famous French banking family. Yehudi sweetly congratulated everyone concerned, yet it was not without pain that the difference in his and Esther's ages had thus been brought home to him. However, there was one great solace. He chanced upon an old friend, with whom he spent many happy hours—Willa Cather, one of the most distinguished writers of her generation. She had been introduced to the Menuhins in Paris by Jan Hambourg and quickly won the affection of Yehudi and his sisters, who called her "Aunt Willa."

It so happened that the University of California bestowed an honorary degree upon her in the spring of 1931, at precisely the time that Yehudi was giving concerts on the west coast, and the two spent much time together, meeting with no opposition from Moshe who, like Marutha, had been completely won over by Miss Cather. She, in turn, was so taken by Yehudi and his sisters that she had thought of dedicating *Shadows on the Rock* to them, but she hesitated when Sam Marantz cautioned her on the sensitiveness of the elder Menuhins to any display of attention to their children. In a letter of March 3, 1931, Willa Cather told Marantz she had learned early in her life that, whenever in doubt, the answer had better be in the negative. Inside the envelope was a separate sheet on which she had typed out the intended dedication: "For Yehudi, Hephzibah and Yaltah." Those words were crossed out in pencil, and underneath she had written: "This is off, understand."

Many more meetings between Yehudi and Willa Cather
were to follow in the years to come, the boy sharing Aunt
Willa with his sisters, but during that spring he had her all to
himself, and the two made a strange pair as they took their
long brisk walks, oblivious of the curious glances of passers-by
—she, solid, strong, with the broad, keen face of a peasant; he,
a handsome, bareheaded youth in shorts, with a sensitive
face and disarming, expectant eyes. He was to say later about
"Aunt Willa": "She was the most wholesome person I've ever
known, crystal-pure and simple, and with a sharp intelligence.
She was honest and straightforward, never shrinking from
saying things even if they hurt, so long as they were true
things and were spoken with affection. She had the strength
of the American soil which she loved so much and understood
so well."

Still averaging one concert a week, Yehudi had sufficient
time that spring to do much reading including several Shakespeare plays, *David Copperfield, Oliver Twist, A Connecticut
Yankee in King Arthur's Court, The Hunchback of Notre
Dame,* and Montaigne's *Essays,* as well as a comprehensive
comparative study of American and European political sys-
tems.

His performances were uniformly successful, the reaction
of the critics being best summed up by one of many headlines
in a similar vein: "Wonder of Yehudi Grows With Time."
Offers continued to pour in from all corners of the world, so
that before he once more sailed for France, to join his mother
and sisters, Yehudi was booked up for the next three years in
Europe and in the United States, after which, some time in
1934 or 1935, he was to make his first round-the-world tour.

At last, in time to celebrate his fifteenth birthday with the
entire family, Yehudi reached Paris in April 1931. There, in
his new home at Ville d'Avray, he found Marutha's school-
conservatory in full swing, and, with no concerts to think of
until October, he slipped into its routine quickly and imperceptibly. The white eighteenth-century-style house was charming and spacious, set in the center of a carefully tended garden

and backed by the lovely trees of the Parc de St. Cloud, whose walls flanked the garden on the south. To the north, an iron fence protected the place from intrusion, with a bell suspended above the gate to warn of anyone entering or leaving the premises. On the rare occasions when Yehudi wanted to slip out without Marutha's knowledge, Hephzibah would climb up his back to tie the tongue of the bell, careful to untie it when her brother returned.

The owners, a M. and Mme. Vian, had moved with their five children to a less imposing home on an adjacent lot where —Yehudi could observe with envy through openings in the hedge—the small Vians were recklessly riding their bicycles. He had never forgotten the bicycle he had had to give up and kept asking for one every now and then, only to be refused on the grounds that, as he had no idea of how to ride a bike, he was almost certain to break an arm or leg. With the help of the Vian children, he now surreptitiously acquired the necessary skill after a few falls, and one day presented his parents with a *fait accompli* by riding up the gravel drive when the whole family was set for a picnic lunch on the lawn. Bowing to the inevitable, the Menuhins bought three bicycles, the one for Yehudi boasting three speeds, a speedometer, lights, and free-wheeling foot brakes. In the company of his sisters, he now spent most of his free time bicycling in the park, darting in and out of paths, circling around statues, or rushing head-long down tree-lined alleys.

Yehudi's victory in the "battle of the bicycle" was merely one manifestation of the slowly altering relationships within the family. Seeing that her son, although growing up during the long absences and becoming accustomed to the compara-tive freedom of touring with his father, showed no tendency to challenge her authority, Marutha began to treat him with all the outward equality that can exist between an older, wiser sister and her adored young brother. Practice became his own responsibility, nor did anyone venture any longer to select for him the works he was to perform. Although Moshe continued to attend all of Yehudi's sessions with Enesco, he was in fact doing it as a matter more of habit and pleasure than of duty. To emphasize Yehudi's special position vis-à-vis the girls, Marutha introduced the luxury of breakfast in bed for him, which she herself brought in each morning, remaining in the room while he ate his fruit and eggs and drank the milk, discussing with him his work, reading, and the teachers.

The one matter on which no concession was made even to him was that of the mail. The family custom was that all letters were brought in unopened at lunchtime and read aloud, as were later also the replies. Since most of the friends were shared by the whole family—and indeed many a letter by the Menuhins was jointly signed "MoMaYeHeYa"—this custom was at first embraced enthusiastically by the children. But, as each of them began to harbor special little secrets, and as the comments from those around the table on both writer and recipient were often dipped in acid, the youngsters began to regret this unsophisticated habit, while the infrequent house guests were sometimes amused and more often embarrassed watching them blush or squirm during the lunch-time letter reading.

And yet, all in all, this was probably the family's happiest period together, the happiest and the most comfortable. The Gallic charm of the house was enhanced by Jan Hambourg's one-time servants, Ferruccio and his wife Bigina, who did the household chores with mirth, devotion, and efficiency. Formerly a jockey, Ferruccio was small and wiry, looking somewhat ridiculous alongside his slow, enormous, bosomy Bigina. They adored each other and were not in the least embarrassed at being surprised in an embrace by one or another of the children as they cleaned house or prepared the meals. Once a week, Moshe and Ferruccio, occasionally accompanied by Yehudi, drove up in the Menuhin Délage to Les Halles—Paris's incomparable wholesale market. They would start out at five in the morning, the half-asleep Yehudi aroused by the marvelous sight of mountains of vegetables, meats, and fruits and by

the vociferous liveliness of the crowd, to which was soon
added Moshe's animated haggling over price and quality. The
marketing completed, they would stop at Chez Androuet with
its proud display of hundreds of varieties of cheese, where,
after long hesitation and soul searching, Moshe invariably
ended by choosing his favorite Reblochon, as well as Brie,
Camembert, and goat cheese for the other members of the
family. The meals at home were simple and wholesome, consisting chiefly of meat, fish, salads of tomato or of mixed green
vegetables, cheese, and fruit.

Schooling proceeded as always, per schedule, the girls having resumed piano lessons with Marcel Ciampi and Yehudi
his sessions with Enesco. General studies were concentrated
chiefly on languages and reading, Marutha having added
Italian and, somewhat later, also Russian to the curriculum.

The French language and literature were taught by Professor Félix Bertaux and his young son Pierre, both of whom
stimulated the interest of the young Menuhins also in German
literature. All three of them possessed a remarkable facility
for languages and a feeling for the written word, with Yaltah
writing poetry in French and Italian, and Hephzibah devouring book after book in the four languages she knew, and
doing excellent translations, including, at the age of fourteen,
Hölderlin's romance *Hyperion* from German into French. Yehudi's literary interests did not go as far as that, but he too
read extensively, making particular progress in Russian, the
language in which he corresponded with his mother for years.

Father and son Bertaux fascinated Yehudi. Tall, dark, with
high cheekbones and fiery eyes, they came of a French peasant
family in Lorraine, where love for the native soil was inseparable from bitter hatred for the Germans and their culture.
Félix Bertaux saw danger in that hatred, and he eventually
became a professor of German and the author of books on the
German language as well as editor, together with his son, of
a French-German and German-French dictionary. Like his
father, Pierre intended to devote his life to the bringing about
of an intellectual understanding between his native country

and its strong and dangerous neighbor. Among his most vivid childhood memories were the visits to their house of Thomas Mann, Heinrich Mann, Jakob Wassermann, and other distinguished men of letters, and his father's championship in France of the works of Rainer Maria Rilke and Franz Kafka. A prodigy in his own right, Pierre was at one time the youngest professor in all France. Years later, his liberalism and his pride as a Frenchman were to land him in prison during the Occupation. He escaped and became one of the leaders of the resistance.[1]

The esteem in which Marutha held the Bertaux impelled her to give them a completely free hand in their work with Yehudi, especially as they were soon to direct his attention to fields that were beyond her or Moshe's competence. Aiming to broaden the youth's cultural horizon, the Bertaux augmented the studies of French and German literature with excursions into the classics of the ancient world and into the realm of philosophy.

"Both Father and I," Pierre Bertaux told me, "quickly noticed that Yehudi's gifts were not confined to the world of music alone. His is an unusually keen mind, not of the quick, flashy kind, but alert and implacably logical, cutting a direct path to the core of the problem at hand. He knew something about chess, for instance, and once I proposed to him a rather complicated problem which I was certain would take him a long time to solve, if solve it he could. But, as he worked on it, I was downright terrified by the unyielding quality of his logic, as it manifested itself in each succeeding step, avoiding detours and inevitably arriving at the correct solution. Although kept from free intercourse with others, his travels increasingly exposed him to the raging intellectual and political passions of our times, fascism in Italy, National Socialism in Germany, Soviet Russia's brand of communism. The one thing they had in common was the challenge they pre-

[1]The reader will find a fascinating account of Pierre Bertaux's turbulent life during and after World War II in Theodore White's *Fire in the Ashes.*

sented to the values of Western democracy, first asserted by the French Revolution, then reinforced and amplified by the American Revolution. Our reading and studies with Yehudi revolved around the idea of free inquiry, for my father and I firmly believed that the highest function of any theory is to open up a road in search of another one, still more valid, more profound and leading to yet greater spiritual heights. This creative restlessness, the one great contact between the cultures of all nations, was and is endangered by the demagogues' insistence that their theory is the only true one. Their vehemence, which has destroyed free inquiry in so large a part of the globe, is at the root of the gravest problems of our times."

Under the guidance of the Bertaux, Yehudi read intensively, rereading in a new light several novels of Victor Hugo and also the works of Descartes and Voltaire. Among American writers he read Thomas Paine and Thomas Jefferson, as well as *Heavenly Discourse* by Erskine Scott Wood, the American poet whom he was soon to meet.

The reading and the discussions with the Bertaux stimulated and fed the boy's interest in the fundamental problems of synthesis between good and evil, heaven and hell, right and wrong, etc., all of which he instinctively felt to be indivisible, ultimately leading toward a search for a philosophical concept that would embrace all mankind and the universe itself. That interest, originally aroused by the injustices he had begun to notice at a very early age, was later directed toward the more general philosophical questions as formulated by his father: "Who am I and whither am I going?" A further stage was reached with the Bertaux, especially after Yehudi had read Descartes's works with them, his attention drawn to the celebrated tenet: "*Je pense, donc je suis* [I think, therefore I exist]." As he grew and developed, he read the works of other European philosophers, of the ancient mystics of India and China, especially Lao-tse, ultimately finding many of the answers he had sought in the concepts of Spinoza and of Constantin Brunner, the German-Jewish philosopher who ex-

panded Spinoza's system, relating it to our own century.[2]
Yehudi Menuhin is now an active member of the Brunner
Society, whose headquarters are in The Hague, which has
undertaken as one of its major tasks to reissue the philosopher's
works, which had been banned and burned by the Nazis.

The three years during which Ville d'Avray served as home
base for the Menuhins were years of growth for the children
and happiness and contentment for the entire family. Yehudi
played a steadily increasing number of concerts each year, the
augmented income allowing Marutha and the girls to join
him on the long annual trips to the United States, putting an
end to the partings and to Marutha's fears that her boy might
not come back "the same." Relaxed, her face and figure still
beautiful, she made a wonderful hostess, impressing her guests
as a modest mother and retiring wife. She was inventive at
creating diversions such as a theater party or a picnic (concerts
were an integral part of the established routine) or improvising a drive into the countryside which often ended up with
a week in Switzerland or on the French Riviera. There was
an adventurousness and a happiness about her, converting
even her children's transgressions into a sort of game and
escapade, emphasizing the new camaraderie. One day Yaltah,
now a pretty and coquettish eleven-year-old, decided to follow
the new fashion of short hair for young ladies. Marutha for-
bade her to touch her long, fair curls, but the little girl could
not resist the temptation of snipping off the locks on one side
"just to see how it would look." It looked pretty awful, everyone agreed, and worse still when the angry Marutha shaved
Yaltah's entire golden head. Out of solidarity with their
frantically unhappy sister, Yehudi and Hephzibah promptly
cut off each other's hair in a fashion so frightful that Marutha
had no recourse but to shave their heads as well. To their
surprise, she laughed as she did it, saying that her mother had
always believed in shaving the head every once in a while, to

[2]See Walter Bernard, *The Philosophy of Spinoza and Brunner*
(New York: The Spinoza Institute of America, 1934).

help the hair acquire a new luster. As a crowning gesture in this orgy of haircutting, she had her own hair shaved off and wore a most becoming turban when visitors came.

Apart from those who were especially invited to Ville d'Avray, the Menuhins kept themselves isolated from unbidden intrusion, watching the world through the fence surrounding their beautiful lawn and through hotel and automobile windows. True, travel and studies, especially discussions with the Bertaux, opened the young Menuhins' eyes to much of what went on beyond their ivory tower, and they knew in an abstract way of the world around them, of its passions and compulsions. But the parental curtain separated them from that world, while their youth and the conditioning since infancy prevented them from being tempted to probe the impenetrability of that curtain. When Yehudi once cautiously brought up the maxim that knowledge is gained from experience, through trial and error, Marutha replied: "My mother used to say that only fools learn by their own mistakes. Wise men profit by the mistakes of others."

Despite her relaxed ways, and despite Yehudi's growing up, his fame, and his role of breadwinner, she continued to be the focal point around which revolved the life of the family, the sole source of authority, direction, and control. Instead of having, as does the overwhelming majority of children, a number of such sources of authority—other relatives, the school, the church, friends—the Menuhin children knew only their mother. For all her love and care, she atrophied all initiative, basing the relationships within the family on her intrinsically Russian and, indeed, oriental conceptions, and this could not fail to have its lasting after-effects. She was the queen, Moshe the consort, acting by virtue of relegated authority, and Yehudi the first-born, the prince who accepted in a detached sort of way the role allotted to him, knowing full well that, however pleasant the protocol, with all its attendant superficialities, it implied no real authority, for it was his mother who exercised all control and who always found ways to exact the reverence befitting her real role.

On one occasion, Yehudi unintentionally committed an act the consequences of which proved instructive to him in respect not only to his mother but to feminine ways in general. He had established a charming custom of sending, on the day of a concert, an orchid to Marutha and roses to his two sisters. Aunt Edie and Sonia happened to be staying at Ville d'Avray at a time when Yehudi was giving a concert in Paris. The boy gallantly sent flowers also for the two guests, but he made the innocent mistake of selecting an orchid for Aunt Edie identical in size and color to the one he had chosen for his mother, whereupon Marutha announced that orchids did not go well with the dresses both ladies were wearing that night, and the flowers were left behind. Poor Yehudi was utterly confused, but his younger sisters and Sonia proceeded to enlighten him.

The Ville d'Avray period, lasting from 1931 to 1934, was marked by an ever widening recognition of Yehudi Menuhin as a mature artist, "the youngest of the Olympians." In June 1931 he received the first of the many honors that have been heaped upon him in the course of his career and that were to include the Belgian Order Leopold and the French Légion d'Honneur: he was given an honorary award of the coveted *Premier Prix,* first prize of the Paris Conservatoire, at a dinner of the Association Amicale des Prix de Violons du Conservatoire. The guest of honor was feted by one hundred former winners, including Enesco, Thibaud, and Cortot, who often went to Ville d'Avray, where they played chamber music for hours, Hephzibah alternating with Cortot at the piano. Georges Enesco planned the programs of those unforgettable sessions and assigned the parts. He, Yehudi, and the talented young Jacqueline Salomons alternated at playing the first and second violins; Pierre Monteux or Enesco played the viola, and Maurice Eisenberg the cello. Whenever the works included the piano, Enesco would call on Hephzibah or on the brilliant young Arthur Balsam, who had replaced Giesen as Yehudi's accompanist in 1932. These sessions sometimes lasted until

long after midnight, followed by enormous suppers provided
by Marutha and enlivened by Enesco's sparkling wit.

Hephzibah's occasional participation in the music making
gave Yehudi enormous satisfaction, for he had discovered that
he felt at one with her to a degree not approached by any one
of his piano partners. Soon they were playing sonatas together.
"We understood each other so well," says Menuhin, "that we
were really as one person. We would be playing back to back,
yet each would know exactly the other's feelings and intentions. It was sheer joy to play with Hephzibah, a joy that has
lost nothing of its force through the years. She has a fine sense
of style and is the most disciplined person I've ever known.
I like to think of her as an English garden, the trees and
hedges beautifully shaped, the lawn clean-cut, whereas Yaltah
reminds me of a blooming tropical garden where everything
grows wild."

It might be said of Yehudi that he comes somewhere in between. In fact, on one occasion, reflecting on the serene, self-
contained strength of one sister and the searching restlessness
of the other, he said: "Hephzibah is my outer self; Yaltah is
my inner self." Yaltah was still too young to play sonatas with
Yehudi on any basis of equal participation, and so, for that
matter, was Hephzibah, but the latter's technical equipment
was already equal to the task, while her sense of discipline
and impeccable attention to detail constituted a challenge
even to his high standards. Their devotion to each other during the years of growing together resulted in an almost complete identity of approach, which prompted Yehudi to say: "I
do not believe that there ever existed a partnership more
naturally, instinctively perfect than ours." Hephzibah had
sufficient understanding of and submissiveness to her adored
brother to avoid friction; he had sufficient understanding and
love to avoid causing her humiliation. Added to it was mastery
of their chosen instruments, producing what later was hailed
by the world press as the greatest brother-and-sister team in
the history of music, and one of its most rewarding partner-
ships.

They had begun playing together without any thought of joint concerts until one day Georges Enesco heard them "having a lot of fun" with a Beethoven sonata. Struck by the extraordinary perfection of the playing, he suggested that they appear in a joint concert, but Marutha objected to the idea of another traveling musician in her family as well as to the concert stage as a career for women. There the matter rested, while Yehudi and Hephzibah went on playing sonatas together out of sheer inner compulsion. They worked separately during the mornings, Hephzibah singing the violin part as she practiced her own; later, in the afternoon or evening, they played together, which subsequently proved to be at least as effective as formal rehearsals. In December 1933, they recorded the Mozart *Sonata in A* (K. 526), which received the *Candide* prize as the best disk of the year, as had the Enesco-Menuhin recording of the Bach double concerto the year before.

Yielding to pressures on every side, Marutha finally allowed the first public concert by the brother-and-sister team to take place on October 13, 1934, at the Salle Pleyel. This was Hephzibah's Paris debut and the second concert in her life. The program, which consisted of the Mozart *Sonata in A*, Schumann's *Sonata in D minor*, Opus 121, and Beethoven's "Kreutzer," was soon repeated at the Queen's Hall, London, and in New York's Town Hall. The critics and audiences in all three cities hailed the perfection of the ensemble, even as had Enesco, covering the Menuhin name with new glory. As Yehudi was already an established artist, most of the attention was naturally focused on his fourteen-year-old sister, who behaved on the stage just as she had six years earlier: as if she were merely "practicing in the presence of many people." Appearing on the platform with Hephzibah, Yehudi would pause briefly to acknowledge the applause that greeted them, but she would go straight to the piano and seat herself without so much as a look at the audience, calmly waiting for the noise to subside. Then she would confidently plunge into the first work on the program, passing on with equal authority from movement to movement, from mood to mood, and from composer to com-

poser, playing with an aplomb and a security amazing in a
musician so young. In New York, as previously in Paris and
London, she refused to acknowledge the applause that inevitably followed each movement, and when they were recalled
again and again at the end of a sonata, she held her brother
by the hand and, instead of taking her bows with him, half-
faced Yehudi, occasionally stealing a tranquil glance at the
clamorous audience. The critics, too, were captivated by the
young pair, devoting as much space to their mystification over
the complete harmony of the ensemble as to praise for it. In
a letter written in January 1954, Hephzibah threw a light on
the "mystery" in her own clear-eyed way:

*Yehudi was very kind to me musically, too. Considering
how recently I've woken up to the reality of music, I realise
how carefully he guarded my balance, to ensure that no
doubts crept into my mind prematurely. He used to go over
the scores with me before concerts or recordings, explaining
musical associations, putting life into phrases, filling in wide
outlines with pertinent detail, so that I was intellectually
safe, within well reasoned arguments. As for emotional freedom, he often commented adversely on my cold efficiency
and asked me if I was in fact as unfeeling as I seemed. I
was not, of course, but I was very ashamed of expressing
emotions, and would have sooner died than rehearse them
for the purpose of exteriorizing. Whatever came naturally,
when all else had been planned and practiced, I never held
back at the time of the performance; and I always relied on
him completely to take the lead. I would have followed him
anywhere. Don't I remember how carefully he told me that
one must have an interpretation at one's fingertips and in
one's head so well perfected that in case inspiration fails,
one might still give a fine performance—true to style and to
meaning in every detail.*

*I remember one Mozart Sonata at the Metropolitan Opera
House in New York, 1938, and it went so beautifully, of
its own accord, that we were both quite thrilled with it.*

In fact, just at the Coda I was listening so spellbound that I forgot to play, and only came in, a split second late, by a tremendously shocked effort of will. We both laughed at this, and then very much enjoyed the after-concert crowding of well wishers, because we felt we had for once deserved their praise.

How well I remember the time in Sydney in 1940, when we played the Kreutzer Sonata, and in a fit of absent-mindedness I left out the repeat of the first half of the minor variation of the slow movement! We were such a team that Yehudi automatically took the cue and came in at the corresponding place, only to register the gap several bars later. I was so amused by the smooth deception that I began to giggle to myself, and was hardly able to control the con-vulsive bursts—I had no means of knowing at precisely what moment he had woken up to the accident—all I knew was that with such a partner one simply had nothing to risk.

In truth, Yehudi was more to Hephzibah than an adored older brother or the more mature musician. She looked up to him with a wonder and awe which time has not outworn, prompting her to exclaim in a recent letter: "To be related to Yehudi means to be part of the endless miracle of life."

Yehudi and Hephzibah were so happy with their joint appearances that many more would soon have followed had their mother not withdrawn the girl from the concert stage once more. "A woman's place is in her home," Marutha said, adding at a later date that she "always praised Hephzibah far more for a well-balanced, well-executed dinner cooked by her than for any concert she ever played with her brother. . . . Hephzibah yearns for Paris and solo recitals and a career of her own. I say it is better that she be happy than famous. I tell her that the only immortality to which a woman should aspire is that of a home and children. Career women lose the most important things of life and do not realize it until it is too late."[3]

[3] San Francisco *Chronicle*, August 11, 1936.

Thus it came about that joint concerts were few and far between after the Town Hall sonata recital, but brother and sister went on playing together for two hours or more each day whenever Yehudi was not away on the road. His tours were becoming ever more extensive, with the orchestras and conductors of Europe and the United States vying with each other for the privilege of playing with him. The sole exception was Toscanini, who inexplicably remained aloof despite the admiration he had voiced for the young violinist. Yehudi, on the other hand, was yearning to play with the Maestro, and was soon to see his dream become a reality. In the meantime, he was to have an inspiring encounter with another great musician, the English composer Sir Edward Elgar.

ELEVEN

Elgar, Toscanini, and a Battle Lost

The grand old man of British music was living in retirement on his country estate near Worcester, tending flowers, backing horses, caring for his dogs, and looking every inch the country squire. He would probably have remained away from musical activity had not Frederick Gaisberg, of His Master's Voice, in London, conceived a plan for recording Elgar's violin concerto in honor of his seventy-fifth birthday, the composer himself conducting. Yehudi Menuhin, Gaisberg decided, should play the solo because of the contrast in age and because the sixteen-year-old violinist "would be pliant and would respond best to his [Elgar's] instruction."[1] The arrangements included also an Albert Hall concert on November 20, 1932, at which the work would be performed. Yehudi arrived in London three days in advance, to have ample time for rehearsals, but hardly had he played the first thirty bars or so (with Ivor Newton, who is one of Britain's two finest accompanists, the other being Gerald Moore), than Sir Edward exclaimed, according to Gaisberg: "I can add nothing. It cannot be done better. You need not work on it any longer, and let's go to the races, instead. It's a fine day, and I shall show you something of London."

The concert that followed assumed the proportions of a national celebration, with a representative of the royal household, the Prime Minister, and his cabinet joining the thousands who thronged the Royal Albert Hall. Yehudi looked young and

[1] F. W. Gaisberg, *The Music Goes Round* (New York: Macmillan & Co. 1942), p. 246.

touching in his first double-breasted black suit, staying in the background as much as he could, to allow the venerable composer to receive the happy tribute of the audience.

Delighted with the success of his venture, the indefatigable Gaisberg sought to repeat the performance in Paris with a French orchestra sometime early the next year. On November 23, 1932, the composer wrote to Moshe Menuhin:

> *I sent a short note to the dear boy at the Grosvenor House immediately after the concert. I will not repeat to you here what a wonderful event the concert was; you will be tired of this sort of thing; but I must tell you that I was overcome by the 'majesty' of Yehudi's playing. His tender and affectionate candour of me (this I prize perhaps more than anything) and your great consideration and kindness are very happy memories.*
>
> *As to Paris in May: I find now that I am free on the date you named, 31st May, but I must be quite candid and ask you to consider if it will not be a risk for Yehudi's immense fame and position to be associated with me. Please understand that I deeply feel the honour and pleasure of accompanying Yehudi, but, while the musicians of all countries (I am happy to say) are on friendly and fraternal terms with me, the Press and, with it, the public do not believe in English musicians, and I fear my appearance in Paris might do more harm to you than good.*
>
> *The attitude of the Press, I feel sure, would be that dear Yehudi was making a mistake in appearing with a musician of very inferior calibre (me). I am much too philosophical to feel any hurt at the well-meant slighting of my abilities, but I cannot bear to think of Yehudi being held responsible for anything not of the first rank.*

Needless to say, this unusual letter had no effect whatsoever on the Menuhins. The extreme modesty of the composer was actually embarrassing to Yehudi, who, like most performing artists, has always held men of creative talent in great reverence. The violinist felt then, as he does now, that "what

Tchaikovsky is to Russian music and César Franck to French music, Sir Edward is to British music. If, being English, he is more stately, it is the more remarkable that he created a work of such melodiousness and warmth. Its orchestration is wonderfully subtle and rich." Yehudi would have felt even more embarrassed and touched had he known that Elgar had risen in defense of the violinist's Albert Hall performance, which was disapproved of by Ernest Newman, dean of the British music critics. Although an admirer of Menuhin for many years, Newman felt that the Elgar concerto was played *too* beautifully, sounded too rich and sensuous, thus robbing the work of its "English reserve and austerity." Elgar, however, was happy that Yehudi captured the sunniness and sensuousness of his disposition, and he resented the ultra-British attitude of those who censured his "dear boy." The music critic Neville Cardus later reported Sir Edward as saying to him: "This is how I heard the slow movement when I was composing it. Why does Ernest Newman object that Menuhin makes the second subject of the first movement lovely and luscious—it is a lovely and luscious tune, isn't it? Austerity be damned! I am not an austere man, am I?"[2]

As in London, the Paris performance of the Elgar concerto assumed the aspect of a state tribute to the man who was in the eyes of the world the *doyen* of British music, but despite all the "bravos," Sir Edward realized, as he told the Menuhins, that his premonition was right: the French responded to the occasion and to Yehudi's performance, but not to the music itself. Hoping for a better reception in the United States, he considered participating in a Boston festival of his works and was negotiating with Koussevitzky, but, alas, the composer died before he could carry out his plans. Yehudi's life was only beginning, but to this day he cherishes the memory of that contact, and not only because the violinist continues to admire the composer, but also because Elgar remains to Menuhin the very personification of England, a country which in the course of years has become a second home to him.

[2]*Herald*, Sydney, Australia, April 26, 1940.

As Yehudi made his annual trips to the States, the newspapers faithfully reported each inch or two he had grown; the change from knee pants to knickers to long trousers; the down that eventually appeared above his upper lip; and his first razor, a gift from Marutha. Similarly, music critics noted a maturity in him, a growth of interpretative powers, a deepening of the imagination, an integration in his performance of all the essentials of a creative act. Redfern Mason, who had been the first to hail him as a prodigy, was now the first to declare that "today Yehudi plays like a man! . . . He left us as a lad; he comes back to us with a man's vision of that baffling mystery which is life. People felt a touch of regret for the wonder that is gone; but it was replaced by an equal wonder for the mature phenomenon which has come in its stead."

It was during that transition from boy to young man that Menuhin's path crossed Toscanini's once more. This time, chance played a decisive role when, on April 30, 1932, they met on the deck of the eastbound *Ile de France* and happily plunged into a discussion of music. Suddenly aware of the crowd that had gathered around them, they withdrew, together with Moshe and Balsam, to the music salon, on the door to which the chief steward posted a "No admittance" sign. With Balsam and occasionally Toscanini at the piano, Yehudi played two or three hours every morning. The Maestro seemed to be the happiest person on board, as he prodded the boy to keep on playing, shouting: *"Bravo, Yehudi caro! Bravissimo!"* Or he would pat him on the head, saying: "How you have grown since I heard you three years ago!" With a wistfulness which would have seemed theatrical in anyone less spontaneous than the Maestro he once exclaimed: "Oh, how little good music I hear in my life! Come, my child, play, play!" Yehudi kept asking for criticism, but Toscanini interrupted him each time with an impatient: "You don't know how to make a mistake! Just go on playing!" Play he did, fired by Toscanini's exuberance, as was also the pianist Balsam, who says he'll never forget the impetuousness of his exalted page turner. Toscanini put so much of his creative restlessness into the dreary business of turning pages that it seemed as though he were conducting, transmitting to Yehudi and Balsam the fire of his own temperament.

As usual on ocean-going liners, a benefit concert for the Seaman's Fund was held on the night before the ship arrived in port. At Toscanini's suggestion, the entire program was filled by Yehudi, who played on one condition: the concert was to be open to the passengers of all classes. Next morning, the conductor and the violinist exchanged parting gifts: a bronze medal bearing the Maestro's head in relief and a photo of Yehudi with Adolf Busch.

More than a year and a half was to pass before the two met again, Yehudi never missing a chance to attend a Toscanini concert, while the Maestro seemed to have forgotten him once more. Sometime in December 1933 Moshe and Yehudi arrived in Toscanini's own Milan, where the violinist was to give his first recital. The Maestro contacted the Menuhins and took them for a stroll along the boulevards of Milan, extolling the city's landmarks, talking about music, and pouring invective upon Mussolini's fascist regime. He cajoled Moshe into letting him "be Papa" that night, stayed backstage throughout the concert, cheered and applauded, rubbed Yehudi down with alcohol, and helped change his shirt during the intermission, muttering to himself in a stage whisper: "Tonight I am Papa!" After the concert, he whisked away the Menuhins to a big reception at his home, where, in parting, he embraced the violinist and whispered in his ear: "We simply must play together, Yehudi *caro!*" Soon after, Moshe received word from Evans and Salter that Yehudi had been engaged to appear in an all-Beethoven program with Toscanini on January 18 and 19, 1934, the opening concerts of Yehudi's forthcoming American tour.

On board the New York bound S/S *Rex* the Menuhins discovered aboard what the other passengers were soon to term "a wild cargo of musicians": Toscanini, Vladimir Horowitz, Nathan Milstein, Gregor Piatigorsky, and Bernardino Molinari, among others. The crossing was rough, keeping most of the passengers in their cabins, but, like Toscanini, the young Menuhin seemed to thrive on the bad weather, and he played several times in the Maestro's suite, accompanied by the latter's erratic whistling and falsetto. They also talked: about their forthcoming joint performance of the Beethoven and, even at greater length, about the boycott of Germany by most of the world's noted musicians in retaliation for Hitler's persecution of the Jews. Shortly before Yehudi had embarked, he had received an invitation from Wilhelm Furtwängler, director of the Berlin Philharmonic, to play with his orchestra. Although Yehudi regretted missing this, his first opportunity to play with Furtwängler, he refused by wire, "unless the ban against the memory of Mendelssohn were raised, or the ban against Bruno Walter and other musicians of Jewish blood." Yehudi now learned from Toscanini that the Maestro, too, had declined to appear in Germany.

On arrival at New York, Yehudi called on Toscanini in his Hotel Astor suite to go over the Beethoven concerto with him. The Maestro was in an exuberant mood, talking, clowning, and whistling, but finally settled down at the piano, and all went well until, as they were nearing the end of the second movement, the telephone rang. Toscanini, who had left word that he was not to be disturbed, shuddered at the sound, but went on playing as if expecting the heavenly serenity of the music to still the phone. The second ring was longer, more insistent, yet Toscanini went on. But when the third ring sounded he took several long, wild steps toward the telephone, seized the wire with both hands, and tore it out of its moorings, plaster and all. Without a word he returned to the piano and resumed playing, completely relaxed, as if all his rage had spent itself on the struggle with the wire. The moment they finished, the hotel manager, accompanied by Mme. Toscanini, came in, offering humble apologies for the disturbance. When would it please the Maestro to have the wire reinstalled? Far from making the expected scene, Toscanini treated the whole matter as a great joke.

Recalling the story, Menuhin said: "I had never seen anyone

obey his impulses without a second thought or regret. Taught
from babyhood to keep my emotions under rigid control, I
early learned to sublimate into music making everything that
was in me of the dark free world of impulse. But here, before
my own eyes, a person obeyed his impulse, and the others
thought it natural. *They* apologized. The right or wrong of it
did not interest me at the time—the revelation and the discovery was that a lack of inhibition can exist to the point
where nothing would be suffered, suppressed, or regretted.
Therein, to a large degree, lies the secret of Toscanini's greatness: complete abandon on the one hand and, on the other, an
implacable inner discipline that sets the highest standards. I
had never even imagined the possibility of yielding to impulse.
Responsible for it was not only the upbringing my parents had
given me. My three teachers—Persinger, Enesco, Busch—were
too kind, too considerate and civilized to follow their elemen-
tal instincts to the degree which Toscanini found natural. The
closest I ever came to a similar indulgence happened some
two years later, when, in a fit of irritation, I slammed the door
of our automobile, breaking the glass. I was so shocked at
myself that I never again allowed my emotions to run out of
control."

The Toscanini-Menuhin concert was one of those rare musical events whose glory does not diminish with time for those
who were present. The orchestra, the soloist, and the conductor
paid homage to Beethoven's genius with both reverence and
mastery. The critics praised the orchestra and extolled Toscanini, but most of the inspired lines were reserved for the
soloist, particularly those of W. J. Henderson, of the New York
Sun:

> *What the child had performed in 1927 with the sheer
> rapture of a gifted nature, the youth played with a passion-
> ate adoration born of new vision and manly emotion. There
> was not a moment of carelessness, not a phrase wanting in
> meticulous finish, yet one never felt that there was an in-
> stant of restraint. The boy projected his spiritual immersion*

*in the music with an art that defied analysis. The perform-
ance was violin playing of the first order, ranking with anything the present recorder had ever heard in his long years
of listening, and an interpretation of the concerto that combined depth, tenderness, and the eager service of the artist
soul. One was convinced that Menuhin loved and revered
Beethoven.*

With the touching sincerity of youth, Yehudi showed his
love and reverence for Toscanini as well—in the way he looked
at him and bowed to him before acknowledging the tribute
of the audience. Afterwards, in the privacy of the Menuhin
apartment at the Ansonia, his mother reprimanded him for
what she considered an exaggerated display of humility. But
this is *Toscanini*, he protested. But you are *Yehudi Menuhin*,
she replied angrily, a Yehudi not worthy of his name!

At the repeat performance two days later, Yehudi was reserved when he and Toscanini appeared on the stage and
forced himself to look straight ahead during the long *tutti*, instead of watching the Maestro's every movement, as on the
previous occasion. Gradually, the music absorbed him, forcing
him to abandon his self-conscious efforts and to contribute his
share to a performance in which the orchestra, the conductor
and the soloist again surpassed themselves, as though borrow-
ing from each other's greatness. With the conclusion of the
concerto, however, Yehudi reassumed his reserve toward
Toscanini, displaying, in marked contrast to the preceding
night, the self-confidence of a triumphant star.

The Menuhins returned to Europe for the summer, spending
part of it at Ospedaletti, Italy, where Yehudi received a note
from Toscanini, inviting the entire family to visit him at his
country home on Lago Maggiore, a comparatively short distance away. Anticipating a renewal of friendship and another
orgy of music making, Yehudi was enchanted with the idea,
but Marutha vetoed the project: "If the Maestro wants to see
you and play with you, he will be welcome here." Toscanini
was advised accordingly in a polite, formal letter, and the

reunion did not take place. The two musicians have never again appeared in joint concerts, nor did they reclaim their friendship until the summer of 1954, when Menuhin visited the aged Maestro in his voluntary retirement to Pallanza on Lago Maggiore.

As he sat on the lovely terrace overlooking the lake, Toscanini at first seemed to breathe tranquillity and contentment, but little time was to pass before he revealed his restlessness. Speaking Italian, he said: "I wanted really to see if I am as old and useless as some people think I am, and this morning I played the recording I had made with the NBC Symphony last March of Beethoven's Fifth Symphony. You know that I have always been my own severest critic but upon listening to the recording I had to admit that the old man still has much to say."

Yehudi had capitulated to his mother in connection with Toscanini mainly because he had challenged her will only a short while earlier over an issue of even greater meaning to him, and had gone down in defeat. Henry Goldman, who had given him his incomparable "Prince Khevenhüller," had just undergone his last, and unsuccessful, eye operation, and was now deprived, among other things, of the pleasure of attending Yehudi's concerts, but, accompanied by Moshe, the boy often visited his ailing friend during his short stays in New York. One day Dr. Garbat told the Menuhins that Goldman was asking if Yehudi would some day play for him, to which the youth responded eagerly, but Moshe, embarrassed, said that they would have to think about it because it involved a principle laid down by Marutha years ago, that her son would not play anywhere except in a concert hall, and neither royalty nor riches had ever succeeded in inducing her to make an exception. Yehudi braced himself for a hammering out of the issue, but neither he nor his father had expected the violence with which she voiced her opposition. Her pride, she said, would not permit her to let her son be enslaved by gratitude for the rest of his life. She'd rather he returned the violin! In vain did Yehudi remind her that she did not object to his playing in the Ehrman home. That was a different matter, she said, the Ehrmans were friends, not benefactors. In vain did he claim that Goldman, too, had become a friend, and that surely the Ehrmans themselves had begun as benefactors. It was not so, she retorted, creating by her vehemence two unspoken yet clearly conveyed alternatives: to leave his violin at home; or to play for Goldman and face a rupture with her. Yehudi dared not test her firmness for, unbelievable though it may seem, even at that late hour no reality existed for him outside the reality of his family, and the very possibility of breaking away was to him unthinkable. So, there was no choice, after all. Sick at heart and desperate with remorse and guilt, Yehudi visited his ailing friend the next day, having left the violin behind. If Mr. Goldman sensed the cheerlessness in Yehudi's voice, or if he was pained by the youth's failure to respond to his wish, he said nothing. Henry Goldman died several years later, little realizing that he had caused the first major crisis in Yehudi's life, a crisis he has never forgotten.

Nineteen years later, in the spring of 1953, I accompanied Menuhin on a trip to The Hague, where he was to devote an entire concert to three of Bach's monumental works for the solo violin. The manager in Holland, Dr. de Koos, met us at the airport with the mail which always awaits Menuhin at each of his stops. Among the letters was one from a stranger, signed C. van der Werff. His eighteen-year-old daughter Tineke, the Dutchman wrote, was a pianist who had looked forward to attending his Bach concert but was now bedridden, dying of leukemia. "Maybe you find my request to play at her bedside ridiculous, yet what but ridiculousness can you expect from parents in their endeavour to give their child's last days the light that your art can give her? . . . We will understand when you cannot fulfill our request but I know that you will excuse my letter, which has been caused by my conviction that sometimes miracles occur. Not the miracle that will save our child but a miracle that can be done to her spirit."

We found Tineke lying on a cheap iron bed in a living room heated by an iron coal stove, although the day was warm and sunny. The girl was blue-eyed and fair-haired, her face all bone and yellowish-gray skin, her wasted arms weirdly artificial. Menuhin played the *Chaconne* for her, and then the *Gavotte*. "This *is* Bach. I feel I've touched him," the girl said in a hardly audible voice.

On the way back to the hotel, I asked: "Will you ever forget Mr. Goldman, Yehudi?"

"No, I cannot, and I fear I never will!"

At his request I promised to mention this incident to no one, but, overcome with gratitude, Mr. Werff gave the story to the newspapers, which released me from my promise. Tineke died several weeks later, having willed her only earthly possessions, three little silver bracelets, to Menuhin's thirteen-year-old daughter Zamira.

The clash over Goldman was the first contest of will between Yehudi and his mother, although it had been preceded by a series of vague minor skirmishes the import of which had escaped him. Yehudi was emerging into an adolescence whose urges, however thoroughly sublimated in the daily grind of study, travel, and music making, were making themselves felt. Without himself being aware of it, Yehudi was wearying of his father's constant presence at his side. While still finding joy in Hephzibah's and Yaltah's company and devotion, he often wished he could see more of, and as freely, his cousin Sonia or Rosalie Leventritt or Lydia Perera, daughters of family friends and prominent patrons of music. He frequently found himself daydreaming, bold in pursuit of romance and adventure, but, coming into actual contact with other youngsters, he revealed a timidity and a lack of worldly knowledge which truly astonished them. As Rosalie told me years later: "All we could say, looking at him, was: 'Oh, no, it cannot be!' and left it at that. We somehow could not get through to him even when his parents weren't around." During a New York sojourn in 1933, when he was seventeen, he rushed headlong into a reckless adventure: he crossed the street for the first time with no one at his side; having gone alone to lunch with the Leventritts, he took Rosalie to a matinee afterwards without first consulting his parents. Marutha, aghast at this unprecedented action, wrested a promise from him that he would not do any such thing again. Yehudi kept his promise, but his very resignation carried with it its own punishment. He grew listless, tired, apathetic to his continuing triumphs on the concert stage. The parents, happy in his success and in the togetherness of the family, seemed to notice nothing. Nonetheless, some of their friends did, and they must have spread the word, for every now and then, a newspaper story would be headlined: "Yehudi, Violin Dictator, Does Not Answer His Father Back." One interviewing journalist, Raymond Dannenbaum, asked Moshe: "Is Yehudi ever alone?" and the father walked straight into the trap: "No, never! We are always with him—to take care of him." Whereupon the reporter mused:

> *Where are those hours when a youth dreams in the sun?*
> *Where hide those moments of delicious loneliness, when a*
> *boy sits by himself beside a river? . . . Yehudi is not ordi-*
> *nary to contemplate. The fine aquilinity of his face, his sen-*
> *sitive nostrils, the bridge of brow across the apex of his*
> *nose, set him apart as a kind of youthful faun. 'Papa'*
> *Menuhin galloping about him, superintending his learning,*
> *his every thought, is like the elderly satyr instructing the*
> *precocious son in the wiles of forest and brook. Sometimes*
> *Moshe is more centaur than satyr or faun. Then he watches*
> *Yehudi as Nessus watched, edging about his son in super-*
> *vision, describing a semicircle with his hinder hoofs.*

Dr. and Mrs. Garbat were watching with grave concern Yehudi's cheerlessness, especially during the weeks that followed his frustrated attempt to play at Goldman's bedside. Although directly involved in the incident, and deeply hurt,

Dr. Garbat held himself aloof, but his wife did speak to Marutha, with the result that the two families began to see less and less of each other, until all contact between them was severed.

Another crisis arose when Enesco, touring the United States, learned about the Goldman incident. The very soul of gentleness and discretion, Enesco had never interfered with the ways of what he called the "Biblical Family Menuhin," but now he chastised Marutha in the presence of her husband and children. Yehudi expected his mother to explode and was bracing himself to side with his master. As though sensing the danger of the moment, Marutha diverted it with feminine adroitness by suddenly making light of the whole matter. Laughing it off, she said that, thank God, Yehudi would soon reach majority and make his own decisions, and then his first independent act she hoped, would be to choose a girl and get married. Thus the ground was cut away from under his feet, as everyone made merry at his expense, with an exuberance born of relief that a crisis had been averted.

The annual trips of the Menuhins to the States allowed them to renew their acquaintance with Willa Cather, which gradually grew into a deep friendship between her and the three children and lasted until she died, in 1945. On a more impersonal level, she also established a close relationship with the elder Menuhins, particularly with Marutha, whom she respected for her strength and courage. Miss Cather knew nothing of the events connected with Goldman, and, on the whole, sympathized with Marutha's efforts to make her family inaccessible to outsiders. Herself trapped by her growing fame, Willa Cather found her freedom increasingly hampered by the innumerable pressures exerted upon all celebrities which threaten to deprive them of that solitude without which the artist ceases to grow. In what she called an effort at self-preservation, she withdrew from the world as much as was humanly possible in order to reduce the wear and tear of

matching her will against that of society. Marutha's similar
effort at withdrawal was rendered more difficult by the nature
of Yehudi's art which, unlike Willa Cather's, reaches its cul-
minating point in the very presence of the multitudes whose
acclamation, so absolutely essential at the time, endangers the
growth and the integrity of an artist when it invades his
privacy.

Marthua lowered her guard where Miss Cather was concerned not only because of the similarity of their views on the
problem they both faced. Miss Cather possessed a strength
and an honesty which banished every suspicion of ulterior
motive in her desire to be in the company of Yehudi and his
sisters. Always fond of children, she was strongly attached to
her youngest brother and sister and subsequently to her nieces
and nephew. She never tired of children, wrote her lifelong
companion, Edith Lewis, playing with them "not as if she were
a grown person, but as children play—with the same spirit of
experiment, of adventurousness and unreflecting enjoyment."[3]

Now, in her later years, she transferred her affections to the
Menuhin children, of whom Miss Lewis wrote:

> *They were not only the most gifted children Willa
> Cather had ever known, with that wonderful aura of charm,
> presence, inspiration, that even the most gifted lose after
> they grow up; they were also extremely lovable, affectionate
> and unspoiled; in some ways funnily naive, in others sensi-
> tive and discerning far beyond their years. They had an
> immense capacity for hero-worship, and Willa Cather be-
> came, I think, their greatest hero.*[4]

The admiration and the enrichment were far from being
one-sided. Another friend of Miss Cather wrote:

> *I had noticed on a table a melting, even angelic photo-
> graph of young Yehudi Menuhin, of whom she had spoken
> sometimes since his appearance at the age of twelve at*

[3]Edith Lewis, *Willa Cather Living, A Personal Record* (New York:
Alfred A. Knopf, 1953), pp. 168, 169.
[4]*Ibid.*, p. 170.

Carnegie Hall. She had a rapturous admiration for his musical gifts and, she now told me, had met him in Paris in 1930 with his family. At last it seemed she had a youngster in her life, marked by fate for genius and a great career as a violinist. Yehudi for Willa opened vistas into the world of the masters of music to which her own passion had ever led. She made a story of this prodigy and his fascinating and gifted little sisters, and of his parents, as if she had at last, by proxy, a family exactly to her taste. Not at all like her beloved father's family with its pioneer tradition; in this brilliant Jewish milieu, erudition and art were primary, and everything else of secondary importance.[5]

The Menuhin children intuitively felt Miss Cather's strength, rocklike in its steadfastness, and gentle because of her deep, warm understanding. In matters of principle she was uncompromising, yet her power to discern deeply buried fears, hopes, and motives endowed her with a tolerance they rarely witnessed at home. "Her love was not easily won but, once given, always had," Yehudi said. "She was a rock one could always turn to, and I often did."

There were probably no happier youngsters in New York than the three Menuhins on those days when Aunt Willa took long walks with them around the reservoir in Central Park, Miss Cather's favorite walk because nowhere else in New York could one tread on earth instead of pavement. The three always remembered to take turns in walking at her side, however deeply involved in the conversation, which ranged from art, literature, and philosophy to clothes and jewelry, of which, incidentally, the girls were becoming increasingly aware. Once Hephzibah declared with all the passion of a twelve-year-old: "To me, a woman without jewels is not a woman!" As they recall those walks and conversations, the young Menuhins remember their particular gratitude to Aunt Willa for never having talked down to them or indulged in

[5]Elizabeth Shepley Sergeant, *Willa Cather—A Memoir* (Philadelphia and New York: 1953), J. B. Lippincott & Company, p. 253.

wearisome praise of their gifts. Practically alone among the
few adults who had the opportunity of being alone with them,
she ranged the gamut of all their and her interests, impatient
of superficialities and pretense.

One result of this association with Willa Cather was the
children's deepening interest in literature. Without appearing
to pursue any aim, she repeatedly introduced the subject,
excited over some book of fiction or poetry. Among Menuhin's
most cherished possessions is a volume of Heine's verse in the
original German with her inscription: "For Yehudi on his six-
teenth birthday, April, 1932." She also gave him his first copy
of Goethe's *Faust*. Disturbed by the rapid acquisition of one
language after another by the Menuhin children before they
had taken a proper hold of English, Miss Cather asked Marutha for permission to organize a Shakespeare Club, with membership reserved only for the two girls, herself, and Miss
Lewis. Marutha readily consented, but as soon as Yehudi heard
of the project, he asked Aunt Willa if he might join. "She
smiled her wonderful smile which always made one feel as if
one had done something special for her," he recalls, "We
started with *Richard II,* continued with *Macbeth, Henry IV,*
and *Hamlet,* all four of us reading in turn. Whenever we came
upon a passage we particularly liked, we asked Aunt Willa to
reread it for us. I sometimes go back to those plays, and can
actually hear her voice when I come upon passages such as
Mowbray's complaint upon being banished by Richard II:

> 'The language I have learn'd these forty years,
> My native English, now I must forego;
> And now my tongue's use is to me no more
> Than an unstringed viol or a harp,
> Or like a cunning instrument cas'd up,
> Or, being open, put into his hands
> That knows no touch to tune the harmony.'

And so on, until the last piercing lines:

> 'What is thy sentence then but speechless death,
> Which robs my tongue from breathing native breath?' "

These lines stirred Yehudi because Shakespeare had drawn upon music for his imagery and even more because, after years of nomadic life, the young Menuhin suddenly realized that he, too, missed the exhiliration of "breathing native breath." Far from satisfying him, his annual trips to the States awakened a longing within him to stay on, putting down roots and sharing the life of the land where he was born. In the first article to appear under his name, he said with characteristic youthful ardor:

> *I am always up in arms against that American inferiority complex, that self-effacement, self-belittlement that we Americans manifest almost to a pathological point whenever we speak of European versus American! . . . All that talk about 'atmosphere of European culture and art' . . . it is not the European atmosphere but the personal Enesco atmosphere that helps me and always inspires me. The Baedeker is one thing for travel, sightseeing, but quite another thing when your soul craves for spiritual and artistic inner development. There, it is the individual alone, as well as the contact with other individuals, that counts. It is only the atmosphere of your own soul, your own home, your own life's philosophy, outlook and ideals that counts.*
>
> *And so far as the outside atmosphere counts, in our youthful, healthy, socially minded, peaceful country, with a people that is anxious to learn, to improve the general material and spiritual life of everybody; in our country where there still is to be found a spirit of pioneering, we have a healthier atmosphere in which to develop our art, if we have the talent.*[6]

Willa Cather was to Yehudi the very personification of that pioneer spirit which contrasted so favorably in his eyes with the atmosphere prevailing in a Europe darkened by Hitler and Mussolini. She had a freshness about her which comes from a people born on the land, and in a land unburdened by history and traditions so many of which seemed to him either

[6]*Musical America,* April 10, 1934.

empty or suffocating. She was the most American of all people he knew, with her directness, simplicity, and wholesomeness. Her letters were always full of descriptions of nature and the countryside, even when written in New York or devoted to entirely different topics. Unfortunately, Miss Cather's will forbids the publication of any of her letters or of passages from them. She knew and loved music and rarely missed a Menuhin concert, rejoicing in his steady growth, excited after listening to him, and tired "with a happy tiredness."

In spite of his closeness to Willa Cather and a faith in her that verged on worship, Yehudi could not talk to her about his personal problems—in fact, he could still talk to Hephzibah alone—if only because of his mother's injunction made years ago that family affairs were never to be discussed with outsiders, however close and intimate. Much time was yet to pass before either he or his sisters found it possible to disregard that rule. Willa Cather herself was too discreet and too jealous of her own privacy to invade anyone else's. The only time in the many years of her friendship with Yehudi when she ever attempted what bore but a distant resemblance to such an invasion she received a reply which only strengthened her reticence. In the spring of 1934 the elder Menuhin publicized Yehudi as: "The Prodigy of Yesterday—the Master of Today," for which Willa chided the youth as unbefitting the dignity of his art and exposing him to ridicule. Yehudi replied: "I'd rather be ridiculed by the whole world than hurt my father's feelings." She said nothing to that, but her objections strengthened the distaste he himself had felt, and he quietly prevailed upon his managers to eliminate the phrase. When, two years later, his father reintroduced it in the even less dignified form of "The Prodigy of Yesterday—The Genius of Today—the Immortal of Tomorrow," Yehudi again avoided a direct struggle but eventually weeded the sentence out.

The summer of 1934, the last of the Ville d'Avray period, was unlike all the preceding ones, although outwardly everything seemed the same: sessions with Enesco; chamber music every Saturday night; endless hours of sonata playing with

Hephzibah; dashing bicycle rides in the St. Cloud woods; lazy, sunlit weeks at Ospedaletti in Italy and Fexthal in Switzerland. But some of the carefree spirit of the previous summers was gone. Yehudi continued to be sweet and devoted in his obedience, but he was more silent than ever, talking less even with Hephzibah. When the Australian impresario Mr. Tait visited the Menuhins to work out the details of the forthcoming round-the-world tour, Yehudi attended his conferences with Moshe but took no active part. The arrangements provided for the entire family to accompany him on the tour, after which they would return to California, to settle down on the hundred acres of virgin land which Moshe had in the meantime bought, adjoining Cathedral Oaks, the estate of their friends, the artists. There, in a house which they would build for themselves, Yehudi would retire for at least a year, an idea that emanated from Marutha. "Make me a gift of that year," she had asked, "before you walk into the world a grown man," and it was thus that the period of his retirement entered into the annals of Yehudi Menuhin's life as "Mother's year." However, there still lay before Yehudi a full season of concerts to play. This accomplished, and with a round-the-world tour soon to begin, the Menuhins indulged in three weeks of rest at Cathedral Oaks.

TWELVE

"Mother's Year"

Those three weeks with Dennison and Ingerson were to Yehudi and his sisters an enchanting festival of music making, talks with their hosts about art, and daily walks from Cathedral Oaks to the adjoining hundred-acre plot on which the Menuhin home was to be built. A friend of the artists, the well-known architect Paul Williams of Los Angeles, submitted a preliminary sketch and estimate of the main house and a guest cottage, which were enthusiastically approved. To please Marutha, the place was to be named "Villa Cherkess."

One day, two visitors called: Colonel Charles Erskine Scott Wood, attorney, writer and poet, and his wife, the poetess Sara Bard Wood, who had faithfully followed Yehudi's career while, for his part, he had known Wood through reading *Heavenly Discourse* and *The Poet in the Desert*. The eighty-two-year-old poet was an arresting figure, tall, erect, with a magnificent head and flowing white beard. He and Yehudi spent most of the afternoon in quiet conversation, and not even Moshe disturbed their absorption in each other. All the Menuhins accompanied the Woods to their nearby home, "The Cats," high in the hills overlooking the town of Los Gatos and the Santa Clara Valley, where Yehudi, Hephzibah, and Yaltah were to spend many a cherished hour.

This, their first taste of California country life, was a brief, happy interlude which filled them with excited anticipation for the time when they would return to their own house in that lovely part of the world.

It was early autumn in Australia when the Menuhins arrived in Sydney sometime in late April, 1935. Two very young men whom they soon met succumbed to Hephzibah's and Yaltah's charms, and won Marutha's approval to accompany them on their walks and to concerts. No girl, however, caught Yehudi's fancy, and he had no inkling that at his first concert one Nola Ruby Nicholas, who was later to change the course of his life, was urging her companion, her brother Lindsay, to study Yehudi's face as well as listen to his music: he was so handsome! When Lindsay suggested that they go backstage to meet him, she became flustered and refused. Next morning Nola wrote to her father in Melbourne about the "magnificent Yehudi," enclosing a reprint that Lindsay had given her of his article on the musical climate in America.

During the sojourn in Melbourne, Moshe received a large envelope from the architect, containing the blueprints for Villa Cherkess and an estimate for $60,000. Backed by her enthusiastic children, Marutha urged Moshe to cable instructions for the work to begin, but Moshe, who had dreamed of a place in the country with a greater wistfulness than any of them, suddenly wavered as he contemplated the cost, which, incidentally, did not greatly exceed the tentative estimate he had been given. Prodded by Marutha and the children, Moshe could not procrastinate for too long and made a compromise: for the time being, the architect was to put up only the guesthouse. "We'll supervise the building of the main house ourselves," he temporized in an effort to redeem his action in the eyes of the family, little realizing that he was laying the foundation for much heartbreak in the future. However deep the disappointment, the incident was soon overshadowed for the Menuhins by the rigors of the Australian schedule, but back in the States there were two people upon whom this decision had a more unfortunate effect. "The boys," who had gone to considerable trouble in securing the services of the architect and had heard Moshe agree with him on design and cost, were now placed in an equivocal position, and they lost no time in saying so. Moshe's sharp reply only served to aggravate the situation, and in the end the long friendship with the two artists was broken.

From Australia the Menuhins sailed to South Africa, where Yehudi repeated his Australian triumph, and from there to France, a voyage remembered primarily by the surprise birthday party the young Menuhins gave their father, Yehudi acting as master of ceremonies. The long speech he had written was annotated with musical terms to guide the degree of expression in his voice: *crescendo, diminuendo, fortissimo, piano subito,* etc. That year, 1935, Yehudi worked as never before, having given by December a total of 110 concerts in sixty-three cities of thirteen different countries.

While in Paris the Menuhins had seen much of Edmond and Madeleine Fleg and their sons, Maurice and Daniel, the two families having been brought together by Bloch and Enesco, for whose operas *Macbeth* and *Oedipus,* respectively, Edmond Fleg, a distinguished French *littérateur,* had written librettos. Before leaving France, the Menuhins secured a promise from Daniel to visit them at Villa Cherkess that summer.

Only two concerts awaited Yehudi upon his return to the United States, winding up his Herculean labor. Judging by the reviews and by the volume and tenor of his fan mail, he continued to be in magnificent form, but many of the letter writers expressed concern over his pale, drawn features and over the indifference with which he acknowledged the applause in stiff, formal bows, his face unsmiling and withdrawn. Two entries in Lydia Perera's diary throw a sharp light on these last concerts before "Mother's year" began:

March 22, 1936. Concert in Town Hall. Toscanini in mother's box. Yehudi looks tired and weak. Mobs rushing through the center aisle, shouting their acclaim.

March 29, 1936. Last concert before Yehudi's retirement. Russian music. Yehudi looks tired, indifferent and sad. The music fits his looks and mood. I had to grit my teeth as I left the Hall, to keep from crying.

The vacuum that entered Yehudi's life immediately following that last concert proved to be more trying than the grueling routine of the preceding months. He had to linger in New
York for a fortnight while Moshe was winding up his business
affairs, and time hung heavily on Yehudi's hands with no rehearsals to attend, no trains to make, or concerts to give. He
was like a runner stopped dead in his tracks. Apart from taking
lessons in ballroom dancing—the only activity organized for
him and his sisters—he had all the free time in the world, but
little liberty and still less initiative to do with it as he pleased.
Whatever freedom he might have wrested he had no idea how
to use. His routine scrapped, he felt as if he were living in a
no man's land: his accompanist and friend Marcel Gazelle had
remained in Europe; no teachers had been hired; visits to the
Garbats were banned; Willa Cather was away. He did see the
Leventritts and the Pereras but felt awkward and alien in the
presence of their children, who, like most young people
brought up in a big city, had enjoyed freedoms which Yehudi
found incomprehensible, however enviable. Even the open,
twelve-cylinder, secondhand Cadillac which Moshe had bought
for Yehudi failed to still his restlessness or banish the humili-
ating feeling of being adrift.

One day, driving through Central Park, the Menuhins
stopped for a short walk. For no reason that he could fathom,
Yehudi was irked by this interruption and, as he followed his
sisters out of the car, suddenly slammed the door with a force
that shattered the glass. After a moment of uneasy silence,
all of them eying an embarrassed and confused Yehudi, they
climbed back into the car with a kind of funereal dignity and
returned to the hotel.

At long last, Moshe wound up his affairs and the Menuhins
left for San Francisco, where they picked up the two cars that
had been shipped from New York, piled the baggage in the
back, and set off for the long-awaited Villa Cherkess. Rejoicing, they drove past the tiny community of Alma, nestling near
the entrance to their land, took the winding drive uphill, and
found themselves in front of the guesthouse. One look at it

and their hearts sank: three bedrooms, a small dining room, a still smaller kitchen, and a tiny music room with a low ceiling. This, for the whole family which needed three pianos and room enough for the youngsters to practice! It was even worse when they inspected the grounds. The warm weather having set in, the surrounding hills were gay with greenery and flowers grew in abundance along the roads, but there was not a tree around the house, not a green blade of grass. Broken and tortured by bulldozers and trucks, the soil was bare, brown, and alien. On the verge of tears, the young Menuhins' first impulse was to run down to Cathedral Oaks in the valley below, but with Aba no longer on speaking terms with "the boys," the visit was unthinkable. The children could also see that their father's despair was deeper than anyone's at the all too late realization of what he had done.

Marutha alone seemed unsurprised. Assuming command, she swept up her family and took them down to Los Gatos, settled them at the Lyndon Hotel, roamed the city for several days, and finally invited her husband and the children to look at the place of her choice. It was a sprawling yellow clapboard house standing in a large garden; an auxiliary building nearby contained two bedrooms and a big music room equipped with a stage and boasting, to boot, a wide terrace looking over the Santa Clara Valley. An ancient oak dominated the grounds that were large enough to allow the building of a swimming pool. As soon as they moved in, this project became the center of much joyous activity, as did also the putting up of a badminton court behind the main house. Gradually the place began to grow on them and became home.

A few minutes' walk above the house were the vast grounds of the Sacred Heart Novitiate. The rector, Father Dunn, hospitably invited the Menuhins to consider the novitiate's orchards, vineyards, tennis courts, and mountain trails their own. Yehudi and his sisters and the friends who were soon to arrive spent many happy hours at the novitiate, with its colony of eucalyptus trees standing guard on the highest point of the grounds, the goal of most of their walks. From there the young people had a view extending on one side all the way down to the bay of San Francisco and embracing the whole of Santa Clara valley. On the other side, the Santa Cruz Mountain range huddled protectively over Alma, Cathedral Oaks, and the barren acres of Villa Cherkess.

With the arrival of the rugs and furniture from Ville d'Avray and the rented pianos, and with the hiring of two Chinese servants, the Menuhin household became a smoothly running affair. A police dog named Alupka was soon acquired, along with a goat—a surprise present from Yehudi to his mother ceremoniously christened Feodosia, adding one more name to remind Marutha of her beloved Crimea. By summer the family was firmly established in the new home and was ready for the house guests who now began to arrive: the pianist Beveridge Webster of Pittsburgh and young William Stix of St. Louis, both of whom had met the Menuhins in Paris; Rosalie Leventritt and her brother Victor; and Daniel Fleg.

The first of the visitors, Daniel, who had been sickly since childhood, was so frail upon arrival that Marutha proceeded to nurse him with what he nicely described in his diary as "angelic patience and implacable will." During the first two or three weeks, when he was plagued by insomnia, Marutha often rose in the middle of the night to bring him a glass of warm milk. To increase his appetite and give him a feeling that he was earning his keep, she "hired" him for three hours every morning to work on the swimming pool. The fresh air, the sun, and his own youth did the rest, and he was soon able to participate in all the activities, which, besides sports, included dancing and dramatic productions, the most ambitious of which was *Cyrano* in French, with Yehudi in the title role.

Daniel's diary records the loveliness of the moonlit walks in the novitiate park; the gaiety of the dances and charades, a game of which they never tired; the sessions of chamber music, with Yehudi's old San Francisco friends, Nathan Firestone and John Paterson, playing the viola and second violin, while Hephzibah and Yaltah alternated at the piano. Daniel loved in Yehudi "a strength and a radiance which we all feel

. . . Madame Menuhin presents an entirely different manifestation of force, will power and dignity beneath her frail
appearance. Several times she discussed with me her marriage,
Yehudi and the way she conceives life for him and the two
other children. *Quelle maternité!*

"I find, there is something excessive, almost offensive in the
way in which this adolescent artist is hovered over, and is to
such a small degree master of his moves and life . . . This
sweet passiveness, respect and admiration for his parents I
find noble, but it irritates me; rather, it worries me, and yet,
were it not for its proportions, I would have found it sublime.
It becomes excessive when it reaches such a menacing degree.
And at all times, in all places, with all people, Yehudi's direct,
inexhaustible kindness manifests itself. Here is true greatness!"[1]

That entry was made on August 8. Five days later, Daniel
drove out with Yehudi, Hephzibah, and Yaltah to Carmel,
where Victor and Rosalie Leventritt were vacationing with
their parents, to bring the brother and sister back with them
to Los Gatos for a lengthy visit. Moshe had been planning
to go with them, but, as there would not have been sufficient
room on the return trip, Marutha suggested that he stay behind. This meant that Yehudi would be out of both parents'
sight and, what is more, in a car. Moshe agreed only after
Daniel had promised that he would drive both ways. But
Yehudi took the wheel on the way back and remained in his
seat even after he had caught sight of Aba nervously pacing
up and down in front of the house. Describing the incident
in his diary, Daniel solemnly concludes: "Today Yehudi has
made, symbolically speaking, a great step toward the independent and normal life of the adolescent of our times!"

Along with Daniel, Rosalie and Victor were appalled by the
unquestioning obedience of the three young Menuhins, in the
face of few, if any, external manifestations of domination. Both
Moshe and Marutha kept at a discreet distance from all the
activities of the young people, intending to give Yehudi and his

[1]Daniel Fleg, *Carnets* [Avignon: Rullière, 1941], p. 82.

sisters a feeling of growing out from under their parents' wings, but the young visitors were scanning the spread of those wings with a mixture of awe and unbelief. "Yehudi's mother is very beautiful," Rosalie wrote from Los Gatos, "with those wonderfully blue eyes of hers and the dusty-blonde hair one can see from under the big straw hats she wears. She has the loveliness of a kitten. She rules the household with an iron hand, but pretends not to: only the velvety hairs are brushed against you, and yet you are always aware of the steel claws you cannot see. Anything she says, she needs to say only once."

Another of the youthful group wrote: "Marutha reminds me of a little Lady Buddha, very delicate and fine and, unlike Buddha, deliberate and powerful. She always finds a place to sit on that is quite high, so she can keep an eye on everything, to guide, to dominate. She never raises her voice, but everyone does as she wants them to."

Despite the invisible wingspread felt by all the young people, friendships inevitably flowered into romance, with the Menuhin children the most romantic of the lot, the least experienced, and the most easily frightened, even the rebellious, impulsive Yaltah. She blossomed out that summer and, at last, grew closer to her older brother and sister on some basis of equality. Full of sentiment and visions of freedom, the fifteen-year-old girl was in love with every one of the young men around her alternately, secretly writing poetry to them in French, English, and Italian, but, like Yehudi and Hephzibah, she shrank from the more concrete manifestations of an embrace or a kiss. As though bewitched, the other young people acted in like manner. Despite the romantic setting, the feasting of eyes, and the loss of hearts, no couple attempted to seek seclusion. As if by a tacit agreement, they walked in pairs during their moonlight excursions to the novitiate, but always in a crowd of pairs.

Yehudi was drawn to Rosalie, a slim, vivacious girl with clear brown eyes and finely chiseled cheekbones. He loved to listen to her deep voice, stayed at her side during the walks, played Mozart sonatas with her, danced with her more than with anybody else, and insisted that she be the first to dive into the swimming pool when it was completed. When the time came for her to rejoin her parents, he drove her to the station, with his sisters and friends piled in the back. He could not muster the courage even to kiss her good-by.

Yehudi's uncertain courtship of Rosalie and, in general, his awakening to the world of romance brought afresh to him memories of Esther, now far away in Paris with her husband and children. In what was an unconscious farewell to his puppy love, he wrote her a long letter about the affection in which he had held her all his life, wanting her to know about it now that he was parting with his childhood and adolescence. Esther's reply was gracious and conventional, its distant friendliness releasing him from the last remnants of bondage. From that time on, he knew, he would be seeing her merely as an old friend, an older friend. When they met again a year later, in 1937, he discovered that he could talk to her more freely than at any time before, and she was the first in whom he confided his plans of getting married soon, although he had no particular girl in mind.

Yehudi was past twenty-one by then. He had been given command of his money—and made generous use of his checkbook; he was free to read reviews of his concerts—a freedom he exercised but little; he could choose his friends and go anywhere, but the entire conditioning of his previous years had made it unthinkable for him to live away from his family or have charge of his career. Feeling, like all growing things, a necessity to branch out, and knowing that he was free to do so, he found to his despair that he lacked the wherewithal. Simply to get up one morning and walk off was in his eyes a step so violent, ungrateful, and fraught with unforeseen consequences that everything in him rebelled against it. The only course open, it seemed to him, was marriage. Not unlike a nineteenth-century girl growing up in a "good" family, he thought of marriage as the only natural and conflictless means of emancipation.

Newspapermen, of course, plagued him with questions

about possible romantic attachments, which he denied, but he did go so far as to say that he would get married if he found the right girl, whereupon ambitious mothers and enterprising young ladies launched activities that led Yehudi to appreciate his father's busy protectiveness as he had never appreciated it before. The only attempt to lead him to the hymeneal altar which actually endeared itself to him, because of its disarming simplicity and directness, came from a girl in Tennessee who wrote on a post card: "Dear Friend: I saw in the papers where you wanted to get married. When you receive this card you can send me your picture and I will send you mine. I am 16 years old, and a brunette." Signature and address followed.

In her own way, Marutha had arrived at the same idea of marriage:

> *We are very anxious for Yehudi, Hephzibah and Yaltah to marry young. We hope that Yehudi, especially, will marry very soon. It may be a little difficult for them to find their proper mates because they are not sophisticated in the way in which many young people are sophisticated today. Yehudi says that if only he could find someone a little like Hephzibah, and Hephzibah adores her brother and compares all other boys to him.*[2]

Mrs. Menuhin said nothing about her own plans in the eventuality of her children's marriage, but when her husband was asked about it by a reporter of the San Francisco *News*, "the answer was unequivocal: 'A little colony of Menuhins on the Los Gatos hills.' "[3]

Yehudi did not touch his violin for the first three months of his retirement, which lasted for about a year and a half. The release from all obligations and the blue skies of California combined to bring about a pleasant laziness, a *dolce far niente*. Scores were gathering dust, and the violins rested.

[2]*Woman's Home Companion*, March 1938.

[3]July 5, 1937.

From time to time a feeling of guilt and worry, so well known to the professional musician on a holiday, would steal upon Yehudi, leading him to set a tentative hour for some practicing, but then someone would think of a drive to the hills or to the ocean or suggest a game of badminton, and the resolution to play would melt with the speed of an ice cube forgotten in the California sun. Nonetheless, the novelty and delight of the unheard-of business of doing nothing were wearing off, and completely vanished when the sieges of guilt and worry were gradually reinforced by a reawakened longing for music. One morning, Yehudi took the "Prince Khevenhüller" out of its case, only to discover that the violin behaved not unlike a proud mistress punishing her wayward lover. The sounds he produced on his incomparable Stradivarius horrified Menuhin, and he had to fetter his impatience and woo the "Prince" as if they had been complete strangers. Ysaye's admonition to work on scales and arpeggios came back to him again, but this time with an added insight that had escaped him all these years. He had recalled Ysaye several times before, each time going over all the intricate technical exercises he could find, but would invariably sparkle his way through them with such ease that he would put away the scores and forget about them until some chance remark or incident would remind him of Ysaye again. Now, as he struggled with the violin, he realized how little he knew about it in its relationship to his body, his limbs, forearms, and fingers. Having until now glided his way past this ignorance, he had grown accustomed to take for granted both the instrument and the functions of the various parts of the body in connection with it. It now occurred to him that Ysaye might have had in mind not so much a literal command of scales and arpeggios as a masterful knowledge of the violin, not unlike that of a surgeon's knowledge of the human body and of the instruments he employs. But no sooner did Yehudi have the vision than his youth and his immense talent enabled him to ram through the initial technical difficulties, forcing the "Prince" once more to respond to him with yielding adoration. Once more Yehudi turned from problems of craftsmanship to the great compositions he had played all his life, with the intention of subjecting his entire repertoire to a critical restudy.

"Up to that time," he recalls, "I was quite instinctive in everything I played, both as to technique and interpretation. The sources of whatever insight in my playing were as much of a mystery to me as to outsiders. Whatever knowledge or understanding I had shown had been absorbed by me as the earth absorbs the fertilizer given to it by man or nature. There was in me an awareness of beauty and of the glory of emotions, but it was an awareness that remained unaware of itself. As I was growing from boy to youth, and from youth to man, I matured very slowly, at least emotionally. Isolated in my day-to-day existence, as well as on the stage, I was slow in achieving a consciousness of life that comes comparatively early to most people, exposed as they are to contacts in schools, at parties, athletic games, or work. The awakening, rebellion and readjustments that came to them naturally and gradually had passed me by. At the same time my physical and intellectual growth were taking their normal course, eventually leading me to the realization that I must shift from my instinctive approach toward music to a conscious awareness and a readjustment, if need be. I felt that if I did not make this transition I would be finished as an artist, sooner or later, in the way so many prodigies have failed when their instinct faltered. Not that mine was faltering yet, but I was aware of the danger.

"There was something else. In making this decision to realign my musical values, I was paying tribute to our modern age, which has become increasingly dependent on scientific checks of intuitive findings, affecting in its progress even the arts, even religion, which had started as the purest act of faith. Following the pattern of man's inquiry into physical science, with its checks and justifications, my mind had to measure and reinforce the promptings of my heart, leading me in my late adolescence to seek a reason for the values I had sensed in Beethoven, Bach, and other great musicians. In the process, I passed through various stages fraught with danger to me as an artist: the reckless triumph of discovery, the arrogance of dogmatic knowledge, the loss of self in the intricacies of analysis. How grateful I was for a sabbatical during that period of drunkenness with inquiry!

"The most significant result was to me the acquisition of the *knowledge* of something which I had previously *felt*, namely, that all great musical works have a unity, structural and expressive, an organic relationship of parts toward each other and toward the whole. This unity found its consummation in Bach, and, most revealing to me, in his six *Sonatas and Partitas for the Violin Alone*. In them, as in a conception of Leonardo da Vinci, science, mysticism, and art are blended in a Holy Trinity. The harmony and unity of those Bach works are such that each sequence is akin to a sculpture fitted into a niche which, in turn, forms part of the nave of a cathedral, the cathedral itself planned as an integral part of a square in the heart of a city which blends with the surrounding countryside.

"The profundity of a mind may be measured by the extent to which it sees universal phenomena as part of a vast whole, and not merely as the indulgence of a benign deity or the work of an evil genius bent on pranks. The more completely one sees a process or an event in its inevitability, the more fully one has comprehended it, and the more truthfully and inspiringly one is able to recreate it in a work of art. Only a great mind, such as Da Vinci's or Albert Einstein's, could conceive and execute the unity and harmony that had gone into the creation of Bach's *Sonatas and Partitas for the Violin Alone*.

"With apologies to the lay reader for technical details, I should like to illustrate my thought. As is known, Bach preferred to compose his series for various instruments in as many different keys as possible. Witness *The Well-Tempered Clavichord*, which contains passages written in every key of the chromatic scale, the keys following each other in a deliberate, inevitable order. The sequence of keys in the sonatas for the violin is similar to the intention and scope of the sequence in *The Well-Tempered Clavichord:* G minor (Sonata); B minor (Partita); A minor (Sonata); D minor (Partita); C major

(Sonata); E major (Partita). This sequence goes in thirds with the one exception that after A Bach jumps to D, but not without a good reason. Had Bach adhered to the sequence by following A with C, he would have been compelled to continue with B, which was already represented. The sequence begins with G, the lowest string on the violin, and ends with E, the highest.

"Another fact: this sequence includes two 'natural' keys, which require neither sharps nor flats in the signature; two keys with two flats and one flat respectively—the G-minor and the D-minor; and two which require in the signature two sharps and four sharps respectively—the B minor and E major. Between them, these six keys offer to the violin the greatest resonance, and to the composer the greatest possibilities for polyphonic writing. In the B-minor and E-major partitas, Bach uses the two sharp keys, these with the largest number of accidentals and, by the same token, keys with the smallest number of open-string notes. Therefore, these partitas contain the least polyphonic writing.

"Significantly, Bach reserves his two greatest fugues, the C-major and the A-minor, for the keys with no accidentals whatsoever. He likewise reserves the *Chaconne* and the *Sarabande* of the D-minor partita for the key with only one accidental.

"The only other keys represented in this series of six works for the violin alone are the three keys of B flat major (relative to G minor) in the *Siciliano* of the G-minor sonata, the C-major *Andante* (relative to A minor) in the A-minor sonata, and the *Largo* in F major, a key very closely related (subdominant) to C major of the C-major sonata.

"It is this kind of technical analysis of great musical works, supplemented by reading about the lives and times of composers, that kept me busy during my retirement. The heartening and downright miraculous thing about it all was that each time I restudied a musical work I made a complete circle, returning to my original intuitive conception, but on a new level."

There were other facets to Menuhin's inquiries. The reverence in which he held creative genius and his eager curiosity about the original intention of the composer had led him to libraries and private collections in various parts of the world, where he could browse over the *Ur*-text editions. He felt closer to the composer when he could see a work written out in the composer's own hand, revealing as it were the flow of the creative impulse, character, and mood. Now, as then, Menuhin is apt to display at the slightest opportunity a photostat copy of a manuscript, pointing out how moods are betrayed by twists and flourishes, the handwriting showing the stately progress of a Bach work, with its flowing curved lines, or Beethoven's inner struggle in the bold, impetuous symbols which he crossed and recrossed. Or he will delight in pointing out the precise musical symbols delicately drawn by Chopin or Debussy.

Menuhin also came to know the excitement of making big and little discoveries and of introducing compositions that had been neglected or lost or were written especially for him. The latter include Bloch's *Abodah,* Franko's arrangement of the Vivaldi concerto, Paul ben Haim's *Sonata in G,* Bartók's monumental *Sonata for Unaccompanied Violin,* and William Walton's *Sonata for Violin and Piano.* This sonata was written for Menuhin and Louis Kentner, a pianist of tremendous range and power yet to be discovered by music lovers of this country.

Among the works discovered or rediscovered for the public by Menuhin are Mozart's "Adelaide" concerto, Schumann's "Lost" concerto, and Mendelssohn's D-minor concerto, as well as several of his sonatas for violin and piano.

While Menuhin happened to be restudying Schumann's *Phantasie,* during "Mother's year," Schott, the music publisher at Mainz, sent in the score of the "Lost" concerto, asking for an opinion. Menuhin played it through with Hephzibah and, stirred, wrote on July 22, 1937, to his old friend Vladimir Goldschmann, conductor of the St. Louis Symphony Orchestra: "The Schumann concerto is the historically missing link of the violin literature; it is the bridge between the Beethoven and the Brahms concertos, though leaning more toward Brahms. Indeed, one finds in both the same human warmth, caressing softness, bold manly rhythms, the same lovely arabesque treatment of the violin, the same rich and noble themes and harmonies. There is also a great thematic resemblance. One is struck with the fact that Brahms could never have been what he was without Schumann's influence!"

Thus convinced of the intrinsic value of the concerto, as well as of its historical significance, Menuhin informed the publisher that he was prepared to play it in America and Europe throughout the next season, and asked for its history. What he learned from the reply and from subsequent research of his own brought to light the weirdest, most pathetic and mystifying of all histories of a major musical work.

On September 21, 1853, Schumann entered in his diary: "A piece for violin commenced . . ." A few days later: "I am diligently working on the violin concerto . . ." The speed with which he composed was so feverish that on October 1 he recorded: "The concerto for violin completed." Two days later he sent the score to his good friend, the great violinist Joachim, with a letter: "Here is something new. It reflects a certain seriousness, with moments of cheerfulness lurking in the background . . . Often I saw you in my imagination when I wrote the concerto." And again, ten days later: "I believe it is easier than my *Phantasie*. The orchestra, too, is more effective . . . Oh, how happy I will be if we can perform it at the opening concert of the new season. . . ." (Schumann was at the time conducting the Düsseldorf orchestra.) But Joachim repeatedly postponed a public performance of the work and in fact never did perform it, yet his correspondence indicates that he liked much of it. On October 22, 1854, he wrote to Clara Schumann: "I cannot imagine spending my time more profitably than in studying the concerto with Brahms and yourself." The following November 17, he wrote to Robert Schumann, who had in the meantime been confined to an asylum: "I am now ready to play it for you. I understand it better than at the time when I performed it for you in Hanover so unworthily, to my great sorrow. It sounds so much better now." On October 15, 1857, less than a year after the composer's death, Joachim wrote to Clara Schumann: "Your Robert's violin concerto we must often play together in Dresden. The last movement is so difficult for the violin, but I begin to master it in my fingers. There are such glorious and wonderful passages in the first and second movements. . . ."

Fully thirty-one years had passed before the work was mentioned again. Replying to a query from his pupil and biographer Andreas Moser, Joachim wrote: "You ask me for information about the manuscript in my possession of a violin concerto by Robert Schumann. I cannot speak about it without deep emotions, for it is the creation of the last half year of my dear Master and friend, immediately prior to the sad outbreak of his mental troubles." And he went on to describe the concerto as *"echt Schumansch"* (real Schumann), inspiring and rhythmical in many of its parts, though in some places "unviolinistic" and "ineffective." Joachim died in 1907, requesting in his will that the Schumann be neither played nor published until one hundred years after the composer's death. It was accordingly entombed in the Prussian State Library in Berlin, spoken of by musicologists as the "lost."

One day in March 1933, a weird new chapter opened in its history. During a spiritualistic séance in London in which two grandnieces of Joachim, the sister violinists Jelly d'Aranyi and Adila Fachiri, participated, a "sender" from the spiritual world who identified himself as Robert Schumann, requested Miss d'Aranyi to find a posthumous work of his for the violin and give it a public performance. Miss d'Aranyi declared she knew nothing of such a work. But, encouraged by a second "message," the sister violinists resourcefully secured the services of Joachim's spirit, which directed them to the Prussian State Library. Here Miss d'Aranyi must have encountered unsurmountable difficulties, for nothing further was heard about the concerto until four years later, when the music publisher from Mainz, having completed all legal arrangements, cabled to Menuhin: "SCHUMANN ALL RIGHT." Thereupon the rejoicing violinist arranged for performances of the concerto, giving San Francisco the honor of the world *première* on October 3.

At this stage, Miss d'Aranyi reappeared on the scene with her story of the spiritualistic messages, claiming the right of first performance. Before Menuhin could deal with this bewildering complication, the Nazi government announced that the world *première* would be held in the Third Reich and that all previously announced performances were to be canceled. Menuhin had no choice but to conform, since the Germans held the world copyright to the concerto, and had to wait until after November 26, on which day Georg Kulenkampff played the Schumann with the Berlin Philharmonic. Accompanied by the pianist Ferguson Webster, Menuhin gave the concerto's first American performance in Carnegie Hall on December 6, playing it again seventeen days later with the St. Louis orchestra and Vladimir Goldschmann. The third violinist to introduce the *"Lost"* to the world was Miss d'Aranyi, playing with the BBC orchestra in London.

American music critics were unanimous in their praise of Menuhin's efforts to acquaint the world with the Schumann, as well as of his mastery, but were divided in their judgment of the intrinsic value of the concerto itself. Olin Downes found it "weak and futile," and Jerome D. Bohm insisted in the *Herald Tribune* that "it should have been permitted to lie undisturbed in the Prussian State Library of Berlin." At the same time, Samuel Chotzinoff of the evening *Post* felt that the concerto's "long interment in a German museum seems altogether inexplicable . . . deeply felt, passionate and darkly brilliant," and John Rosenfield, Jr., of the Dallas *Morning News* declared it "a work of beauty and inspiration, for all its imperfections." Musical opinion in Europe likewise lacked uniformity, but most of the critics agreed with Menuhin on the beauty and loveliness of the first two movements, feeling at the same time that the third sadly let the whole work down.

The fantastic and tragic story of the Schumann concerto almost obscured the adventure of Menuhin's return to the concert stage after an absence of eighteen months. The last traces

of the prodigy in his appearance had vanished. Taller and
slimmer than before retirement, and wearing tails and white
tie for the first time, he made a handsome figure. Samuel
Chotzinoff found that "Menuhin's romantic, youthful appearance won all hearts even before he played a note. It was, indeed, a triumphal return, and enthusiasm was at fever heat
throughout the evening." More significantly, the music critics
sensed "a growth and a maturity," "a glowing personal affirma-
tion," "intensity and poetic insight," "rich ripening," "a deepening of the emotional interpretation," "a glowing splendor
and opulence which were truly ravishing." Casting all caution
to the world, some critics proclaimed Menuhin "at the head
of the list," "the greatest of them all," and "immortal."

The new wave of recognition and the violinist's youthful
handsomeness aroused Hollywood's interest but, still acting
as his son's spokesman, Moshe refused to consider any offer,
because "between Yehudi's musical art and Hollywood, as it is
constituted today, there is an abyss that cannot be bridged.
The pure, simple, integral, and complete art of Mozart, Bach,
Beethoven, Schumann, Brahms, and Hollywood's synthetic,
commercial, made-to-order art, are two different, irreconcilable
worlds which no fakir, no money, and no whitewashing can
bring together."

Compared with Moshe's outburst, the reply by a representative of Paramount was sweet reasonableness: "When musical
geniuses like Leopold Stokowski, Kirsten Flagstad, Werner
Janssen, Lily Pons, Gladys Swarthout, Grace Moore, and innumerable others are content to entrust their talents to motion
pictures, I think we need have no fear as to the technical and
artistic qualities of the screen. The young maestro might well
make a major contribution to his own art by elevating the art
of the films through appearing in them himself."

The Menuhins ignored the challenge, but Hollywood tried
again, offering a two-million-dollar contract. The answer again
was "No!" Interviewed by a reporter, Yehudi declared that
the emissaries sent from Hollywood to New York "actually
thought that I was crazy or else that I wanted more money.

They could not understand it." The reporter said that he did not either, and would the violinist explain, but at this point Moshe stepped in: "We would not sell our soul for all the money in Hollywood. Artistic integrity means more to us than riches!"

Recalling the incident, Menuhin remembers resenting the violence of his father's utterances, just as he regretted the superlatives with which Moshe peppered the announcements of his appearances. But he was not really paying much attention to anything at that particular time, overcome as he was by a feeling hitherto unknown to him, a feeling of anticipation, of self-reliance. When he mentioned this to Hephzibah, who was four years his junior, she remarked that she had known that feeling for some time. He also talked about it to Willa Cather during their walks around the reservoir that winter of 1937–38. She was happy, she told him, that he seemed to have found a way of making a stepping stone into the future out of the days gone by. And she reminded him how profoundly he was impressed when he came upon the phrase in *The Tempest* during a session of their "Shakespeare Club": "What's past is prologue."

"Throughout the weeks preceding our departure for London," Menuhin recalls, "I felt a spring fever in my bones, and so did Hephzibah and Yaltah. There was a nostalgic quality about those days in New York, as if we were revisiting the city for the last time, and we certainly were never to see it again with the same eyes. Everything assumed a particular significance, and we were insatiable in our curiosity, tireless, laughing, and reckless, that is, reckless for us. The outer shell was still intact, but inside of all three of us things were fermenting, ready to erupt."

THIRTEEN

"The Marrying Menuhins"

Menuhin's tour of the British Isles repeated his American triumph, the audiences behaving as though they had a personal stake in the violinist's safe transition from prodigy to young manhood and were now rejoicing in the happy consummation of the process. And so were the critics, whose reaction may be best summarized in the words of the London *Evening News* reviewer: "What did Menuhin bring that was not in his hands before? Finely posed weight of style, controlled fire, his blend of the pure and the romantic . . . We bowed our heads in thankfulness for heavenly radiance of tone, for great music perfectly expressed."

The Royal Albert Hall was filled to capacity on Sunday afternoon, March 20, 1938, for Menuhin's second concert that season. To the apprehension of the audience, instead of the violinist and his accompanist, a representative of the management appeared on the stage and in the ensuing hush announced that the pianist had left all his music in a bus on the way to the hall, and that telephone calls to the terminal, Scotland Yard, and police headquarters had yielded no results. He appealed to those who might happen to have with them the score of any of the works on the program, to lend it until the end of the concert. One man produced Tartini's *Devil's Trill Sonata,* and Aunt Edie contributed Lalo's *Symphonie Espagnole.* Five pounds was then offered to anyone who would go home by taxi and return with the score of any of the other works in the program, but no one budged, fearing to miss part of the concert. Backstage, Ferguson Webster, the accompanist, kept wringing his hands and threatening to throw himself into the Thames, and Harold Holt, the manager, moaned: "My God, how can I refund eight thousand people! . . ." Running from one to the other, Moshe urged Webster to postpone his suicide for the moment and begged Holt not to cancel the concert. "But what are we going to do?" demanded the manager. Moshe did not know, but Yehudi calmly announced: "I'll play unaccompanied Bach."

The concert was forty minutes late in starting, yet the audience did not seem to mind. Mr. Webster, as one paper later wrote, "made ample atonement for his absent-mindedness," while Menuhin's Bach met with a profound response, heightened, if truth be told, by gratitude for the loss of the scores of Paganini's *Moses* variations and Locatelli's *Labyrinth*. Demands for encores were prolonged and insistent, and the line of grateful well-wishers after the concert was the longest Menuhin had ever had to cope with. Slowly advancing toward the artists' room, along with the other people in the line, was Sir Bernard Heinze, conductor of the Melbourne Symphony, with whom Menuhin had played in Australia, in the company of a tall young man about Yehudi's age and an attractive girl with red hair and laughing hazel eyes.

"My friends, Nola and Lindsay Nicholas," said Sir Bernard. Despite the wear and tear of a full recital, Menuhin was always happy to see friends and strangers call on him in the artists' room, but now, as he looked at the girl, he wished the crowd were not so big. Seeing that she, along with Sir Bernard and her brother, had started to inch her way toward the exit, Yehudi asked them, a sudden urgency in his voice, to please come to the Grosvenor in a half hour to have tea with him. "And don't be offended if I am a few minutes late."

"Don't mind that," said Lindsay, "we too are staying at the Grosvenor."

That was the first time Menuhin had ever invited anyone to join his family circle without first consulting his parents, but no one seemed to resent it, least of all Marutha, who was gay and gracious. After the tea, the Nicholases and the three young Menuhins went for a walk, then for a ride in Nola's smart convertible Jaguar, which she handled with a skill that did not fail to impress Yehudi. He had a few brief days before departing with his family for a tour of Holland, and contrived to spend the afternoons and evenings with his sisters and the Nicholases. With the unspoken connivance of the others, Yehudi maneuvered awkwardly but always successfully to trail behind in Nola's company.

He seemed to be bursting with things to tell her but actually said very little, while Nola marveled with gay unconcern at the grave, strange, adorable young man walking beside her, and talked with ease about herself and her family. She was in Europe that summer on a holiday trip which her father allowed her to take with Lindsay. Their mother had died when the children were very young, before she could fully enjoy the fortune her husband, a chemist, had made by developing Aspro, a substitute for aspirin, during World War I. Nola and Lindsay, the girl was telling Yehudi, attended his concerts in Melbourne, and had planned their European trip in such a way as to be in Britain in time for his Albert Hall appearance. They were shortly leaving for the country to spend the Easter holidays with relatives. Would she give him their telephone number? Yehudi asked. Of course she would, but what use would it be to him in Holland?

As always, Yehudi's room was part of the Menuhin suite, and he waited up the first night in Holland until everyone was asleep, locked his door, and put through a person-to-person call to England. Barely saying hello, he blurted out to Nola:

"Will you marry me?"

"What?"

"Will you marry me?"

"But we hardly know each other. . . . It's so sudden. . . ."

Night after night he kept calling her, Nola pleading for time. Yes, she loved him too, but she had to think about it, and she had to ask her father. She was only nineteen and could not get married without his permission. Finally, yes, she said, she would marry him, only if he would please wait, wait until they met again, until her father replied. He'd probably come to England to meet Yehudi before giving his consent.

As the Menuhins were checking out of their hotel, Moshe challenged the clerk on the unusually large telephone bill, but Yehudi, flustered, said: "I made those calls," and quickly leading his father out of earshot, "I proposed to Nola Nicholas."

For once, the elder Menuhin found nothing to say, and neither did Marutha, who received the news with a faint smile which somehow conveyed the impression that she had known about it all along. When they returned to London, she saw to it that her children were free to spend much of their time with the Nicholases and did not seem to mind Yaltah's frequent refusals to join the various outings. She was busy shopping, the girl said, as well as catching up with her mail, the bulk of which consisted of letters to William Stix of St. Louis.

At long last, Mr. George Nicholas arrived from Australia. Yehudi called on him at his suite and formally requested his daughter's hand in marriage. It was a heavy responsibility Yehudi was asking him to assume, Nicholas said. His daughter was, after all, under age, and he would never forgive himself should the marriage prove an unhappy one. Still, since she wanted it, and as they seemed to be in love with each other, there was nothing he could do but give his consent.

Moshe and Marutha having added theirs, it was with an almost dramatic and certainly neat sense of fitness that Hephzibah and Lindsay announced their intention to follow suit. And, as though the lifelong obedience to routine were not to be abandoned even in matters of the heart, Yaltah promptly fell into line with the news of her engagement to William Stix. So, all three Menuhin children, by getting engaged at about the same time, escaped the necessity to fill the void that would have been made in the unit had they married one by one.

Accompanied by Nola and Lindsay, the Menuhin family spent two happy weeks in Sorrento, Italy, in close proximity to the vacationing Hambourgs, in whose house they spent many hours making music and playing games. During the parties

and the long moonlight walks arm-in-arm with Yehudi, Nola
again marveled at the strange, shy youth she was about to
marry. Indeed, the whole family seemed odd to this modernly
brought-up Australian girl, as though it came from another
planet, ignorant of and indifferent to so many things most
people knew and liked and all stirred up about persons and
ideas one surely paid little attention to, working so hard as if
music were the only thing that counted, and then playing a
child's game like charades with an infantile kind of self-
forgetfulness. They were closely knit and devoted to each
other, but the way they did everything, absolutely everything their mother told them had to be seen to be believed. Of
course, it was good to have a mother, any mother, especially
one so young and pleasant to look at. Nola herself did not
remember hers, and had never had anyone particular to order
her about, so it was quite fun to do the little things Marutha
kept suggesting, such as to tone down a bit the gaiety of her
clothes, and to learn languages, because life with Yehudi
would mean traveling to the different countries and she did
not know anything but English.

Nola gradually found herself spending more time with
Marutha than with Yehudi, finding a novel pleasure in abiding
by her wishes, which Yehudi did not mind in the least, although he teased her about it and pretended to be jealous.
He loved her, she could see it by the way he looked at her,
and he sometimes talked the way all young lovers do, but he
remained shy and never even attempted to embrace or kiss
her. Even more baffling, during a party at the Hambourgs one
night he had so delighted her with a witty remark that she
impulsively hugged him, but he disengaged himself and whispered: "Not now—after we get married . . ."

The betrothal of Nola and Yehudi was the first in the Menuhin schedule of marriages—set up, one might add, with the
precision of a concert tour. The European press announced
the forthcoming weddings with its customary reserve, but the
American newspapers gave themselves a field day, sensational-
izing the story with such headlines as "The Marrying Menu-

hins," "They All Got Married," and "Pop Go the Menuhins!"

Yehudi's wedding was to have taken place on May 27, 1938, to be followed in the evening by a family dinner, but when he learned that Toscanini was to conduct Verdi's *Requiem* on that day he advanced the ceremony by twenty-four hours so as to be free to attend the concert with his bride. Thus, on the morning of May 26, Nola and Yehudi were married at the Caxton Hall Registry in London, in the presence of a few friends and the immediate members of both families. The ritual was accompanied by the clatter of carpenters at work on an air-raid shelter under construction in the basement. Asked whether he had the wedding ring ready, Yehudi hastily drew it out of his pocket and, seizing Nola's hand, almost got it on her finger before the registrar gravely stopped him, requesting him with British imperturbability to place it on the open service book from which he had been reading. The bride and groom smiled at each other, and the tension was broken.

The Menuhins sailed for the States on the *Ile de France*, leaving Lindsay and his father to follow later. Moshe had arranged for the largest suite available, which the newlyweds shared with the rest of the family. Nothing seemed to have changed, except that the family group had expanded sufficiently to absorb a new member, the younger Mrs. Menuhin. As before, they did not mix with the other passengers, and, as always, meals were brought in to the suite. During the first dinner, the chief steward came in to inquire of Nola whether she wanted any of her trunks in the cabin, but it was Marutha who answered:

"They will all remain in the hold."

"But my evening clothes are in those trunks . . ." Nola ventured.

"You'll have no occasion to wear them on this trip."

Bewildered, the bride shifted her eyes to Yehudi, who seemed to find nothing unusual in the exchange and did not even look up. From this point on, the process of absorbing the young bride into the Menuhin world, a process imperceptibly started at Sorrento, was to become more deliberate, although a cold which had chained Nola to her bed for two or three days after the *Ile de France* had come out into open sea tended to slow it up somewhat. Yehudi was loving and solicitous but, reminded of his usual long morning stroll immediately after breakfast, he would hurry obediently to the deck, while Marutha roused her daughter-in-law, encouraging her in the pursuit of her French studies by calling in a waiter and requesting that Nola order her breakfast in French. Upon Yehudi's return, Marutha would withdraw, leaving behind an injunction that he read Pirandello with his wife so that she could the sooner master Italian.

As for the cold, only Nola's desperate stand spared her a mustard plaster, but she was powerless to save herself from Marutha's next-best cure—unbearably hot baths. "That scorching water certainly killed the cold, but at the time I thought that I'd go with it," Nola later recalled. In the meantime, she had inevitably passed on the cold to Yehudi, and for this her mother-in-law reproved her in a brief, stinging lecture.

In the first wave of affection, Nola had accepted Marutha's criticisms and suggestions with gratitude and a kind of good-natured curiosity. She laughed when the older woman exclaimed: "How plebeian of you to eat double-decker sandwiches!" and stopped ordering them. She accepted placidly the sarcastic remarks about the five hundred hand-embroidered pieces of lingerie she had received as a wedding gift from her father and had even swallowed the resentment aroused in her by the order to leave her trunks in the hold. But the implication carried in the reproof for having passed on her cold to Yehudi actually frightened her, and she pleaded with him to change the plans for settling down in his parents' home at Los Gatos. Why not, before it was too late, Nola pleaded, move to Villa Cherkess, which Moshe had given them as a wedding present? Miserable and loving though he was, Yehudi now found that all his preconceptions had failed him. Aged twenty-two and married, he discovered he still could not break away. At any rate, not so abruptly. They had to move in with his parents, he said to Nola, if only for a short time.

William Stix met the Menuhins at the pier, and on the next day, June seventh, married Yaltah, and they both went off to Washington, where he had just been appointed to a government post. Yaltah, not yet sixteen, looked lovely and forlorn as she bid good-by to her family, holding on pathetically to the familiarity of her brief case, in which she always kept some musical scores, several volumes of her favorite French poets, and a notebook or two of her own verse.

Hephzibah and Lindsay were married on July 16 under the huge oak tree that guarded the Menuhin home in Los Gatos, in the presence of the bride's family, the groom's father, and a small group of friends. Erskine Scott Wood offered a toast to the happiness of the newlyweds, who were to make their home in distant Australia. The decision to settle there was complicated for Hephzibah, as steps had been taken to launch her on an independent career, but she did not waver. In a letter to Bruno Zirato, of the New York Philharmonic Society, she canceled her first scheduled concert as a soloist with the orchestra, saying in part, and in characteristic Menuhin style:

> *I am sure you have heard, my dear Zirato, that my fiancé is an Australian shepherd, supreme owner of several thousand sheep, innocent little animals which 'baa-baa' in chorus, impatient to know their future little mistress. I will be married soon and, as a good wife, I will sacrifice everything I have loved up to now, to go with my husband where he has his own house, to cheer his solitude, to play the piano for him, to teach him the Italian language and animate the monotonous plateaus of his immense property with winged vision, with thoughts gathered from other countries, other people, other times.*
>
> *This is the career that I have chosen. To follow it I am compelled to leave behind my brother whom I adore, as well as my dear little sister, my mother and my father. The concert I was to play with the Philharmonic Symphony under Maestro Enesco in February is a part of my sacrifice which I offer to the man I love. He appreciates it so much that you must not scold him or scold me either.*

The elder Nicholas left California soon after the marriage ceremony, but the newlyweds lingered on. As if unable to part with her brother, Hephzibah played sonatas with him for hours every day and made plans for joint concerts in Australia as soon as possible. At last, on September 12, Lindsay and Hephzibah Nicholas sailed on the S/S *Mariposa* from San Francisco, where all the Menuhins saw them off. Holding her husband by the arm, Hephzibah waved and waved to her dear ones on the pier, then, as if remembering something that had remained undone, she rushed down to her cabin, gathered up all her heavily boned corsets, wrapped them in a news-paper, and, holding onto her husband with one hand, hurled them into the bay.

Only three weeks were now left before the beginning of Yehudi's tour, but time hung heavily on Nola's hands. She was in love and was being loved, happy whenever alone with her husband, but those moments were all too rare in the busy, well-ordered life in Los Gatos, to which she was a stranger. It was a dedicated, hard-working life that the Menuhins led, each one of them, even the gentle, solicitous Yehudi, expecting her to adapt herself to it silently and uncomplainingly, apparently oblivious of the fact that she missed her freedom, the glitter of big-city life, the chance to wear her beautiful clothes. She tried. She read while Yehudi practiced, and she studied lan-guages. Not French any longer, for the lessons with Marutha were somehow discontinued without a word's being spoken about it, and she feared to offend her mother-in-law by asking Yehudi to teach her the language. Instead, she read Italian and German with him, particularly Heine, the volume Willa Cather had given him. One morning, to please her husband, she learned a whole poem by heart and, upon hearing that he had finished his practicing, rushed into his room to recite the love poem, but there she found him already at the desk, reading a Russian book with his mother. Arrested in her impetuous, loving gesture, Nola apologized and hastily withdrew, Yehudi shouting after her: "I'll soon join you, darling." When he did eventually, Nola could not bring herself to recite the poem. Instead, she pleaded: "Let us go away for a holiday, alone! We haven't even had a honeymoon. . . ."

In a few days, the two drove off for a short trip to Yosemite, Yehudi's first excursion without either of the parents, an act which seemed to him so unnatural, somehow so bespeaking ingratitude, that he was overcome by a feeling of guilt, and spoke of it to Nola. She was driving at the time and stopped the car: "Shall we turn back?" But that he would not, and on they went until they reached their destination. Early evening they picnicked on a huge bold rock beyond Glacier Point, watching the sun sink in fiery abandon while a full golden moon rose in the east, long dark shadows forming all around them in the silence. The two young people sat, happy and alone together, so undeniably belonging to each other that Menuhin recalls, "the feeling of guilt that had plagued me completely disappeared, never to come back again. It was that evening when I realized that my life had become divorced from my previous existence in a way I had never thought it could be." The next morning he wrote to his parents that he and Nola would go straight to Villa Cherkess from Yosemite and settle in the guest cottage until the time came to begin his tour, and so the young couple drove straight to Alma and up the winding road to Villa Cherkess and happily worked for two days to convert it into a real home of their own. Neither Moshe nor Marutha showed any signs of disapproval.

Yehudi was accompanied on his American and European tours that season by Nola, Moshe, and a young Dutchman, Hendrick Endt, the last accompanist his father was to hire for him. The elder Menuhin continued to have charge of all arrangements and dealings with managers, and he also did most of the talking to reporters, but he tactfully left Yehudi and Nola to themselves as much as possible. On board ship he arranged for a separate table for them and during stops for concerts he firmly refused their invitations to have meals with them or go to an occasional film or play, joining them only on visits to old friends whom Yehudi wanted Nola to meet— Enesco, the Bertaux, the Flegs.

In Paris the young Menuhin learned that he was going to be a father.

The European trip over in the spring of 1939, Nola and Yehudi stayed on for a brief vacation at the Beauvallon summer home of the Flegs in the south of France, while Moshe went back to the United States alone for the first time, grateful for the company of Daniel Fleg, who traveled with him to Le Havre and there saw him off. Little did Moshe know that his young friend would no longer be alive before the end of that fateful year 1939: despondent over the refusal of the air force to accept him, Daniel committed suicide on November 27 by drowning in the Seine. His older brother, Maurice, died in battle the following June. In memory of their sons, Edmond and Madeleine Fleg subsequently permitted the publication of Daniel's diary, passages from which were quoted in an earlier chapter.

The months that followed their return to California were full of excited happiness for the young couple, alone in their new home near Alma waiting for the baby to arrive and taking regular trips to Nola's doctor in San Francisco. Nola's unaffected manner and her happy, easygoing ways released Yehudi from some of the reserve in which he had been brought up. Although her English did not sparkle with polished wit, it was natural and fluent, awakening a response in the normally tongue-tied violinist. He also lost his nervousness with the telephone and learned to manage his own timetable, granting or refusing interviews, making appointments, and, with Nola's help, taking care of his voluminous correspondence.

She gradually released Moshe also of other chores connected with Yehudi's life as a concert artist, including the alcohol rub and shirt-changing routine which Toscanini alone had on one occasion wrested from Moshe. For so long completely absorbed by his son's career, indeed his entire life revolving around it, Moshe failed to sense the inevitable despite all these signs and was thus unable to spare Yehudi the embarrassment of having to tell his father that he need no longer accompany him on concert tours. Moshe bowed to the decision with pained resignation not unmixed with genuine worry over how Yehudi would fare on a concert tour without him. On the eve of his son's departure for the first time with only Nola and Hendrick Endt, Moshe handed the pianist a list of instructions written out by hand, telling him in minutest detail how to take care of Yehudi during the tour: he, Endt, should see to it that Yehudi take at least one long walk a day; that he, Endt, always have ten dollars in change ready for tipping; that no one be allowed to touch the violin case except himself, Nola, and Yehudi; that there should always be Eau de Cologne in the artists' room for a rubdown during the intermission; and a shirt to change into, etc., etc.

Nola received a list of similar instructions, and the poor worried father had no idea that when Yehudi saw the lists, he angrily confiscated them, and, at the first attempt on the part of his companions to do anything for him, he would sarcastically refer to article so-and-so in the list of instructions. To this day, Menuhin's reaction against the excessive care with which he had been surrounded makes it difficult for anyone to help him with the many chores connected with his intensive travels. On the contrary, he goes out of his way to be of service to his companions, men and women alike. To return this service is difficult, even so far as getting him to allow someone to carry his heavy violin case containing two violins, sheets of music, correspondence, and even an odd shirt, and therefore a dangerous strain on his wrists. Unless it be his accompanist or a trusted friend, he prefers to carry the case Indian-style, on his head.

Moshe's duties in connection with his son's affairs have since that time been limited to keeping track of his accounts, which he does with zeal and great skill. Most of his free time the elder Menuhin now devotes to gardening and fruit raising, and the grounds around his and Marutha's home in Los Gatos are indeed lovely to behold.

Both Moshe and Marutha found it difficult to make an adjustment to a life not centered around their children, an adjustment more difficult than that which their children faced, who, after all, were carried along on the wave of romance and discovery. It took many years before the elder Menuhins renewed their pilgrimages to join the children for brief periods —a visit with Hephzibah in Australia or a trip to New York to attend some of Yehudi's concerts and renew old friendships.

On September 29, 1939, Nola gave birth to a baby girl, whose name Zamira was derived from the Russian word for peace and the Hebrew for songbird. Wearing a surgeon's gown and mask, Yehudi remained in the delivery room by special dispensation of her doctor so that he could witness the birth of his first child. The concert season was opening the next day with a recital in San Francisco, and, as Yehudi hurried from the hospital to a rehearsal with his accompanist, he was cornered by journalists, some of whom had been reporting his comings and goings ever since he was a little boy in knee pants.

"No," the young father said in reply to a question, "I shall not insist upon my child having a professional music career. It is a fine career and I've enjoyed mine, but I shall not insist. The less conscious the effort to plan any human being's life, the better."

Menuhin also told the reporters that his sister Hephzibah was expecting a child soon, and that he was planning a tour of Australia early next year, where he would perform with her, while Nola was looking forward to a reunion with her family and old friends. He likewise confirmed the reports that Yaltah's marriage had been annulled and that she had now returned to live with her parents in Los Gatos.

Several years later, Yaltah married Benjamin Rolfe, of Los Angeles, and has been pursuing with distinction a career as a pianist.

To coincide with the birth of her child, Nola presented

Yehudi with a surprise gift, a Joseph Guarnieri del Gesù made in 1742. Ever since he had received his Stradivarius from Henry Goldman, Menuhin had been hoping to acquire a companion violin so as not to overwork his precious "Prince Khevenhüller," and he actually did find such a violin, a Guarnerius, in Emil Hermann's collection, but, with the baby on the way and the plans to enlarge Villa Cherkess into a full-sized house, Menuhin decided against making a heavy investment at the time. After an exchange of letters with her father and a few surreptitious huddles with Moshe, Nola purchased the Guarnerius for her husband.

Among the joys of Menuhin's new life was a renewal of friendship with his neighbors, "the boys," and long sessions of chamber music which attracted to Alma many of his friends in the musical world. At first, those sessions were merely impromptu affairs, with musicians driving in for an afternoon or an evening, often finding the young father busy washing dishes or changing Zamira's diapers, but after the main building and the two guest cottages had been completed the musician-guests stayed on for weeks and sometimes an entire summer season.

Those were wonderful days of clear skies and invigorating mountain air, divided between hiking, swimming in the pool and music making, with Yehudi proving to be a modest, gracious host, and Nola carefree, gay, and tireless.

In 1940, accompanied by Yaltah, Endt, Zamira, and "Nanny" Louise Blochman, they sailed for Australia. There, Yehudi spent endless hours playing sonatas with Hephzibah on her husband's ranch, and there Nola gave birth to her second child, a son whom Yehudi named Krov, which means "blood" in Russian and "battle" in Hebrew, a name inspired by the glorious and terrible news of the Battle of Britain.

FOURTEEN

The War Years

By the time Yehudi Menuhin had returned from Australia World War II was ravaging the Europe he knew and cherished. Much of it, including France, had been overrun; the Battle of Britain was subjecting the island to its cruelest test; and the Jews, his own people, were being exterminated in concentration camps and death factories. In the United States itself there was no escaping the knowledge that time was running out and that the peace and well-being in the land could not last forever, as frustration mounted during the long wait for the inescapable—America's participation in the war with Hitler Germany.

It was during that long, restless period of waiting that Menuhin met the distinguished pianist Adolph Baller, who was to become his accompanist and close friend. A native of Poland and a former child prodigy, Baller had made his first appearance at the age of eight with the Vienna Philharmonic Orchestra, followed by concerts in other European capitals. When the Nazis came to power, they incarcerated him, subjecting him to torture by breaking his finger joints one by one. In 1938, Baller made a miraculous escape and emigrated to the United States, after having undergone medical treatment which enabled him to make a comeback as a pianist.

Heavy-set, dark, with the long hair of an old-fashioned musician, he presented a striking contrast to Menuhin, but his piano merged so naturally and authoritatively with the latter's violin that listeners and critics became at once grate-

fully aware of being in the presence of two men who possessed that rare intimacy of musical understanding that makes
for ideal partners.

They began playing together in the summer of 1941, soon
after Menuhin had returned from his first South American
tour. During his absence, the architect Gardner Dailey had
converted the old guest cottage of Villa Cherkess into the
roomier and exceedingly pleasant home which Menuhin now
occupies, having renamed it "Alma." At the foot of the lawn,
one hundred-odd feet below the house, a large games-and-
concert room was built with two guest rooms underneath,
as well as a fully equipped guest cottage which Baller made
his home for several years to come.

Reporting to the draft board after Pearl Harbor, the twenty-
five-year-old Menuhin was deferred as the father of two
children, but he volunteered his services as a violinist to the
war effort, increasingly devoting his time and energies to it,
so that by V-J Day he had given over five hundred benefit
concerts for troops and relief organizations all over the United
States. Traveling alone or with Baller, he came in contact during those wartime appearances with the boys and men of his
generation, with whom he had had until then so little contact,
and was happy to discover that he felt at home with them and
could participate, in however limited a way, in their horseplay,
join in jam sessions, understand their jokes, as well as fathom
the depth of their nostalgia. There was pathos in the way
the men tried not to show their homesickness yet would invariably turn the conversation to things divorced from war,
asking questions about the humblest matters that spelled
home and besieging the departing Menuhin with requests to
deliver messages upon his return to the "mainland," and this
he did as a welcome and sacred duty.

What surprised and gladdened him most was the profound
reaction of the men to his music. There were no orders to
attend his "high-brow" concerts, nor was there the pressure of
tradition, yet the GI's always filled the halls and stadiums to
overflowing, responding to the music with spontaneity and in-

tensity, as if something vital, which had been submerged in the discipline and impersonality of army life, had been released inside them. Menuhin made no particular concession to popular taste even in his encores, and apologetically had to refuse occasional requests for popular songs, most of which he had never heard of. One night, amused by demands for "Pistol-Packing Momma," he asked that someone whistle the melody for him. Practically the entire audience obliged. Baller picked up the tune on the piano, Menuhin joined in, and "Pistol-Packing Momma" was played as she had never been played before.

The major part of his programs was devoted to the great classics—Beethoven, Brahms, Mendelssohn—whom so many in his audiences were now hearing for the first time. On one occasion, Menuhin and Baller found themselves on a USO assignment in the severe cold and darkness of a secret war base in the Aleutians. The concert was held in a sprawling hospital building where the piano, the musicians discovered at the last moment, had half its keys stuck, and those which did work were hopelessly out of tune. Left without Baller's assistance, Menuhin decided to risk an entire program of unaccompanied Bach, which represents a formidable challenge even to an audience of music lovers. He started, rather timidly, with the *Praeludium* from the A-minor solo sonata and with the *Gavotte*, then, emboldened by the reception, went on, concluding the concert with the *Chaconne*.

In its own way, that performance remains one of Menuhin's most stirring experiences in all his years as a concert artist. Just like the detachment of marines for whom, on a later occasion, Menuhin played in Honolulu after they had received their embarkation orders and, isolated from all others, were living in the tense prebattle atmosphere, those wounded men in the Aleutians displayed no hilarity, no easy exuberance. Each lost in his own thoughts and pain, they listened with a quiet, worshipful release, as if finding in Bach the answers they needed and the hope they had been in search of.

At the outset, the violinist thought of his concerts primarily as his contribution to the war, however small, hoping that it might bring pleasure to thousands of the young men serving their country, but their reaction, the hushed attention, and the sentiments voiced in the many letters he was receiving bore witness that he was giving more than pleasure: he was giving the men an escape back to the world of normal human emotions, of tenderness, romance, warmth, and also of exaltation. One letter was particularly eloquent:

> *I am the chaplain of a regiment of marines preparing for combat. The men come to me with all sorts of problems. I know that if these men could have the Lord of the Universe speak to them through music, as was done for the thousands last evening, that theirs would be a greater strength and a stronger determination to fight the forces of evil in the world. In times like these we need this strength, for then through the light of music the 'big things become small and small things become great.' All things take on a mystic value.*
>
> *Wherever I shall go I shall be strengthened as I recall the moments spent listening to your violin. It was as though I had worshipped in one of God's great temples.*

Menuhin was coming back from the Aleutians, sharing a priority flight with sick and wounded stretcher cases returning home. "I've known the pangs of leave-taking from my loved ones since early childhood," he remarked, "for my life as an artist has been one endless series of leave-taking and home-coming, but my wartime wanderings had brought strongly to my consciousness the universality and the deep tragedy of that experience which I had known only as an intimate one, not untinged with glad anticipation. Indeed, the heartbreaking departure of millions of young men to the front and the return home of the wounded are probably among the few universal symbols of our century, the first denoting the tragedy of man's inability to cope with his world, the second seemingly a miraculous gift.

"It was an extraordinary sensation to live, even as I did

for only twenty-eight days, in those bleak Aleutian outposts
where nature knows no gentleness, and where there is no past
with which one could associate human life. There was nothing
there that could fit into a frame, and it was extremely interesting to observe how the men tried to make up for the deficiencies by falling back upon their inner resources: carving
fossilized tusks, painting, reading, listening to music. Unfortunately, very few actors, singers, or musicians came there.
Several Hollywood stars had tried, I understand, but had to
be flown back after a day or two. The only one of them who
stuck it out for two weeks was Olivia de Havilland, whom I
met at one of the hospitals, but in the end her body proved
more frail than her spirit, and she had a breakdown upon her
return home.

"Baller and I, being of the tougher, if not the stronger sex,
managed to pull through somewhat better, with the help of the
Navy, which did its best for us. It was a fantastic feeling to
leave those hopeless, frozen wastes and know that when our
plane would next touch land it would be in Seattle. All of us
were overwhelmed by a tremendous expectancy, a kind of
holding one's breath during the entire trip. With all their
pain and inability to move, the men strapped to their stretchers
all had beatific, happy expressions on their faces.

"Those who have never been away from what we call civilization cannot know what it means to be able to take a taxi
again, see an electric sign, enter a restaurant, or go into a
telephone booth where, after a few brief moments, one can
hear the voices of those one loves. And later, the bliss of
that commercial flight to San Francisco, sitting in an uphol-
stered chair and looking into the pretty, smiling face of the
stewardess.

"In contrast to the Aleutians, my wartime concerts in Hawaii
seemed to be taking place in a kind of semi paradise, where
my guardian angel was Maurice Evans, then a captain in the
U.S. Army in charge of special services. He was a wonderful
and very popular m.c. whose job it was to unearth all men
who had any entertaining talents, were they hillbilly singers,

musicians, jugglers, or clowns. Although I played two or more times a day, I managed to squeeze in two good, long swims daily—one in the morning before my work started, the other late at night when the last concert was done. And often I would take part in jam sessions lasting past midnight, punctuated by singing, juggling, playing or, best of all, Evans' recitations from Shakespeare."

From the day the war began, Menuhin's thoughts kept constantly returning to Europe, where, after all, he had spent so large a part of his childhood and adolescence. With all of Western Europe except England under the Nazi heel, it was naturally impossible for him to make plans, but he never relinquished the idea. He happened to be in Australia at the precise moment when the Battle of Britain was raging, in a country geographically as far removed from the battle as it was emotionally involved in it. The people of Australia reacted painfully and instantaneously to each German plane over England, to all victories and losses, with Menuhin sharing their anger and sorrows, determined to get over there as soon as possible. Therefore, not long after his return to the States, he wrote to Harold Holt, his concert manager in London, offering his voluntary services as violinist to the relief organizations and the armed forces of Britain. Holt made inquiries, but the immediacy of the danger and the pressing need for an ever greater flow of supplies from America made the trip by a visiting violinist completely out of the question.

Nothing daunted, Menuhin tried again in the summer of 1942, having enlisted the good offices of the British Embassy in Washington, in addition to prodding Holt to renewed efforts on his behalf. At about the same time, and completely unknown to Menuhin, Winston Churchill was discussing with Archibald MacLeish of the U.S. Office of War Information the possibility of a visit to Britain by an outstanding American concert artist, preferably Yehudi Menuhin, as a cultural complement to the supplies and arms from the

States—in other words, to add music to guns and Spam. Thus, when he was on the point of giving up hope of ever getting to Europe, the delighted Menuhin was informed by the Office of War Information that a priority flight to England had been arranged for him. He flew to New York immediately, only to be told on arrival by an embarrassed OWI official, Roger Starr, on whose story this account is based, that the priority had been canceled because a rush shipment of a secret nature had been urgently requested by London. Yehudi suggested telephoning the White House, hoping that the President, whom he had met, might do something in the emergency, but Starr replied with all the finality befitting the situation: "On the basis of what the Air Force tells me, I assure you that Mrs. Roosevelt herself would not be able to obtain passage to London tonight or any time this week."

Deflated, Menuhin took the next plane west. A front-page headline in the next morning's papers revealed the nature of the mysterious cargo: "Eleanor Roosevelt Flies to London." Roger Starr received a laconic wire later in the day: "Hope you read today's newspapers. Yehudi Menuhin."

Still he continued his dogged efforts through all possible American and British channels and, finally, in the spring of 1943, was flown across the Atlantic in a bomber of the RAF, to become the first foreign concert artist to visit England in four years. There he found his old-time friend and accompanist, Marcel Gazelle, who had escaped at the time of Dunkirk and was now serving with the Belgian forces in Great Britain. On Menuhin's request, he was released to accompany him on his tour, which raised more than thirty thousand pounds for wartime charities. The tour was divided, as Yehudi had suggested, into three parts: concerts for British audiences in concert halls and factories; for the allied military forces—the British, French, Belgian, Polish, and others; and for U.S. Army special services, so that he might play for his compatriots in their camps.

Yehudi found in England an even greater receptiveness and intensity of reaction than ever before. After four years of war effort and common danger, the audiences seemed to be eager to show their appreciation and gratitude to a visiting artist, especially to one whom so many of his listeners remembered as a small golden-haired boy. One London newspaper reported that "Yehudi Menuhin's playing of Bach unaccompanied was the biggest success ever known at an aircraft works luncheon-hour canteen concert," and that most of the workers had neglected their meal so as to listen with undivided attention. "Menuhin is paid," said another paper, "in gratitude that cannot be reckoned, and earns the wages of immortality."

He repeated the tour the next year and the year after, traveling by bomber, warship, jeep, and, on occasion, in a submarine, experiencing, in addition to a sense of duty fulfilled, the excitement of a personal adventure, particularly in London, as he groped his way in the blackout that had brought to the grim, embattled city a mysterious and lyrical loveliness all its own. The many hours which he spent in the underground stations with thousands of people who slept through bombardments so they could do their job in the factories the next day filled him with a new and undying admiration.

Considering the uncertainties of war's fortunes and of his own many commitments for concerts in the States, Canada, and Mexico, it was most extraordinary that Menuhin happened to be in England during the Normandy landings, as he had secretly hoped he would. He had no official status, nor was his passport validated for travel on the continent of Europe, yet, with a resourcefulness amazing in one who had but recently emerged from a relentlessly sheltered existence, with good luck, uncanny intuition, and the impetuous assistance of sundry admirers, he achieved the seemingly impossible —he landed on the continent on the very heels of the attacking U.S. and Allied troops and gave the first concerts in liberated Brussels, Antwerp, and Paris. Marcel Gazelle, as reckless as Yehudi, and even more eager because a long-overdue reunion with his family awaited him in Brussels, accompanied

him on that tour, which began at the Palais des Beaux Arts
of Belgium's capital.

Some of the outlying parts of Antwerp were still in the
hands of the Germans, but the mad musicians "commandeered"
an army car and set off towards the city. The guards who
stopped them at each of the many checking points wore uni-
forms that ranged from the battle dress of the regular army,
through the smart garb of the military police, down to the
ragged clothes of the underground fighters who had then
emerged to take their rightful place of responsibility and
honor in the liberation of their country.

The concert at Antwerp was scheduled for late afternoon
because the Reichswehr, still in control of fortified positions
in the outskirts, nightly subjected the central part of the city
to a methodical bombardment, beginning, with characteristic
German regularity, at exactly nine o'clock. An artillery duel
somewhere in the distance provided a dramatic accompaniment to the concert as well as to the dinner that followed at
the blacked-out home of the newly installed mayor of Antwerp.
One of the first acts of his administration, the mayor was
telling Menuhin, was to send twelve collaborators to their
death. "Ours are not only days of triumph and rejoicing," he
said, "but also of bitterness and retribution."

The musicians were sent back to Brussels immediately after
the dinner, because their hosts did not want the responsibility
of keeping them in embattled Antwerp overnight, which
proved to be a wonderful piece of good luck. When Menuhin
and Gazelle set off for the Brussels airport the next morning, with no idea as to what was in store for them there, they
found an American DC-3 ready to take off for the Le Bourget
airport of Paris. The first moments of suspicion were dispelled
when someone recognized Yehudi, all regulations were waived
aside, and the adventuresome pair was seated in the plane.
The half-deserted streets of Paris were strange, almost un-
recognizable, stripped as they were of automobile traffic, except for an occasional military vehicle and the still rarer
sight of a taxi. There were a few bicycle rickshaws and quite

a number of people on bicycles, including a lady here and there, her Parisian elegance unimpaired by her flying skirt.

Menuhin startled his agent, Maurice Dandelot, who hadn't seen him in five years, by calmly walking into his office and suggesting a concert with a Paris symphony orchestra for the benefit of war victims. At the Opera House, of course. It surely can be reopened in two days. Yes, in two days, Yehudi blithely asserted, on Saturday afternoon, to be exact, because he had to be back in London for a Sunday rehearsal and broadcast with Sir Adrian Boult and the BBC symphony orchestra. Dandelot rolled his eyes, shrugged his shoulders, and with a rueful smile said: "You mad Americans!" Then he happily threw himself into the routine of arrangements—tickets, advertising, programs—having first secured the delighted agreement of Charles Munch to conduct the Conservatoire Symphony Orchestra, and of the Minister of Arts a permission to hold the concert, as well as a promise to have the Opera House cleared of cobwebs, the marble washed, and the ushers collected for the first concert in liberated Paris.

Turning next to the problem of transportation to London, Yehudi contacted the commanding officer of the U.S. military airport at Villacoublay. In exchange for a readily given promise to give a recital at the airport grounds, the officer undertook to fly him to Britain immediately after the concert, provided he left the Opera House not later than five, for he had no authorization to fly his transport planes across the Channel after dark, because of the isolated German ack-ack batteries still active at night.

Pursuing his very effective strategy, Yehudi arranged to give a recital at the largest U.S. military grouping near Paris, at Versailles, in "payment" for which a taxi was placed at his disposal for the duration of his stay in Paris, enabling him to call on his old friends. When the great French violinist Jacques Thibaud discovered that Yehudi had brought with him only his replica of the "Prince Khevenhüller" (for fear of risking the precious violin), he generously loaned him his own Stradivarius. From Thibaud, Yehudi learned, much to his elation, that Georges Enesco was safe in Rumania, as was Pablo Casals in the South of France.

The box office of the Opera House was opened Saturday morning, and within two hours there was not a ticket left. During that same time Yehudi was inside, rehearsing with the orchestra. The program consisted of the Beethoven concerto, the Lalo *Symphonie Espagnole* and the Mendelssohn concerto, which had been banned by the Nazis. The French musicians had likewise not been allowed to play the *Marseillaise* during the long years of the Occupation, and they now spent on it more rehearsal time proportionately than on the other compositions, not so much, Yehudi suspected, because they had forgotten it as because they could not have enough of the sounds of their magnificent national anthem.

The curtain rose on a packed house that afternoon, the entire audience on its feet as it sang the *Marseillaise*, which Menuhin, the American, played with the orchestra. Charles Munch was so carried away by the emotion in the hall that, in giving the signal to begin the Mendelssohn concerto which followed, he shouted: *"Allegro molto apassionato!"*, although conductors normally do not read aloud the tempo indications.

The ovation at the end of the concert was frenzied, the people acclaiming not so much the men on the stage as the symbol of the moment.

It was already five o'clock when Menuhin, coming off the stage after his third or fourth bow, perceived standing in the wings Marcel Gazelle and two U.S. Air Force officers who had come to escort both musicians to the airport. In an effort to prevent Yehudi from giving any encores, the officers forced him to put away his violin, but the audience continued to clamor so insistently for "Yehu*di*" that he borrowed the concertmaster's instrument and played a short piece. Then, caught between the impatient officers and the continued demands for encores, he gave a little speech, explaining his dilemma and saying that he was proud to have had the privilege of participating in the jubilation, and that he hoped to be coming back again and again to his beloved Paris. Two minutes later he was

holding on for dear life in a careening army jeep, racing
against the setting sun, and was soon boarding the plane
whose motors were already warmed up, their roar blotting out
in his ears the last lingering echoes of the ovation at the Opera
House. In his knapsack were several bottles of champagne to
share with his friends in England and in the States and a round
of Reblochon for his father.

The plane was halfway across the Channel when dusk set
in, and then, to add to the pilot's predicament, the electrical
equipment broke down, silencing the radio and jamming the
landing gear. On top of this, a blanket of fog was forming in
the gathering darkness. The plane circled for a while, took
the plunge and, luckily, there was still just enough light left
for the pilot to catch sight of a friendly pasture on which he
managed to land with little damage to the plane and none
whatsoever to its passengers. Thus, two hours after the emo-
tion-packed scene at the Paris Opera House, Menuhin found
himself with Gazelle and two GI's on a sleepy meadow in
southern England. The two civilians said good-by to the men,
picked up their belongings, and trundled off. Their luck held,
and they soon struck a main road where, after a while, the
prosaic bulk of a suburban bus loomed into sight, and the
adventure was over. The day's work was done.

The BBC broadcast was held as planned the next day, and
on Monday morning Yehudi Menuhin was in a plane once
more, en route to the United States, where more concerts
awaited him and a grave crisis in his private life.

The war years saw the end of Menuhin's marriage to Nola.
His immense effort and the trips away from home, on which
she was unable to accompany him, contributed their sad share,
helping to erode the soil in which their marriage had been
rooted. Yet they merely accelerated a process made inevitable
by basic differences in character, interests, and background.
While music was to Menuhin much more than his daily bread
or even a means for self-expression—it was his entire existence

—Nola had little of music in her blood and could not possibly allow her life to revolve around it without protest. For music made implacable demands: hard work, sacrifice of comfort, constant travel, partings, while she adored the life of carefree gaiety and heartily disliked the discipline, whether in work, food, drink, or rest, which music making exacted from her husband and, however tolerant he might himself be, made impatient demands of her as well. She had lived all her life by flair and charm, and when she was flooded with happiness and fulfillment the flood could submerge all differences and problems, but she had never been taught self-discipline, nor was there ever implanted in her a need for constant learning and growth. To her, marriage was a continuation, with a handsome and famous mate, of the good times she had had as a young girl, and she thus proved to be a genuine consort to Menuhin on the social level alone, which from the very beginning predestined the drifting apart of the two young people, so that neither the bonds of love nor devotion to their two children proved strong enough to prevent the final rupture. Nor was Menuhin's gratitude for the happiness and the help she gave him in the begininng, particularly in the pursuit of his emancipation from paternal discipline and its lingering psychological influences, sufficient to uphold the marriage for any length of time. Nola helped him to reach out for a freer and more natural contact with the world, but the widening quests and interests inherent in that very contact proved to be adventures which she could not or would not share with him.

Hardly aware at the time of the reasons for the estrangement, they unhappily watched their marriage disintegrate before their very eyes despite the desperate attempts they were making to keep it intact, ranging from solemn vows to pathetic efforts at finding some common activity they might share. Thus, she bought a set of golf clubs for her husband, an undertaking that proved doomed to failure from the very outset, while he, trying to meet Nola on her own ground, took her to the theater night after night during one sojourn in New York, and afterwards to supper and night clubs, dancing and

watching floor shows. As can be imagined, this resort to outside stimuli to fill the emptiness that had invaded their happiness was bound to boomerang, and after a week or ten days
of it they found themselves more of strangers to each other
than ever before.

Each time Menuhin was about to leave on tour he knew
that upon return he would discover a still further widening
of the gulf between him and his wife, and, by the end of 1944,
had to admit to himself that their marriage was beyond re-
demption. The time had come for them, he understood, to go
their separate ways, and yet he did nothing about it, finding
it hard in those days to take initiative on all matters except
those connected with music. "That inability was my greatest
offense against my destiny," he says, choosing in this assump-
tion of responsibility to disregard the fact that he had never
been exposed in his childhood and protracted adolescence to
the necessity of making decisions, which plays such a crucial
part in the shaping of character and habits. Yehudi Menuhin
had but rarely known the experience of choosing friends,
books, games, or of meeting challenges by boys and girls of
his own age. This almost total absence of the give-and-take
of human relationships during the character-shaping years had
stamped him with an "unworldliness" which people still notice
in him and his sisters, despite the fact that they have learned
by now to come to terms with life. This they have done the
hard way. However disarming and enchanting that unworldliness might have been, it often complicated what were already
desperate issues. The apartness, the unawareness about them,
had all too often rendered them powerless to elude easily
avoidable punishment or indeed to prevent them from causing
anguish they had not meant to inflict.

Hephzibah, who, like Yehudi and Yaltah, has had her share
of heartbreak, including the ordeal of divorce, has written
movingly in a letter:

> *Perhaps the worst was that lack of contact with life as it*
> *is generally lived amongst those who are not absolutely*

sheltered from everyday's troubles, as we were. It made awful fools of us all when we faced our first life situations. We were incapable of functioning as creatures of free will; we were mentally cognizant of every problem, but only as a theoretical dilemma. We had overcome *ourselves, and* readjusted *ourselves to inevitable problems many times before, but we had never* solved *a problem. Other people had never entered our lives before as definite factors to be contended with; there had been no fluidity in a life built on the achieving of mastery in one well defined field. There had been work—holy, absolute work performed in a spirit of extreme self-giving—and the rest was not important. As soon as our structure became invaded by the utterly different values of other people, we were helpless in coping with the conflict it set up between what we* had been *taught, and what we* were being *taught.*

We had to become disloyal to one standard or to the other, and, as we had never dealt with problems to which the solutions were not well known ahead of time, we did not discover until it was too late that one could compromise and still retain one's dignity; *that one could love a person or persons and still disagree with their views on life or their tastes in clothes. We had been beautifully trained to operate with spectacular precision and quite unchildish reliability in one particular field, but out of this field we were just not at home. We had neither experience nor precedent to guide us through unforeseen developments . . . and learned through untold suffering to accept as inevitable the fact that the Twentieth Century was not to be run according to the Commandments that had governed our childhood. We had to learn that, for all the glamor of concert life and its extreme importance, there were other factors that helped to determine one's life—factors of personality and temperament, and of environment and cultural patterns, which made other people as helpless before our helplessness as we were helpless before theirs. In such cases, nothing and nobody is of any avail, 'till one has gone through the trial and failed completely. All our music helped not at all to build a humane life. Before the wreckage of those early dreams, we had to admit that our claim to success was infinitely smaller offstage than onstage. Before the responsibility for our growing children we had no other standards than those against which we had had to measure up ourselves. And these had partially failed us.*

After all this time, I feel that the best is still ahead of us. We have had much misery to shed, for in spite of nursing the world's finest intentions, we have done more harm to people we loved than we ever believed ourselves capable of doing to people we didn't love.

Weeks and months went by, with Menuhin's procrastination merely multiplying the problems he and Nola faced, until final rupture came one day in the spring of 1945, ultimately leading to divorce.

FIFTEEN

Retooling

'Tis God gives skill, but not without man's
hands;
He could not make Antonio Stradivari's violins
Without Antonio.

STRADIVARIUS

It was a beautiful day in the spring of 1943 when Menuhin
and Baller were returning home from their tour of the U.S. Air
Force bases in the Aleutians. Baller alone knew how compel-
lingly Menuhin needed a rest, for he had shared with him
the toil and hazards of most of his wartime concerts, the cumu-
lative effects of which had been particularly telling in the
frostbitten darkness of those bases, where they had given
sixty-four performances in twenty-eight days, flying at least
once each day in an unheated DC-3, sitting in bucket seats,
which, as the musicians discovered to their great discomfort,
are perfect conductors of vibration. Each time he landed,
Menuhin was aware of the cramped numbness in his body, the
stiffness of his limbs, the forced position of head and shoulders.
His walk was wobbly and his fingers ached with cold. Like
Baller, he did not complain, snatching moments of rest on top
of mailbags in the planes or on the floor alongside the wounded
men lying on stretchers, but his whole being craved for rest
when he finally returned to California.

The excitement of homecoming carried him briefly on its
evanescent wings and then, as suddenly, evaporated. He was

left to face the immediate, familiar routine of concert giving, without either the spiritual elation which he shared with the people in the bombed cities of Europe or the invigorating force of a challenge such as the grimness of nature in the Aleutians to make up for fatigue and for the lack of daily practice. The full extent to which his violinistic and physical form had suffered ever since Pearl Harbor was forcibly brought home to him during a short charity broadcast in San Francisco a few days following his return: in order merely to keep going he had to pour into the comparatively easy music on the program every ounce of energy left in him. Like the ballet dancer, the violinist is forever aware of his potential, and this time Menuhin realized that he had no reserve left in him. He sensed a tension spreading itself across the back of his neck, affecting his posture, and he had to strain for his right arm, fettering the elbow and robbing his motion of some of its precision and authority.

There had been other moments in recent months when he had had to struggle against this tension and fatigue, which tended to deprive his tone of its customary roundness and volume, but this time he could not, as he had done on other occasions, call upon even those hidden reserves which all of us possess. True, there had been times when he had actually been too tired or too upset to make the effort. Whenever this happened, it was usually at the beginning of a concert, before the music had moved him or the unfailing warmth of the audience had braced him, so that, as a result, the performance was marked by unevenness. Thus, Howard Taubman had written in the New York *Times:*

> He [Menuhin] *seemed almost two violinists in the course of the evening. At the beginning, his playing was tame and lusterless, and thoroughly surprising for a musician of his attainments. Then, after the opening work, he underwent a sudden change. His performance became alive, incandescent, full of the quality of excitement that has made him one of the most popular fiddlers of the day.*

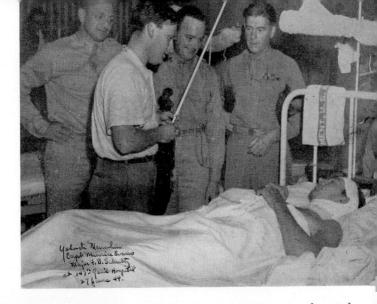

Yehudi and Maurice Evans, in a hospital
ward in Hawaii, 1944.

In the Aleutians, with Adolph Baller
at the piano.

In a hospital ward in Kodiak,
Alaska, 1944.

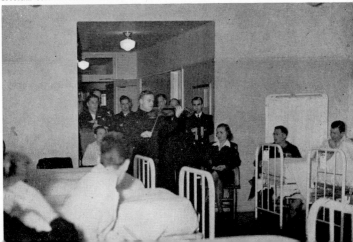

With Adolph Baller, listening to their recording
of the Bartók First Piano and Violin Sonata.

With the late Georges Enesco at the Bucharest airport, 1946.

Alma.

CARL COATE

Presented to Yehudi in recognition of his wartime services by the China Concert Committee; the Red Cross and St. John Fund; the Belgian Red Cross; the Jewish National Fund; the Association of Friends of the French Volunteers; British Factory Workers; British, American, and Allied Troops. London, March 1943.

With Leonard Bernstein, Eleanor Roosevelt,
and Henry Morgenthau III, in New York.

With David Oistrakh
in Moscow, 1945.

With Shostakovitch, Kathleen Harriman,
Kemenov, and Ambassador Averell
Harriman, Moscow, 1945.

ANGUS MC BEAN, LONDON

Diana Gould in "Pavane."

With Louis Kentner, Furtwängler, Griselda,
Elisabeth Furtwängler, Diana, in Switzerland.

With Furtwängler, following a performance
for the Jewish Community of Berlin, 1947.

With André Philippe and Pierre Bertaux,
following the presentation to Yehudi
of the Légion d'Honneur.

With Jacob Epstein in his studio, London, 1945.

With Nehru and Diana in the Botanical Garden, Calcutta, 1952.

Yehudi admiring Japanese mask, in Tokyo, 1951.

With Zamira, Jeremy,
Diana, and Gerard.

Gerard and Jeremy,
London, 1953.

Conscientious artist that he is, Menuhin regretted his less distinguished performances, but he was not deeply disturbed, for he had attributed them primarily to the "mass production" necessitated by his wartime effort and thought that all he had to do was to take time off for a good long rest and some serious practice. But on that day of the charity broadcast in San Francisco he realized as in a flash that there was far more than that to his difficulties; that, although he had somehow pulled through the concert, he was very much like a racing machine run ruthlessly over grueling tracks, its lines clogged and its bearings long since fouled. In his own words: "I saw myself as a child and adolescent, forging ahead with a wild kind of intensity, and even later, during 'Mother's year,' battering my way through technical difficulties, relying on my will power and vitality rather than on the knowledge of what was wrong and what was to be done."

It is imperative at this point to run somewhat ahead of the story and say that Menuhin sought to avoid the recognition that all his problems were interrelated and that not only his mastery of the violin but his entire being, all the issues of his life, including his past, the Cherkess so resolutely nurtured in him by his mother, and his marriage, which already hung in the balance, were all on trial, as well as his courage, his stamina, his convictions, and his faith in himself. Ever since childhood, Menuhin had always sought to keep his music isolated from the conflicting physical and emotional tensions that harassed him, as they must all mortals, turning to the violin as a refuge, release, and solace. He had escaped into his music, but now, when life had finally immersed him in its harsh realities, even his sanctuary, the violin, seemed to be rejecting him.

The war was to end, a new love and a new marriage were to come, and much hard work as well as sustained struggle gone through before he found that peace and serenity, the emotional equilibrium and physical well-being which are now his. But on that day of the San Francisco broadcast they seemed perilously far away when he turned to face the first of his battles to come, the battle of the violin.

The immediate problem, as it had crystallized in Menuhin's mind, was to assimilate consciously that which he had done subconsciously with such amazing results. The irrepressible urge in him to make music during his childhood and adolescence, he now knew, had led to efforts so extravagant that they might easily have harmed him had not his physical growth and its accompanying rejuvenescence furnished him with the requisite strength and energy to overcome whatever ill effects his unorthodox methods produced. Once this growth ceased, however, this compensation was no longer forthcoming, and, as he continued to ignore correct body function in relation to his instrument, there arose a need for yet greater exertion, which, in its turn, made still further demands upon his reserves of energy and still further aggravated the effect of the wrong habits he had acquired in his technique.

Having thus analyzed the first stage of his problem, Menuhin resolved to begin by reacquainting himself with his body in terms of the violin, by determining the proper functioning of joints and limbs, and by exploring the pull of gravity as it affects the movements involved. ("At last I understood," says Menuhin, "that the body must be so relaxed as to enable the weight of the head alone to hold the violin, and the fingers must of their own negligent weight fall on the finger board, with pressure applied only afterwards.") Trying to summon the technical knowledge he had acquired, he was astonished that, although his limbs and fingers knew instinctively, and superbly at that, he consciously knew almost nothing of the physical and technical processes involved. Had he been asked how exactly he solved a particular problem, he knew that he could hardly answer better then than he could as a twelve-year-old boy when Mishel Piastro, who had replaced Persinger as the concertmaster of the San Francisco Symphony Orchestra, inquired:

"Do you keep your little finger on the bow as you approach the tip? Or do you take it off? Do you use the wrist or the arm in producing a vibrato? Where do you keep your thumb as you change positions?"

Menuhin remembers those questions so clearly because he was bewildered by his inability to answer them. He did not know. He simply played, and the rest did not matter. In fact, it mattered so little that he neglected even to mention the conversation to his teacher Persinger.

The only other conversation with a colleague along similar lines that Menuhin recalls took place some ten years later during a chance encounter with Joseph Szigeti, that sensitive artist of rare charm and brilliance, who, like Menuhin, is a former child prodigy. The conversation led to a fascinating common search but, alas, not to any facile discoveries or cast-iron solutions.

In his pursuit of the subject of violin technique, Menuhin soon learned that his ignorance was rooted not so much in the isolation in which he had functioned nor in the failure of his teachers to concentrate on technique as in the general dearth of knowledge in that field. Although other instruments, particularly the piano, have been subjected to thorough scientific study and analysis, the violin has resisted the purely rational approach, remaining in large degree elusive to this day. He found astonishingly few references and still fewer answers to problems posed by technical processes, by the fundamentals, the step-by-step movements, even in such authoritative works as Dounis' *Technique of the Violin* and *The Independence of Fingers*, or Karl Flesch's *The Art of Violin Playing*. Like all violinists, he is indebted to these two master teachers and cherishes with, for him, a rare sentimentality his chance meeting with Flesch during a stroll in the woods of Baden-Baden when Yehudi, aged thirteen, was introduced to the master and had a brief conversation with him.

This deficiency in literature on the violin, Menuhin thinks, is accounted for primarily by the inalienability of the instrument's link with the human body: "the violin is therefore much more dependent on the moral and physical condition of the musician and is a far more elusive instrument to reduce to terms of cold technique than, say, its major counterpart in the concert world, the piano.

"Like the human voice, the violin possesses no keys nor pedals nor any other mechanical means of sound production, in complete contrast to the piano, an instrument which, moreover, stands on its own three legs, eliminating from the player's mind all worry as to position or balance. Naturally, one would not seek to minimize the extremely subtle and complicated technique by which great pianists transform their instrument, but they at least do not have to seek their notes, nor is the ivory key as appallingly sensitive to the touch as is the temperamental violin string. To make the comparison clearer, even at the risk of oversimplification, one might add that the piano requires one motion—the vertical hammer action, either harder or lighter, slower or faster, the fingers striking at a keyboard on which the notes of the scale are in a permanent position, and the octaves, therefore, an equal distance from each other. Added to which the pianist relies on an intermediary mechanical process to set the strings in motion, a process that lends itself to step-by-step analysis. With the violin, in contrast, even as simple an action as the playing of a single note requires a variety of techniques that must be mastered and co-ordinated. Not only does the violinist handle the string at both ends, but the instrument itself must be held in a way that is at one and the same time firm and free. In order to select the notes, the left hand must find its way unerringly over divisions and subdivisions of a space which varies as does a slide rule. At the same time, the right hand technique is governed by its own rules, which vary with each part of the bow, with each string, each changing position of the left hand, and, finally, with the type of the bow stroke used.

"This is why months of patience, work, and faith must be invested before even one good clean sound can be produced on the violin. The conscious mind can hardly be expected to guide the violinist through the complexities of the independent actions involved, but while it allows the subconscious, the automatic, to take over, the mind can and must seek for itself the right of approval. To do so, it must be armed with a solid knowledge of violin technique, based on a minute analysis of the many factors involved, on a splitting of the action into its smallest essential elements. This the violin resists stubbornly, but it must be achieved if an adult musician is to give a sustained, controlled performance of artistic merit.

"Of course, the gypsy fiddlers of Rumania and Hungary have played unconsciously since time immemorial, as do the indigenous fiddlers of Scotland, Norway, or our own Kentucky mountains, without ever having undertaken such analysis. But they have never been asked, nor have they ever asked themselves, how it is that they play, even as the centipede does not pause to reflect on exactly which foot he moves first, or why. Likewise, they are not obliged to play great works, either classical or modern, cast in a precise mold.

"Every concert violinist has groped for the knowledge, understanding, and mastery of his instrument. Some have succeeded, some have floundered, but at no time has there been evolved a method or methods for the training and self-training of violinists as foolproof as those which have produced and continue to produce many excellent piano players."

Menuhin has always been reluctant to admit even to himself —and this I have gathered from him indirectly, through a chance remark or an abrupt pause—that circumstances beyond his control could have the power of defeating him in his function as an artist. He is convinced that the performing musician, like the writer, painter, composer, or actor, must be possessed by a feeling of invulnerability as he practices his art, which lends him the pride and the inspiration to transcend the limits set by his everyday existence. Thus, to find himself handicapped by technical difficulties was to Menuhin as frustrating as it was bewildering, while the very decision to pit himself against them required great humility and still greater courage. As against the artistic conception, which lies in the realm of intuition—with its wondrous flashes and miraculous short cuts—the technique of violin playing yields only to prolonged periods of humble groundwork and grueling conscious effort. Having neglected to acquire the proper approach to technique during his prodigy days, and having discovered that the short cuts he had devised—the "battering ram" method —had only led him deeper into the maze, he now undertook the job of complete retooling, as it were, determined to study and work until he was again able to play immortal works as naturally as he could draw breath.

Menuhin decided to take advantage of the few weeks of respite from travel and concerts that followed the broadcast in order to make a solid start on what he knew was bound to become an extended period of daily encounter with his instrument. That much he knew, but little did he suspect that those brief early-summer weeks in his own home, with his family and friends, would be but a prelude to years not only of arduous work but also of loneliness and of tribulations, alternately inspiring and depressing, placing on trial his very essence as a man, his moral courage and physical stamina, as well as his mastery of the violin.

It was probably just as well that he suspected nothing during those blue-skied weeks, the last happy weeks he was to have at home for more than five years to come. Except for the practicing hours, the days were filled with swimming, picnics, and music making with Baller and the house guests, the violinist Roman Totenberg, the cellist Gabor Rejto, and Jenö Lener of the great Lener String Quartet.[1]

The beginning of Menuhin's new "encounter" with his instrument was most auspicious. Upon his return from San Francisco, he spent the entire afternoon playing chamber music with his inspiring partners, and playing with such abandon and masterful ease that the gnawing feeling of dissatisfaction with his broadcast soon yielded to cheerful confidence. Still exhilarated, he withdrew to his room the next morning to

[1]It was during this period of music making that the Alma Trio was formed by Baller, Totenberg, and Rejto, which functions with great distinction to this day, Maurice Wilk having replaced Totenberg.

practice, but, as he was tucking the violin under his chin, he became aware of the familiar tension across the back, a heavy weight in his limbs, and resistance in the joints. Obeying an impulse, he put the instrument aside, lay down on the floor and began exercises in search of basic positions of body relaxation and muscle control. Breathing in and out deeply and evenly, he improvised progressively elaborate motions. This relaxed him enormously, and, as he developed the habit of these exercises, he found that if he added concentration on some abstract thought, were it musical or philosophical, it greatly enhanced the effect. Years later, chancing upon a book on yoga during a sojourn in New Zealand, he discovered to his surprise that he had instinctively developed some of the methods leading toward bodily well-being and inner peace that had been devised by Indian sages thousands of years ago.

Menuhin thus worked away day after day in a spirit of adventure, shedding fatigue and tension and with them the woodenness of body and limb. The weeks flew by in a kind of happy, busy dream, at the end of which he realized that if there ever were a time in his life for canceling engagements, this was the moment, for his retooling had only just begun. But this also happened to be the moment when he felt he had no right to do so, for most of his appearances were to be at army bases, in military hospitals, and for wartime charities.

Plagued by the knowledge that he had left much undone, Menuhin went off on his strenuous tour, and, surely enough, fatigue soon began to accumulate once more, bringing with it tension and unevenness of performance. "At times I felt like a marionette being pulled back, the strings manipulated by a senseless, cruel force," he recalls.

Still, there was so much of the artist in him that despite this partial blockage he managed for the main part to give fine performances, so fine indeed as to enable him to maintain his unique position in the musical world. He kept up this achievement only by virtue of making an exaggerated effort and by having to summon all his musical knowledge and life-long professional experience. As time and travel were taking their toll, this effort was becoming increasingly difficult to make. Contributing to his trial was his refusal to compromise in his programming or to seek escape in flashy mannerisms. Whenever events and mood conspired to give him relative calm and a few days of rest, he displayed a miraculous resilience, playing with regained luster and noble poise. And though, even on his off nights, there was still sufficient magic left in him to please his audiences,[2] the critics unerringly sensed the difference and would deplore "an inadventurous course," noting that "something of the grand line was missing," or declaring impatiently that "Menuhin has not lost his virtuosity but, at least last night, did not seem to worry about impeccably managed detail of tone and color."

Accustomed to the perfection of his past performances, recognizing the successful ones during that period of struggle, and having no way of knowing what lay behind the failures, the critics were understandably baffled and irritated, and so were those conductors and other musicians who played with Yehudi. Antal Dorati once remarked to me: "I must confess that Menuhin's tone, so pure and beautiful that it permits nothing to stand between itself and the listener, has always led me to be more critical of him than of any other violinist I have ever played with." Dorati could not have been more right, but there was more to the question than merely that of tone. Yehudi Menuhin's emergence on the concert platform, which became one of the legends of its time, had aroused expectations, the realization of which required godlike qualities. Speaking of these expectations, Fritz Kreisler said:

"Most of us take the major part of a lifetime to develop the gifts nature has bestowed upon us. It is a slow, prolonged process wherein no human being is able to transcend the limits set by the laws of nature. The miracle of Yehudi con-

[2]Remarking upon Menuhin's unfailing success with his audiences, Bruno Walter said to me: "It is not only that Yehudi plays well even when he is not in top form. Music is a good 'conductor' of personality, just as metal is a good conductor of heat. Through music man himself speaks. The audiences sense the man, and that which they sense in Yehudi they love."

sisted in that by the age of twelve or fourteen he had fulfilled a very large part of what nature had given him, reaching in one leap, as it were, a stage of development he would have normally attained at thirty-five or forty. As a child, he played like a grown man, like an enormously gifted grown man.

"Because the young Yehudi had anticipated so early and so much of what nature had given him, I foresaw that he would have great difficulties. Some of them, fortunately, proved to be rooted not so much within the process of his own development as within those of his listeners who tended to ignore the laws of nature. They expected Yehudi to grow and mature after adolescence at a rate comparable to that of the period preceding it. In other words, as Yehudi had achieved during that early stage, say, seventy per cent of his capacities, those persons expected him to achieve one hundred and forty per cent or more upon reaching manhood.

"There was another source of difficulties for Yehudi. Our age is an age of speed, of impatience, whereas maturity and growth are a slow process, in its own way even more miraculous, more beautiful and rewarding, than the phenomenon of the child prodigy.

"Yehudi has been growing, constantly, steadily, against the heaviest odds, such odds as have actually destroyed most prodigies. He has achieved a maturity of style in his own way —he has achieved the artist's most difficult goal: he remains himself, he is Yehudi no matter what he plays or however faithfully. The tempo of an artist lies not in the metronome but in the pulse beating inside him, for great music is adjustable to the personality of the artist playing it. Listening to Yehudi, I sense a pure, noble mind, understanding, and, above all, constant growth."[3]

Menuhin, in the meantime, continued to grapple with his problems in a wretched kind of isolation. He saw little of his wife, as they had become strangers to each other, and he saw little of his parents, colleagues, or friends, confiding in them even less, convinced that he had to fight his battle quite alone,

[3]From an interview with this author in December 1953.

turning to no one for help, and least of all to those whose very shelter and nursing he needs must shed. This self-imposed inner aloneness made it impossible for anyone to share with him the anguish of that period or shield him from it to some extent. Even his sister Hephzibah, who visited the United States in 1946, found that she could not get through to her brother. Nor could his beloved Aunt Willa. Describing a visit to Miss Cather by Yehudi, Hephzibah and their four children, Edith Lewis says in her book: "Once again the place is filled with children's voices and laughter. Under the gaiety and happiness that morning, there was somehow a sense of heart-break."[4] Miss Lewis refers primarily to Willa Cather's age and ailment (and, indeed, neither Yehudi nor Hephzibah was ever to see her again), but she told me there was endless sadness for her and Miss Cather in the sight of Yehudi and his children calling without Nola, he tense and brooding and betraying a kind of darkness utterly alien to the Yehudi they had always known.

His very appearance was changing under the impact of his ordeal. Unaccustomed to taking care of himself, he had gained much weight and was pale and flabby, moving about like the tired man he was. He kept to himself as much as his profession allowed, and when in New York he lived alone in the empty apartment of Klari and Antal Dorati, who were away most of the time in Dallas, where Dorati was conductor of the Symphony Orchestra. One day Menuhin was cooking a lonely dinner for himself, consisting solely of a huge slice of liver. He who would abide only by the *Ur*-text in his own profession was utterly nonconformist in other fields and, instead of following the time-honored way of preparing liver steak, insisted upon frying it, of all things, in milk. By the time the smoke had reached the ceiling, he was on long distance to Mrs. Dorati: "Klari, what do I do with the stuff now?" he cried. The answer was very much to the point: "Throw it out, open the windows, and order yourself some liver at the nearest good restaurant."

'*Willa Cather Living*, p. 172.

The concert-going public knew nothing of Menuhin's trials and tribulations, and the glamor of his name was tarnished but little by the scattered unfavorable notices some of his concerts were receiving, while his indefatigable war work added a bright new glow to it. The professional musicians who played with him or attended his concerts were, of course, aware of his difficulties, but few had any knowledge of the root of his troubles and still fewer presumed to broach any personal or professional subjects to him. Those who did found no encouraging response and retreated, but when two New York violin teachers, Theodore and Alice Pashkus, called on him one day he listened with interest to their account of the years they had spent in study and experiment, applying to the violin the laws of mechanics that govern the acquisition of any ordinary manual skill. Defining violin playing from this point of view as merely a series of motions intended to bring forth certain sounds, the Pashkuses had sought to determine the exact motions, the proper muscles, and the precise application of finger pressures involved in the production of the desired sounds. Intrigued, Menuhin worked with the Pashkuses on that and many a later occasion, testing the exercises they had devised and working out some of his own, having found in the Pashkuses and their theories "a whetstone against which I sharpened the blade of my technique."

Shedding habits, especially those automatically acquired and practiced for many years, and bringing new habits under conscious control is as grim an undertaking as any adult could assume. Initial failures were unavoidable, and Menuhin would begin all over again, and then once more, and yet again, like a boxer rising from the canvas, despite the merciless punishment to which he was being subjected.

Thus he went on month after month and year after year, giving at the same time countless concerts in the U.S.A. and Europe, unmindful of frustrations and fatigue. His studies and experiments helped him to fathom many a hitherto unexplored problem in the field of violin technique, as well as to gain a new security in his hard-won knowledge, and in the conscious mastery that was gradually becoming his.

The arduous, time-consuming task of retooling, however important, was only the outward aspect of the complex and difficult process of Menuhin's education and growth, merely the visible part of the iceberg, in a manner of speaking. The submerged part was by far the greater and the more decisive in Menuhin's mastery of his ordeal.

SIXTEEN

The Submerged Part of the Iceberg—I

*If a man is to preserve his art, he must have
something else, something more than his
native genius: passions, sorrows, which shall
fill this life and give it a direction.*

HENRIK IBSEN

*Keep thy heart with all diligence; for out of
it are the issues of life.*

PROVERBS 4:23

It was natural, even imperative, for Menuhin to concentrate,
throughout the years of his ordeal, above all on the violin. At
the same time, he regarded his problem as not only, or even
primarily, a crisis in technique; that crisis, he came to understand, was merely one of the many "issues of life." At first he
tended to seek those issues within and by himself, crawling
into a shell and shutting it tightly, but soon, under the impact
of his frustrations and of the contacts he inescapably made in
the pursuit of his profession, he forced his shell open, however
narrowly, and gradually widened the crack, his eyes clear, his
ears alert, and his mind ready to gather and relate each discovery. There was something very touching and humble in
his eagerness to receive, but the sensitive observer could
easily discern a sharp critical quality in him, clinical in its
thoroughness and objectivity, as well as a confidence and a
pride in the few things of which Menuhin was certain.

It was a long, often exciting, occasionally tedious and pain-
ful search, as though of pieces of some magical jigsaw puzzle
the solution of which promised to bring with it mastery and

maturity. He well knew how poorly equipped he was for his search of the solution. His education had never been systematic, his knowledge of languages, conception of world affairs, insight into people, even his music, had all been acquired on the wing, as it were, nor had he much experience in establishing contact with fellow men. On the other hand, his wartime experience had taught him to act freely and energetically, while the lack of formal education had a compensating quality all its own: unconditioned by any group or doctrine, his mind worked, and still does, in a fresh, unorthodox way, reacting to events, ideas, and people with rare naturalness and lack of prejudice. One might say that, just as the greater part of his life has been governed by an instrument which holds no mechanically set notes, forcing him each time to find them for himself, so does he form his judgments not by depending on any set of absolutes but calling, instead, upon his own instincts and sensibility. As the present Mrs. Menuhin once said, half in delight, half in exasperation: "Yehudi's is the least prefabricated and most unpredictable mind I have ever come across." Experience soon convinced him that the accidental and the unexpected often yield richer rewards than the planned and the intended, so that he is now ever open to new ideas and people, a boyish eagerness in his receptivity.

Among the mass of encounters, associations, and experiences that followed Menuhin's opening of the crack in his shell, one can trace certain key events and relationships which were the most instrumental in bringing into focus the issues of his life. There was the brief but poignant friendship and creative collaboration with the great Hungarian composer Béla Bartók, the association with Wilhelm Furtwängler and the dramatic circumstances surrounding it, Menuhin's first trips to Israel and India, and, finally, the new love that had entered his life.

In tracing these events, chronology must be cast to the winds, as they all overlap in time—with the one exception, that is, of Menuhin's relationship with Béla Bartók.

Yehudi first heard about the composer in 1940 from Antal Dorati when they met on board the ship that brought the violinist and the conductor from Australia back to the United States. Menuhin's curiosity was aroused by Dorati's spirited description of the grandeur and originality of his great country-man's works. One day late in 1942 Menuhin received the score of Bartók's monumental violin concerto from Dimitri Mitropoulos, along with a suggestion that they perform it with the Minneapolis Symphony Orchestra. The concerto was introduced earlier in the year by Tossy Spivakovsky and the Cleveland Orchestra under Artur Rodzinski. The score excited Menuhin with its tremendous range of tenderness and violence and with the novel, strangely effective way in which the solo instrument was pitted against a turbulent orchestra. He now set out in eager search of Bartók's other works for the violin, a search that fulfilled his wildest expectations. "No other composer has drawn me as irresistibly as Bartók," Menuhin wrote subsequently. "I felt as one with his implacable and complex rhythms, at one with the abstract yet intensely expressive construction of his melodic lines, at one with his incredibly rich range of harmonies—sometimes simple, sometimes clashing or ironical—and, above all, at one with that streamlined cleanness of design and execution, always without a trace of irrelevance or sentimentality. . . . One other factor which attracted me irresistibly is the oriental quality of his music."[1]

Captivated by the barbaric sweep and beauty of the concerto, Yehudi made it his own and played it with virtuosity and understanding. Subsequently, Menuhin introduced the concerto in London, with Sir Adrian Boult, and in other European capitals. With Dorati he made the first recording of it.

It might seem strange to the Bartók-conscious world of today, but the fact remains that the composer was at the time leading a life of obscurity and near poverty in a crowded apartment in Forest Hills, New York, plagued by ill-health and by a bitter and growing awareness of himself as a neglected stranger in the midst of the bustling musical life of

[1]From a BBC broadcast delivered on November 4, 1945.

America. Menuhin's interest in his work excited and cheered
Bartók, even as Bartók's music had come to hold deep significance for the violinist, and he was eager to meet the composer. At the same time, he was reluctant to intrude on his
privacy. A Carnegie Hall recital with Adolph Baller in November 1943, the program for which included Bartók's *First
Violin Sonata,* gave Yehudi the awaited opportunity, and he
invited the composer for a private hearing of his work two
days before the recital. The meeting took place at the home
of a mutual friend, Mrs. Lionello Perera, an amateur violinist
of distinction, and when Menuhin came in, accompanied by
Baller, he found Bartók already seated in a chair, pencil and
score in hand. After the briefest of preliminaries, he pointedly
directed his gaze at the piano.

The contrast between the two could not have been greater.
One, known throughout the world, was young, robust, fair-
haired, with gentle, smiling eyes; the other, neglected by all
but a few worshipers, was white-haired, fragile, his stern
features given life only by enormous, burning eyes. Both were
shy, and men of few words, but Bartók seemed, in addition,
to make a conscious effort at economy of speech and movement, as though trying to reserve every particle of his dwin-
dling energy for creative work.

"Immediately with the first notes," Menuhin said in his BBC
broadcast, "there burst forth between us, as an electric contact, an intimate bond which was to remain fast and firm. In
fact, I believe that there can exist between a composer and
his interpreter a stronger, more intimate bond, even without
the exchange of words, than between the composer and a
friend he may have known for years. For the composer
reserves the core of his personality, the essence of his self, for
his works.

"As we finished the first movement, he rose, came over to
me, and said the following words—which, for Bartók, were
equivalent to an uncontrolled burst of impassioned exuberance
—he said: 'I thought works were only played in that way long
after the composers were dead.'

"It was on that occasion that I asked him if he would compose a sonata for violin alone."

Actually, a friend of the composer has stated that Bartók had contemplated writing a work for the violinist before Menuhin had made his request.[2] Be that as it may, Bartók replied with a brief "I shall" and composed for Menuhin the now celebrated *Sonata for Solo Violin*, the last major original score he was to complete before his death.

The Carnegie Hall recital that took place after their first meeting was a stirring triumph for both the composer and the violinist. Menuhin gave one of his best performances during that period, arousing a tumultuous ovation which he insisted that Bartók share with him on the stage. Bartók's friends who were with him in the hall that evening, and who had thought him impervious to human frailty, saw with amazement that his eyes were dimmed by tears when he returned to his place after having taken several stiff, awkward bows.

Menuhin, too, was happy that evening, and he would have been happier still had he known that Bartók was to say in a letter to a friend:

He [Menuhin] *is a great artist, he played in the same concert Bach's C-major sonata in a grand, classical style. My sonata, too, was exceedingly well done. When there is a real great artist, then the composer's advice and help is not necessary, the performer finds his way quite well, alone. It is altogether a happy thing that a young artist is interested in contemporary works which draw no public and likes them, and performs them comme il faut.*[3]

On his doctor's advice, Bartók spent the winter of 1943–44 at Asheville, N.C., where, on March 14, he completed

[2]H. W. Heinsheimer, *Fanfare for 2 Pigeons* (New York: Doubleday, 1952), p. 118.

[3]Written to Wilhelmine Creel on December 17, 1943, as cited in *The Life and Music of Béla Bartók* by Halsey Stevens (New York: Oxford University Press, 1953), p. 99.

the violin solo sonata he had promised Yehudi. In forwarding the score, Bartók wrote:

> *I am rather worried about the 'playability' of some of the double-stops, etc. On the last page I give you some of the alternatives. In any case, I should like to have your advice. I sent you two copies. Would you be so kind as to introduce in one of them the necessary changes in bowing, and perhaps the absolutely necessary fingering and other suggestions, and return it to me? And also indicate the impracticable difficulties? I would try to change them.*

Far from being a display of fussy self-consciousness, this concern arose out of the realization that he, the most demanding of all modern composers, had just completed one of his most demanding works. It was created for an instrument which he did not play, although he knew and understood it better than most practicing violinists, as he had abundantly proved in his compositions. Bartók actually experimented with the violin in the course of his work on the sonata, to arrive at the rather discouraging conviction that his musical conceptions were making impossible demands upon the instrument as well as upon the performer.

The music itself impressed Menuhin as the work of a genius, undoubtedly the greatest piece for the solo violin since Bach. He felt that Bartók's powerful, analytical mind had brought out entirely new and completely unanticipated effects on the violin. He immediately wrote to the composer, making a number of suggestions of a technical nature. To this Bartók replied: "Many thanks for the minute work you have spent on fingering and bowing of the sonata, and for everything else you have done. . . . I am very glad to hear that the work is playable."

The two met shortly before the first performance of this sonata on November 26, 1944, to discuss its final form. The composer's luminous eyes seemed to burn with the inner flame that was consuming his life, and he was more than ever sparing of words, his manner alone indicating the friendship he felt

for the young musician. Bartók briefly considered Menuhin's
suggestions in a voice that was soft but had at the same time
a curious finality. When, at one point, Menuhin asked if Bartók
would make a slight alteration in a chord, the composer gazed
at him for a moment or two and quietly said "No." The chord
remained unchanged.

Menuhin gave the sonata a magnificent first performance,
but the critics, while applauding the violinist, reacted nega-
tively to the composition. It must be said, in all fairness, that
they should have been given one or two private hearings in
advance of the public performance. Neither Bartók nor Yehudi
had thought of doing it, and the critics were completely
unprepared for the exacting task of tracing the sonata's complex inner line. This, in the words of Olin Downes, was "a test
for ears, the intelligence, the receptiveness of the most learned
listener. . . . On initial acquaintance, we take none too kindly
to the piece." It should be added that the critics later revised
their first appraisals. Olin Downes even volunteered to me recently that he feels deeply indebted to Menuhin for having
Bartók's masterpiece brought to his attention.

The initial coolness to his work did little to dismay the
composer: he was too confident about it. And he rejoiced in
what he called "Menuhin's wonderful performance."

The friendship between the two musicians grew with each
meeting, and finally Bartók accepted Yehudi's invitation for
himself and Mrs. Bartók to spend the summer of 1945 at Alma.
Up to that time he had been too proud to accept help from any
of his friends. Yehudi's simplicity and modesty disarmed him
altogether. Everything was ready for the arrival of the Bartóks
in mid-June when, at practically the last moment, the composer wrote to Menuhin:

Dear Friend:
   *I am sorry to have to tell you that we cannot come to
California! I do not feel quite well and—for variety's sake—
now Mrs. Bartók was ill for several weeks and does not yet
feel quite well. We simply are scared to try such a long*

*journey connected, especially now, with all kinds of annoy-
ances. I scarcely can tell you how I regret this. I had so
many musical plans connected with my stay there. All this
now comes to nothing.*

Béla Bartók died on September 26 of that year, leaving a
great void in the world of music and in the life of Yehudi
Menuhin.

> *You took my life, like a book from a shelf,
> And blew the dust off it.*
>
> BORIS PASTERNAK

One day in the fall of 1944, on the eve of his departure for
England, Yehudi called at Cathedral Oaks to say good-by to
his neighbors, the artists George Dennison and Frank Ingerson.
They asked him whether he had any personal friends in London. Only Aunt Edie and her family, he replied.

"Is there any use in our giving you an introduction to Lady
Harcourt?" said Frank.

"But who is Lady Harcourt?" asked Yehudi.

A very good friend of ours in London, they said, and added
that as a young woman she had been one of the most distinguished English pianists of her generation, known to the
public under her maiden name, Evelyn Suart. After her first
marriage, to Gerard Gould, she had retired from the concert
stage but kept up an active interest in music, and the Sunday
afternoon concerts at her home, Mulberry House, became
something of an institution in London, attracting writers,
poets, and painters, as well as nearly every musician who
visited England. George and Frank had twice suggested to
Moshe and Marutha in those faraway days of Yehudi's boyhood that they meet the Goulds, whose three children, Gerard,
Diana, and Griselda, were about the same age as the young
Menuhins and had similar tastes and interests—Diana was
dancing in the ballet and Griselda played the piano beautifully. True to her principles, Marutha had stayed aloof.

Yehudi dutifully telephoned Lady Harcourt a day or two after his arrival in London. When he announced: "This is Yehudi Menuhin," the voice at the other end answered with delightful, if disturbing informality: "Is it, indeed? What would you like?" Somewhat taken aback, he blurted out: "May I come and have lunch?" The brief conversation ended with an invitation to lunch on September 29, a date he well remembers because on that day he met Diana. Not that Diana dominated the occasion. True, she was beautiful, with her huge, brown eyes, clear skin, and the swift, graceful movements of a ballet dancer; but there was also the blond, blue-eyed Griselda who was equally radiant and, like Diana, sharp and witty, with seemingly all the resources of the English language at her command. No less interesting and amusing were the others at the table, the actor Michael Redgrave, the film director Anthony Asquith, and, of course, Lady Harcourt herself, the gayest of them all.

Yehudi delighted in his luncheon companions but, held back by his habitual inarticulateness, he kept his silence most of the time. "What struck me," Diana recalls, "was how strangely he belied the dedicated and legendary Yehudi of the concert platform, this plump, prosperous-looking, incredibly young and utterly uncomplicated boy who had walked into my mother's room. When we met again, almost a year later, and I saw more of him, I realized the error of that first impression. He was neither as uncomplicated nor as untouched by life as we all had thought."

Menuhin returned to England the following summer to record the musical score for the London production of *The Magic Bow*, a film based on the life of Paganini. Tempted to see himself on the screen, Yehudi accepted the producer's suggestion that he take a screen test as Paganini, whom Stewart Granger was portraying in the film. Menuhin asked Diana, who was acting in *Jacobowsky and the Colonel* at the time, to coach him for the test.

"Aid and abet you to become a third-rate film star?" she laughed. "Certainly not!"

Cornered, he had to confess to her that all he wanted was to see himself on the screen, and, thus convinced, she entered into the spirit of the thing. They had endless fun with the clumsy script and with Yehudi's make-up, Diana insisting that the wavy wig made him look like a cross between the Lorelei and one of the lions at Trafalgar Square. She mentioned Greta Garbo at one point and stopped in her tracks, unbelieving, when she heard him say: "Who is Greta Garbo?" It was too good to be true. "Say it again," she requested, watching out of the corner of her eye to make sure he was not pulling her leg. "But who is Greta Garbo?" he asked again, this time hesitatingly, his eyes honest and rather troubled, for he had sensed the unbelief in her voice.

"I must have fallen in love with him at just that point," she was to say years later.

When they both found a free evening, they went to see *Ninotchka.* Yehudi was completely enraptured.

One night they were dining together after Diana's show. Both were preoccupied and tired. Diana began to speak slowly, almost irrelevantly. Isn't it anguish, she said, that moment when one is no longer a prodigy and suddenly becomes aware of what one is doing? Now everything that one did naturally and instinctively suddenly has to be translated into conscious terms. It is as though one has come to a river and has to dismantle himself, then take each piece across to reassemble on the other side.

He looked at her with astonishment: "How do you know?"

"Every dancer who has the slightest talent has proven herself by the time she is fifteen or sixteen. Then the upheaval starts, with some earlier, with others later, and still others—later yet."

Yehudi began to speak of his struggle with the violin, at first haltingly, guardedly; then, disarmed by her sensitive understanding, he found himself talking as he had never talked to anyone except to Hephzibah during the years of their growing up.

So the summer went on. Apart from sharing each other's

problems and interests, they found time for walks, drives into the country; they visited art galleries and saw mutual friends, and on the rare free evenings they had together they went to the theater, the cinema or the ballet. To his delight, Yehudi discovered that they shared a love of France and the French language—for Diana's father's family had left Ireland and settled in France in the early nineteenth century, and all the Gould children had spoken French since childhood.

One day Yehudi brought Diana to the studio of Jacob Epstein, who was doing a head of the violinist in the midst of a triumphant disorder. Wearing a crumpled smock (topped with an ancient jacket on more formal occasions) and stained old pants, Epstein would park Yehudi on a dusty chair, study him for several minutes with restless, bulging eyes like two small revolving moons, and then proceed to torment the clay with jovial, untidy energy. "Always bring Diana, won't you?" he said after her first visit. "Your face is quite different when she is there." He fashioned a magnificent head, having captured the sensitiveness and good humor of Yehudi's face along with the determination which the events of the last few years had wrought upon it. But, alas, one of the studio cats jumped upon the head in the middle of the night and knocked it to the floor, where it broke to a thousand bits. Epstein started again, but Yehudi was about to leave London for the continent and could give him no more than two or three sittings. In the short time allotted, Epstein could not do justice to his own greatness.

On looking back upon that happy, fruitful summer, Yehudi finds it dominated by his growing closeness to Diana "who was gradually adding new dimensions to my life. It was not only that I was falling in love with her (I was, God knows, but that feeling and my awareness of it were slow in coming upon me); there was also something else, possibly just as important. Diana was awakening in me a new understanding of myself and of my work, helping me to gain a new perspective which stripped my violin of its exclusive significance but which, magically, did not rob it of its vitality and importance. I had been hedged around and isolated far too long, living under a glass shade and emerging from it for just long enough to give a concert, then returning to its shelter. My life with Nola had smashed that glass shade, yet involuntarily I kept crawling under what was no longer there. This could not but create a chasm between me and the world which I had to bridge if ever I were to be one with my fellow men. My wartime work brought out a self-reliance in me which had enabled me for the first time to gather all the threads of my life in my own hands. With the coming of Diana, I found it possible also to identify myself with other people and other artists, for with her she brought her sense of humor, her love of poetry and painting, the art of conversation, and her friends; she brought with her a whole rich world which my peculiar education and background had denied me. Most of all, along with Diana came to me a new understanding of courage, the courage she had discovered in the struggle and anguish of her own career and was now sharing with me."

And if Yehudi felt that about Diana, she had this to say about him:

"In myself, the liquid, the essence of life, appeared to be constantly in a state of combustion, to be about to send off God knows what emotional gases and uncontrollable explosions. With Yehudi, the essence seemed to have passed through all such chemical processes, to be already fused, the hazards of the volcanic experiments within him resolved or, perhaps, by some deific privilege bypassed, and the inner being so serene, limpid, and of such a steadfastness that whatever cataclysms assailed him, whatever shook the outer him, this essence, like still water, always found its own level and remained tranquil and undisturbed. It is from this that comes that radiance, the unwavering light that can shine only from a single and unselfish heart.

"I, who so often came up against creatures who either spent themselves in an extravagance of actions and reactions, flinging themselves on the four winds until there was nothing left, or who hoarded what they might have given, parsimoniously

doling out a few stale crumbs to those they could have nurtured—to me then this quality that was the whole Yehudi was
something at once so uncontaminated and yet so deeply
human, so self-contained and at the same time so outgoing,
that it seemed to bring to reality the illusion which all men
and women seek in each other and rarely in their disenchantment find, the heavenly contentment of an utterly true heart."

Like her brother and sister, Diana grew up in Mulberry
House. It was gracious and vivid, its rooms filled with lovely
old furniture and exquisite china, glass, and silver collected by
her father. Towards the end of World War I he died, leaving
his wife with three very small children. A few years later, his
widow married Cecil Harcourt, a naval officer who proved to
be a devoted stepfather and helped Evelyn maintain the
charming atmosphere of Mulberry House. That atmosphere
did little, however, to prepare Diana for the competitive, in-
trigue-ridden jungle of the ballet, which she had entered at
the age of eight. As often as not, her one great defensive
weapon—annihilating repartee—would be turned against her,
for she had neglected to acquire the healthy knowledge of how
to choose her targets. Nor had she learned to compromise with
the truth. (She refuses to lie even about her age, "though it
sometimes proves a bit embarrassing to my younger girl friends
of the same age," says she.) According to Agnes de Mille in
Dance to the Piper, her polished sarcasm "would have done
Wilde no discredit," but quite often it aroused the ire of ballet
critics, entrepreneurs, or teachers. Once, as a young girl, she
sadly observed that "the tragedy of life lies not so much in the
fact that it is so ugly as in the idea that it ought to be so beautiful."

Nevertheless, she herself has been a constant slave to this
idea, having begun to pay homage to it as a child, by joining
what had seemed to her the radiant world of the ballet. Her
memories of it go far back to one evening when "my mother
flew ecstatically into the night nursery, tore me out of bed,

and bid a protesting nanny dress me at once, as she was going to take me to the Coliseum to see the Diaghilev Ballet. I can remember little now except an atmosphere of pure fairy tale; that otherworldness with which most of us are born and which gradually fades from the awakening mind as will color before too crude and naked a light. I never forgot that dream of sound and color and smell." (And here, in one of Diana's breathless asides that often outshine the main topic of her discourse, she continued: "For surely you have noticed the ballet has its own peculiar smell—of tarlatan and sweat and rosin and benzine; of size and seccotine and of dust, layer upon layer of dust, stirred and blown about by the legs and arms of countless dancers, and by the draughts of a hundred 'flies,' stamped into cloth and canvas and ironed in, painted over, sealed, forever imprisoned in costume and décor? Once I could have told you in the pitch dark the *Carnaval* from the *Scheherazade* backdrop, merely from the smell alone.")

Diana started her training at Marie Rambert's ballet school, where, along with the other pupils, she spent most of her waking hours in dark, damp studios, put through the paces by Madame, who screamed and rammed poetry and grace into the wooden, large-boned, long-limbed bodies of her English pupils, whose capacity for taking punishment was second only to that of the Russian girls.

Mme. Rambert's wind was not tempered for the shorn lamb that was Diana when she came to the studio, practically straight from the nursery. Her wit, far from shielding her from Madame's spleen, served only to provoke her into singling out the little girl for particular punishment. Diana writhed and chafed but was too strictly brought up to complain or even to weep. Instead, she toiled and plodded on, converting the agonies of muscular pain into allies of her natural grace, beauty, and imagination. At fourteen, she was selected by Diaghilev from among her classmates to join his company in the next season. He introduced Diana to his dancers as a future member and *"la seule jeune fille que j'aimerais épouser* [the only little girl I'd like to marry]."

Diana's next few months were spent in even harder work, and then, one sultry day in August, the newspapers announced Diaghilev's death. Even in her despair she went on dancing, and gave her first recital before she had reached her fifteenth birthday. "Like the divine Karsavina," said one critic, "Diana Gould is a joy to gaze upon." Then followed a season with that "divine Karsavina"—Diana's goddess—a season so successful that no one was surprised when the great Anna Pavlova invited her to join her company. But within three months, like Diaghilev, Pavlova died suddenly. This second calamity almost crushed the girl's will, but she grimly kept up her daily grind under the demanding, all-seeing eyes of Madame Rambert.

The next blow added a note of mockery: Diana suddenly began to shoot upward, and was soon too tall for star roles in the existing ballets. Several new parts were created especially for her (as were Frederick Ashton's *Leda and the Swan* and Anthony Tudor's *Lysistrata*), as well as individual numbers for her repertoire, including Keith Lester's remarkable *Pavane*.

At this time, Diana's gifts as an actress came to the fore, aided by a riotous, wicked sense of the comic. A leading British balletomane, Poppoea Vanda, wrote of Diana: "She is an excellent dancer, yes, but she is also the greatest actress in the history of the English ballet." The leading critic in the field, Arnold Haskell, wrote: "Miss Gould is the finest young artist the English dance has produced." Speaking at a literary luncheon on December 6, 1934, he said: "Again I will select one dancer, and my choice rests on a really remarkable talent, Diana Gould."

After a period of additional study in Paris with the indomitable Kshessinskaya, star of the former Imperial Russian Ballet, Diana, among many other things, worked with Reinhardt and Massine in *The Miracle*, and danced as a soloist in Balanchine's ballet, with De Basil's ballet, with Nijinska, and with the Markova-Dolin company. During World War II, she acted on the legitimate stage in several plays, ran a ballet company, toured army camps in Great Britain, Africa, and Italy with Cyril Ritchard and Madge Elliott's *Merry Widow*, and found time in between to translate a French play in collaboration with Michael Redgrave.

Despite a begininng that held great promise, her career was a difficult and lonely one, in which the illusions she had had as a child and adolescent were ultimately dispelled. In the highly competitive field which she had chosen for herself, she learned all too early that courage and resilience were as necessary as were talent and looks. She possessed all those qualities and had won her way to a position of distinction in the ballet world of England, but she had to fight every inch of the way and paid the price of disenchantment. Then she met Yehudi and fell in love and gave up her career to become Mrs. Yehudi Menuhin. They were married on Sunday, October 19, 1947, at nine o'clock in the morning by two gentlemen of the Chelsea Registry Office, unforgettably named Mr. Marsh and Mr. Stream. Lady Harcourt was there, and Aunt Edie, Harold Holt, and Griselda and her husband, Louis Kentner. The ceremony over, the little group gathered at the Kentners' house to open a bottle of champagne, which the bridegroom smelled wistfully but dared not drink for he was due within half an hour at a rehearsal with George Weldon and the London Symphony Orchestra to be followed by a concert on that same afternoon. In a valiant effort at a honeymoon, the newlyweds spent one day and night at the Ritchards' country cottage, and then set off on a tour of the English provinces.

Thus, from the very moment that she became Mrs. Yehudi Menuhin, Diana found herself swept into the daily grind which constitutes the main part of a hard-working virtuoso's life. She attacked a score or two of letters a day, packed and unpacked with lightning speed, washed, ironed, and darned for them both, and attended to a hundred and one other domestic chores. "I've since gathered," she says wryly, "an infinite knowledge of airports, seaports, railway stations, and hotels on five continents."

SEVENTEEN

The Submerged Part of the Iceberg—II

*God offers to every mind its choice between
truth and repose.*

RALPH WALDO EMERSON

Shortly after Yehudi's memorable conversation with Diana
that summer in 1945, he undertook an extensive tour of the
countries of our wartime allies, including France, Holland,
Czechoslovakia, and Russia, for the benefit of local charity
organizations. The tour was preceded by several concerts he
gave for the survivors of concentration camps and for displaced persons. In Belsen, now the central gathering point for
Jewish survivors of concentration camps all the way from
Czechoslovakia to Denmark, he found the former inmates
wearing with pride the suits and skirts they had fashioned out
of U. S. Army blankets. The concentration camp had been
burned by the survivors, who had moved into the adjoining
infantry barracks, which boasted green lawns, an up-to-date
hospital, and even a theater, in which Yehudi played.

There, as well as in the other camps he visited with the distinguished British composer Benjamin Britten as his accompanist, Menuhin found that the initial joy of liberation had
partly worn off and that squalor and disorganization had set
in among the men and women to whom no country in the
world was willing to give asylum. Menuhin was so moved by
their plight that he wrote a report to the U.S. authorities,

urging them to liquidate the camps with the utmost speed so that the people could be returned to a normal existence, for their insecurity and the uncertainty as to their future were driving them to despair and hatred.

In the camps, Menuhin talked with people of many nationalities, speaking different languages and united primarily by their hatred of the Germans. He was therefore impressed when several musicians in Belsen spoke to him of their gratitude to one German, the conductor Wilhelm Furtwängler, for the struggle he had put up for the Jews in his orchestra, the Berlin Philharmonic. He had shielded them to the point of testifying on their behalf before Nazi courts. Some were arrested, nevertheless, and of these only a few had survived. Other Jews succeeded in fleeing from the Nazis with Furtwängler's help, notably the great Karl Flesch and his wife. The Flesches had been imprisoned in Holland, and Furtwängler had saved their lives by making it possible for them to escape to Switzerland.

Menuhin was particularly interested because he had heard similar accounts from Furtwängler's former secretary, Berta Geismar, a Jewess, who had succeeded in fleeing to London. And in Paris French musicians told Menuhin of the conductor's consistent refusal to accompany his orchestra on propaganda tours of the Nazi-overrun territories or to conduct any of the orchestras of the occupied countries, despite relentless pressures. True, he had remained in the Third Reich and held high posts in his capacity as a musician,[1] but he never joined Hitler's party, nor did he ever comply with the unwritten rule requiring the conductor to make a Nazi salute at the beginning of each concert. The French musicians went so far as to state that they would welcome Furtwängler as a guest conductor, an honor they would not bestow at that time on any other German.

Yehudi reported all these statements about Furtwängler in

[1] In her *Two Worlds of Music*, Berta Geismar says that "Furtwängler was constantly implored by his friends and his public not to forsake them." (Creative Age, Inc.: New York, 1946, p. 140.)

interviews with newspapermen upon his return to the States in December 1945. As a result, he found himself, to his great surprise and even greater consternation, in the center of a most bitter controversy. American public opinion was then aroused by the Nürnberg trials. In Menuhin's own field there was great agitation as to whether or not those artists who had remained in Germany and practiced their art under Nazism were now to be allowed to return to their old posts.

The attack on Yehudi was led off by Ira A. Hirschmann, founder and president of the New Friends of Music, who declared that he was "horror-stricken" at Menuhin for "attempting to whitewash the Nazi official musical director of the Third Reich, Wilhelm Furtwängler.

"At the very moment when the employers of Mr. Furtwängler are facing international trial for mass butchery, that anyone should attempt to give a clear bill of health to one of their conspirators seems incredible."

As to Furtwängler's record "of employing a few anti-Nazis and Jews [from] among the millions who were later murdered by his colleagues," Hirschmann dismissed it as merely "playing an old game," and he added that Menuhin "chooses a rather critical moment in history to suggest the return of one of the Nazi satellites. . . . That it should be suggested for him [Furtwängler] to return to America to purge his strain is so incredible as to be unthinkable. . . . We are outraged at the very thought of this Nazi invading America."

Having inadvertently become involved in a public controversy of a violence that was utterly alien to his nature, Menuhin was particularly disturbed at finding himself under censure by men of his own race. He felt that the accusation was unjustified, and he declared to the press that Hirschmann "misrepresented and misstated me. I never mentioned that Furtwängler should come to this country. . . . It is wrong to mention Furtwängler and those beasts on trial in Nürnberg in the same breath. It is a very easy and cheap way of raising mass feelings. Even those beasts are getting a fair, democratic trial. Surely it is wrong to condemn Furtwängler, about whom there are divided opinions, without a fair trial."[2]

But no trial was given Furtwängler until April, 1947,[3] when he was called before a German denazification tribunal which absolved him of collaboration charges, primarily on the strength of the evidence that he had protected Jewish musicians from fascist persecution. The most effective testimony was given by a violinist, Mark Hindricks Leuschner, who swore that Furtwängler had saved his life and also actively aided other Jewish musicians. The acquittal was ratified two days later by the Allied Kommandatura, and Furtwängler returned to his post as head of the Berlin Philharmonic.

Soon thereafter, the U. S. Military Government in Germany decided to sponsor a series of charity concerts by the Berlin Philharmonic Orchestra under Furtwängler's baton, with the participation of leading American soloists. The first such soloist invited by the U. S. Military Government was Yehudi Menuhin. Robert Murphy, then serving as political advisor to the

[2]For full texts of Hirschmann's and Menuhin's statements, as well as for additional facts relevant to the controversy, see the New York *Times, Post,* and *PM* between December 5 and 11, 1945.

[3]A voice in defense of Furtwängler was raised in February 1946, by Richard Wagner's granddaughter, Friedelind Wagner, who had herself left Germany at the beginning of the war because of her anti-Nazi views. In a public statement made in London, she declared that Furtwängler, although "a weak person," had always opposed Nazism. She recalled a 1936 meeting between Hitler and Furtwängler in the Bayreuth home of her mother "who apparently still liked the Nazis: I remember Hitler turning to Furtwängler and telling him that he would have to allow himself to be used by the party for propaganda purposes, and I remember Furtwängler refusing. Hitler got angry and told Furtwängler that in that case there would be a concentration camp ready for him. Furtwängler was silent for a moment and then said: 'In that case, Herr Reichschancellor, I will be in very good company.' Apparently Hitler was taken aback by the conductor's defiance, because he went into none of his usual rantings but simply walked away."

As for Furtwängler's refusal to leave Nazi Germany, Miss Wagner stated that the conductor felt it was "his duty to stay on and save something." (New York *Times,* February 22, 1946.)

U. S. Military Government, personally urged him to accept. The violinist agreed, and it was on his initiative that one of the events was a concert for the benefit of the Jewish community of Berlin, for which Furtwängler, the orchestra, and Menuhin donated their services. Because of the complexity of the arrangements for that concert (it was held at the State Opera House, in the Russian Zone), it came third in the order of the performances given by Menuhin. The first, on September 29, 1947, was for the benefit of British and American victims of polio and attended by British and Americans only. The second, two days later, was open to the public. Most of the tickets had been bought by Germans who were happy to see Dr. Furtwängler on the podium once more. They were still happier to welcome Menuhin, the first great artist of the democratic world to play for them since 1933.

The third concert, for the benefit of the Jewish community, was also open to the general public. Menuhin offered to give a recital for the two thousand Jewish DP's of the nearby Deuppel Center on the morning of the same day, the only time that had not yet been filled. The U.S. commander of the camp, Captain Fishbein, obtained a cinema theater large enough to hold an audience of two thousand, but when Menuhin walked out upon the stage he found only a sprinkling of people scattered through the hall. Without asking any questions, he proceeded with his program. Later, backstage, Captain Fishbein showed him that day's issue of the camp paper, edited by one of the DP's who called himself Jonas of Lemberg. The lead editorial signed by Jonas urged all its readers to boycott the concert because Yehudi had played for "the murderers of the Jewish people, the Germans." Addressing Menuhin, Jonas wrote:

When I read of your 'human' deeds toward 'distressed German youth' and of how your new worshippers applauded you, I knew that in your audience there must have sat those two passionate lovers of music, Eppel and Kempke—SS men from the Kurewitz camp near Lemberg—who liked to have

us sing while they shot our brothers down. . . . Wherever
you travel, our newspaper will follow you like a curse until
your conscience awakes.

As soon as he read this, Menuhin told Captain Fishbein that
he'd like to speak to Jonas and to all the DP's in their camp.
"That's fine!" said the Captain, "I'll arrange that for tomorrow
morning."

The hall of the camp was so crowded that Menuhin could
hardly make his way to the stage which was flanked by two
husky, armed M.P.'s. Waiting for Yehudi on the platform was
a short, clubfooted man with an alert, intelligent face. "Mr.
Jonas," the captain introduced him. Menuhin extended his
hand. Surprised and embarrassed, Jonas did not move, then
awkwardly shook hands with the violinist. Menuhin turned to
the audience. The women, he noticed, had kerchiefs around
their heads; most of the men were tieless and, like the women,
shabbily dressed. They were all silent, their faces gray, lost,
unhappy rather than hostile. This was the first time Yehudi
had faced a crowd that was animated not by gratitude and
affection, and now he was to speak to them, and in German
of all languages: the only language everyone understood—the
language of the enemy! He remembers saying:

"I've come to speak to you as a Jew, and to tell you that
what I've done, I've done as a Jew."

A voice shouted: "You've played for the murderers!"

No one stirred, and Menuhin went on:

"There are many ways for a person to behave, and I have
behaved in the only way I thought I should, the only way I
could. When the Germans allowed Hitler to come to power,
I refused to play for them. When they were defeated, my first
thoughts were of my own people, and I went to the death
camps with my violin. We cannot and we must not forget the
past, but a time has to come to face the future and to begin
building it.

"To behave toward the Germans the way the Nazis behaved
toward us is to admit that we have grown to be like the Nazis.

Our only way of proving the birthright and the greatness of our race is by asserting its strength and virtues and not by imitating evil. We cannot build our future on hatred. We cannot put an end to war and persecution by acts of revenge."

A tall, thin man rose in the back of the hall and shouted: "Go on, play for the murderers! Play just for them!"

This time hundreds of faces turned toward the heckler. "Shame! Shame!" the people shouted him down.

"I cannot blame anyone for his bitterness," Menuhin went on. "You have suffered too much, you have lost parents, children, brothers and sisters. I have been spared this torture. And still, I do say that you simply cannot rebuild your life on your suffering. You cannot build your future as victims, you can build it as tailors, doctors, shoemakers, musicians, farmers. Your future is in hard, honest work, just as is mine and that of all living people. I cannot change myself. I am what my music, my country, and my race have made me, and I can only act as I feel and think is right. You may not agree with me, but you must believe in me and not think of me as a traitor to my people."

At this he sat down. Nearly everyone in the hall applauded him, and there were shouts: "Our Yehudi!" "Our Yehudi!" Not looking at Menuhin, Jonas rose, his face pale and tortured:

"People come here, look at the ruins of Berlin, and say to us: 'How terrible! Only three houses left intact on this street . . .' Or they say: 'How horrible! So many children have been killed . . .' I say: 'How terrible! Fully three German houses still left intact! How terrible! There are German children still playing in the street . . .'"

But the people in the hall did not let him go on. They surged toward the stage, shouting "Yehudi! Our Yehudi!" Men and women came up to embrace him, asking if he would come back to play for them. Even Jonas went up to Yehudi with an extended hand: "You are dead wrong, but you are sincere— this I believe." To U.S. reporters who later heard of the meeting and interviewed Jonas, he said:

"If Menuhin offered us a concert today, we would all go.

Perhaps it is too much to expect that those who have not experienced persecutions and camps should understand our feelings."[4]

In the hope that his experiences in Germany might be of some interest in Washington, Yehudi wrote down his impressions, in which he emphasized the insecurities plaguing displaced persons, the crushing knowledge that they were not wanted anywhere, and the demoralizing effect of enforced idleness. "Too long has our government allowed conditions to drift," he wrote. "We should have liquidated the DP camps two years ago quite independently of any other problems or their solutions. This is a human problem, and these victims should have been offered a choice of nationalities in various countries soon after the war."

U.S. military and civilian authorities in Germany, and particularly Political Advisor Robert Murphy and, later, High Commissioner John J. McCloy, kept repeatedly and urgently inviting Menuhin back to Germany, hailing him as America's "cultural ambassador" and "cultural missionary." ("In your role as an artist and as a free individual," wrote McCloy, "you have represented America in a unique manner which brings significant credit upon yourself and upon our country. I hope you may be able to revisit Germany often in the future.")

As to the Germans, they responded to Menuhin with hundreds of letters expressing gratitude, remorse, and hope. He has never regretted his action. Understanding full well that music alone is powerless to prevent a resurgence of Nazism, and scanning with concern the political horizon of present-day Germany, he nevertheless continues to believe that cultural ostracism cannot serve as the cornerstone on which the foundations of the postwar world should be built. As he said (on September 26, 1950) to an audience of German university students in explaining his position:

> *I came first to Germany to play to those who had survived the horrors of the camps, and later, as you must all*

[4]*Time*, October 27, 1947.

*know, I continued to come and play to all of you irrespec-
tive of creed or dogma, for I came as one who had much in
common with you, one who shared with you the music of
Bach, Beethoven, and Brahms, the thoughts of such re-
nowned men as Goethe and Heine, and the great wisdom of
Brunner and Einstein.*

*This to me represented the greatness of your race, and
not the distorted miscreations of the Nazi decades. And it
was because of this attitude of mine that I was able to come
as a Jew, who, fully cognizant of the indisputable crimes
committed against his people in this very land, felt none
the less that in these troubled and dangerous times it is
essential to control the passions and prejudices of man and
to judge him as an individual capable of good will and
tolerance to his fellow man and not as a conglomerate mass,
deaf and dumb to all the decencies which elevate him above
the primitive tribes.*

*My concerts, as you know, were at the request of the
American administration and were given without fee, the
proceeds being given to such causes as I stipulated: the
Jewish community, the* Hochschule [*Academy*] *for Music,
in memory of Karl Flesch, the Berlin Philharmonic, the*
Freie Universität [*Free University*], *and so forth.*

*I could do this not only because my country asked me to
come but because it conformed with my own convictions as
a human being and a musician. I felt I was representing in
my triple capacity as an American, a musician, and a Jew
something beyond the narrow, cruel conceptions that bade
fair to warp the German race, and to convey to you all
something of the essential brotherhood of man.*

Despite the acceptance of Menuhin by the Jewish DP's,
despite Jonas' declaration, the public testimonial by Schwartzschild, chief rabbi of Berlin, and despite the appreciation of
Menuhin's activity by official U.S. authorities, some Jewish
newspapers in the States and many in Israel continued to

censure him for having played with Furtwängler and for having performed for German audiences.

Yehudi's Berlin concerts with Furtwängler, and the many more that followed, proved to be a significant musical experience to Menuhin, who found in the conductor "a unique and fascinating power to release the intuitive, 'inspirational' faculties of the orchestra musicians, as well as his own. A conductor's major function is to free these faculties rather than force them into any preconceived mold; he is not a timekeeper nor a metronome. The moments of subdivided time are the arbitrary signposts on the road; they are the flow of the river. We do not live by jumping from signpost to signpost—we live as we fill in the space between the signposts; we live as we accept the flow of the river, both guiding our canoe and yielding to the current. Such was Furtwängler's conception, and no one to my knowledge could follow a composer's stream of consciousness as superbly as Furtwängler did with Bach, Brahms, Beethoven, Mozart, or Schubert. He managed to be the unquestioned leader and yet give the orchestra a sense of being on its own. In other words, he evoked in the men a feeling of individual and collective responsibility while remaining the one in command. On the surface, his conducting appeared anything but precise; there were no sharp angular edges, no stabbing movements. On the other hand, there was also no trace of the smooth, circular undulation so characteristic of Toscanini's finality and perfection. But there was a vital driving reality, a higher reality which seemed to come from spheres that lie far beyond the preconceived and the chartered."

> *I've come to you as a Jew, to tell you that what I've done, I've done as a Jew.*
>
> YEHUDI MENUHIN

Ever since he could remember, Yehudi had wanted to go to Palestine, where his father's family of illustrious rabbis had resided for many generations. He had for years been giving benefit concerts for various causes in that country, and with particular frequency and enthusiasm after May 14, 1948, the day of the birth of the sovereign state of Israel. However, the reports that were reaching him from there spoke primarily of severe criticism of the position he had taken in connection with postwar Germany in general and Wilhelm Furtwängler in particular. The Israeli Symphony Orchestra, which had been a matter of particular concern to him and for the benefit of which he had given many a concert in the United States, Europe, and South Africa, had never acknowledged his help, although the local organizers of these concerts were most eloquent in their praise of his contribution. Nor was there any invitation forthcoming from the orchestra to perform with them, whereas individual organizations and the Tel-Aviv concert manager, Baruch Gillon, were insistent in their requests that he come to Israel for recitals. A tour was finally arranged for the spring of 1950, in which Hephzibah was to join him for a series of sonata recitals.

A short time before he left for Israel, Yehudi received an alarmed letter from Gillon saying that a well-organized campaign against him was raging in the many newspapers of the small country and that threats had been made to place time bombs in the halls where Menuhin was to perform. Some of the terrorists even warned Yehudi to stay away from Israel or face assassination. Menuhin replied briefly by cable: "Precisely because I played in Berlin, I wish to play in Israel. As to threats, they cannot put me off. If there are people who wish to hear me, I'll come and play." Gillon's reply was even more brief: "Come and play."

Menuhin's forthcoming concerts became something of a national issue, a kind of a Dreyfus affair, transcending matters of music, a burning political and moral problem which split families and consumed friendships. Officially, the government stood aloof, but the President and Mrs. Weizmann sent out invitations for a luncheon party in honor of the Yehudi Menuhins and Hephzibah.

The moment Yehudi and Diana stepped out of their plane at the Tel-Aviv airport late in the evening of April 11, 1950, they were surrounded by the largest crowd of newspapermen that had ever met the violinist upon arrival anywhere. But instead of the usual sounds of welcome, there was an icy silence which was not broken until the press conference had started inside the airport building. The questions were couched in polite, ominously formal terms, as though the reporters were interviewing an envoy of a hostile state. Yehudi took up the questions one by one, stating the facts and presenting his point of view. Similar questions were asked and similar answers were given the next morning before an even larger group of newspapermen. In conclusion he said:

"I realize that it might be asking too much of those who have suffered beyond human endurance that they share my convictions now or ever. I also realize that I may have inadvertently reopened old wounds and have caused pain. This I regret most deeply, and I offer my apologies to all those whom I may have hurt. But I cannot renounce the principles by which I live."

The newspapers reported the interviews in full, objectively and with dignity, and this naturally had a calming effect on the general public. There were still enough fanatics on hand to compel the authorities to retain a police guard at the hotel where the Menuhins were staying. One guard sat up all night in the hotel corridor, facing the Menuhins' door, a gun lying across his knees. Another followed them wherever they went the next day and installed himself in the artists' room shortly before the concert. The hall itself was surrounded by a double cordon of police. Yehudi laughed when the management gravely assured him that detectives had gone over the entire building, but Diana, sitting in the front row with Mrs. Gillon, was unable to banish the thought that a bomb might explode at any moment.

Hephzibah and Yehudi played beautifully that night, but the emotional, almost hysterical acclaim accorded them after the concert went beyond the audience's appreciation of the

music. The crowd's need to assure Menuhin of its affection
went so far that the police, originally assembled to protect
him from his adversaries, now had to be urgently called upon
to protect him from his admirers and force a path through
a frenzied wall of well-wishers to get the Menuhins to their
car. Some of the ecstatic worshipers, unable to get to Yehudi,
kissed the doors and windows of the car, while still others
had to be removed from its roof by force.

At Menuhin's insistent requests, his personal guards were
withdrawn, as were also the uniformed policemen who stood
watch around the hotel. This proved a near calamity, for no
sooner was he left unprotected than he was submerged by a
flood of people trying to gain his ear, express their admiration,
or appeal for help of one kind or another. Most time consuming of all were the future Yehudi Menuhins whose parents
proudly presented them in such numbers that "at times it
seemed as though all the violin prodigies in the world had
crowded into my room and the hall leading to it. I had to listen
to them all, of course, and they wore me out, I must admit, but
I was also heartened, because no instrument is as sadly neglected in our mechanistic age as is the violin. It is an individual
instrument expressing individual feelings. Somehow, it has
always 'belonged' to the Jewish people, so that I was not altogether surprised to find so many violinists and violin prodigies
in Israel."

Almost overnight, the entire "Yehudi Menuhin issue" disappeared in Israel. The editorials and articles which followed
the first interviews were extremely favorable. In addition, the
music critics had nothing but praise for the brother-and-sister
team. Since the tickets to the twelve originally scheduled concerts had been sold out long in advance, Yehudi and Hephzibah yielded to requests that they squeeze twice that number
into the period of eleven days. Those were exciting days of
little sleep and feverish activity, for the spirit of urgency that
permeated the very air of the young state kept charging and
recharging the two musicians. Despite the impossible schedule,
which included concerts in military hospitals and *kibbutzim*

(co-operative farms), the Menuhins managed to visit the various members of Moshe's family, meet government officials, foreign diplomats, writers, and musicians, visit an art exhibition, and pay two visits to the residence of President and Mrs. Chaim Weizmann in Rehovot. The founder of Israel was already too ill to attend any of the concerts, so Yehudi played for him in his home.

Like her husband and Hephzibah, Diana was overwhelmed by her first impressions of Israel, by the indomitable spirit of the country, and she once said to Weizmann: "This extraordinary effort, its vigor and devotion, remind me so much of the atmosphere of London in the blitz, in which everyone sank their own in the common good."

Weizmann nodded: "You are right, my dear. It is a wonderful spirit, and my prayer is that we may never lose it."

Next year, and again in 1952, Yehudi repeated his triumphant tour of Israel, and a year later came an official invitation to play with the Israeli Symphony Orchestra. By that time, the earnestness and sincerity of the motives which had determined Menuhin's course after the allied victory in Europe seem to have been recognized by all but his most fanatical opponents. In a newspaper devoted to Jewish affairs, Dr. Camille Honig recently wrote a fitting conclusion to that difficult chapter in Menuhin's life.

Professor Martin Buber of the Hebrew University in Jerusalem, the great religious Jew, has the same feeling of admiration for Yehudi Menuhin as I and many other Jews who refuse to accept the Nazi theory of collective guilt of a whole people.

When Yehudi returned recently from a tour of Israel he was full of enthusiasm and admiration for the work that is being done there, and above all he was deeply impressed by the unvindictiveness of the Jews there. This, Yehudi said, is the true essence of the teaching of Judaism. Yehudi is above all a cosmopolitan artist universally adored for his genius and his divine gifts, about whom Bernard Shaw once said to me: 'Listening to such an artist like Yehudi makes even an atheist believe in God.'[5]

> *Perhaps India will teach us the tolerance and gentleness of the mature mind, the quiet content of the unacquisitive soul, the calm of the understanding spirit, and a unifying, pacifying love for all living things.*
>
> WILL DURANT

Although Menuhin's first trip to India came about as a result of fortuitous circumstances, he would ultimately have made his pilgrimage there irrespective of any accidents of fate. He had been fascinated by the East for as long as he could remember, his yearning gradually crystallizing into a determination to see the very heart of the East, the world called India.

While touring New Zealand in the summer of 1951 he came across a book on yoga in which he discovered an approach toward the human body and its relation to the workings of the mind for which he had been groping. This was an approach which viewed the body, the mind, and ethics as one unit. Strangely enough, at just about the time of that discovery, he received an invitation from Prime Minister Nehru to tour India. The Prime Minister said in his letter that his country, having achieved independence, was now free to choose such cultural and artistic influences as it desired, and he could wish for nothing better than to have Menuhin bring the music of the Western world to India.

The violinist gladly agreed to a series of ten concerts during February and March 1952, insisting that the proceeds be donated to the Prime Minister's fund for the relief of famine.

The response to the performances proved to be so great that Indira Gandhi, Nehru's daughter, who headed the Yehudi Menuhin Concert Committee, was overwhelmed with requests for additional appearances by the violinist, but her father firmly refused, explaining that time must be allowed for Yehudi to see as much of India as possible.

[5]*The Voice,* January 29, 1954.

When the Menuhins, accompanied by Marcel Gazelle, arrived in that absorbing country of violent contrasts, they found themselves guests in the Prime Minister's house. Yehudi remembers with affection that first dinner together, in the course of which Nehru told him how invaluable the practice of yoga had been to him, Gandhi, and the other leaders of the Independence movement during their many prison terms. Yehudi believes that his friendship with Nehru dates back to that evening when, although it was entirely the wrong time of day, they both promptly stood on their heads and compared notes as to their relative skill in the *sirshasana* (the headstand) before a delighted audience consisting of Madame Pandit, Indira Gandhi, and one or two Congress leaders. Yehudi came off second best. He was exceedingly pleased, when, at luncheon a few days later, the President, Sri Rajendra Prasad, told him that, on hearing of his interest in the practice of yoga, he had arranged for him to attend a class given by the oldest yogi in the country.

The stay in India was crowded with travel, concerts, receptions, meetings with leading statesmen, writers, dancers, and musicians, and with representatives of the Western world. Menuhin much enjoyed comparing notes during brief meetings with Mrs. Roosevelt, who was visiting India at the time, and with the U.S. Ambassador, Chester Bowles.

In Bombay, a dignified, sari-clad Hindu lady came to the artists' room after a concert. "I would like you to have this," she said presenting Yehudi with a plaque of Gandhi. She was Psyche Captain, a lifelong friend and disciple of the great Hindu leader. Touched, Yehudi thanked her and expressed his regret that he had come to India too late to meet Gandhi.

"I think he would have liked to have met you, too," she replied. "He once read in the newspapers that you had some trouble with DP's in Germany, and that you went to them in their camp and explained that life cannot be built on hate. I was with Gandhi when he read about it, and he said: 'There is a man who believes as I do in the principle of universal love.'"

Yehudi was eagerly absorbing the sights, the thought, the mood and art of the country, and was to say later: "India came as an overwhelming discovery to me, and I began to see it as a great ocean to which all land and all water is tributary. Other civilizations seem to develop along some branch or another, but India is the mother earth or the mother ocean whose development over a period of thousands of years has a continuity such as no other land knows, not even China. There is not a facet in history nor an aspect of human activity, from its most ecstatic and spiritual to its most primitive, that has not been encompassed in that great subcontinent."

He found the people of India, even the poorest and the most modestly clad, possessing natural beauty, dignity, and elegance. The color of their skin, the grace of their carriage, their cleanliness and gentleness, the music of the English they spoke ("more beautiful than the English spoken anywhere else in the world"), and the richness of their imagination and flexibility of mind—all combined to impress and fascinate him.

The simplicity of everyday life in India impressed itself upon Menuhin with particular force; as in art, everything had been reduced to its essentials. "Of course," he says, "poverty is to a dominant degree responsible for this simplicity and economy, and the long arid seasons have encouraged the art of meditation through all strata, endowing the men and women of India with a dignity and a peace of mind such as are unknown to the mass of the people in any other country. We in the West have rebelled against the blind cruelty of nature and have achieved an almost miraculous independence from it, but we have become enmeshed in the gears of our own progress and have cluttered up our leisure with artificial means for forgetting and escape."

While becoming increasingly absorbed in the unhurried richness of the spiritual and artistic life of India, Yehudi was fully aware also of the well-nigh insuperable practical problems the country was facing. Shortage of food was the predominant one, due to lack of reservoirs to catch the torrential seasonal rains, to insufficient irrigation, primitive agricultural methods, and poor means of food preservation. In his conversations with Indian leaders and scientists, and in subsequent correspondence with them, Menuhin showed a sensitive grasp of the problems, approaching them in a concrete, practical way surprising in an artist and truly American in spirit. Here is one of his typical reactions:

> *Food, of course, is the basic problem. New chemicals which would make the soil permeable to moisture could be tried; large dehydrating plants could be developed for fish, greens and grain leftovers. I do not believe in refrigerating food in the present state of India's industrialization. Dehydration is the answer.*
>
> *Until India has sufficient electrical power and the other basic means of industrialization (they are working on it, but this takes time), we can help them to develop more efficient methods for their own, time-honored cottage industries. There is, for instance, the brick which they bake in mud flats in the south of India; it is brittle and disintegrates too quickly. We can easily show them how to produce a brick more like the adobe we use in California, mixed with oil and various other ingredients which make for a highly resistant, attractive, and insulating material. There is the thatching of houses. We might develop some way of making their thatching fireproof.*

Of all his projects, none was closer to Yehudi's heart than that of advancing the cause of Western music in India. He had found the country "in an almost virginal state" insofar as knowledge of that music was concerned, and at the same time responding to it with eagerness, welcoming and desiring it. Menuhin's theory was that the music of the West awakens in men something which the music of Asiatic countries, and of India in particular, has left dormant, since it is

> *a traditional, crystallized form of expression in which the performers and auditors partake of a resignation to environment and fate. It is a more contemplative, meditative, and*

passive form of music. It does not allow the surges of emotion and fury, the interplay of opposing forces to mar its detachment. It invites the listener to attain a state of meditation, of oneness with God.

The music of the West . . . stimulates, by communication, the personality of each listener in the audience. It spurs him to proclaim his domination over, or at least his wrestling with his fate and his environment.[6]

Further developing this thesis in a letter to the U.S. Ambassador, Chester Bowles, Menuhin asserted:

This impact of Western music on the Asiatic ear is like a sudden awakening of the long-restrained, suppressed, and controlled egos, the personalities and individual self-glorification latent in all human beings. It is, therefore, a music which inspires men to action, to self-expression, to change and what may be regarded in certain ways as 'progress.' It implies therefore a kind of social revolution.

. . . I feel that there is a fast growing interest and demand for the best of Western music and for its exponents. With the advent of the vast communications of our day, as well as of the rivalry between nations, I know that the cultural missions of Russia and China will try to do a great deal to take root in India. I believe that in the face of the very strong and well-founded Indian traditions, the only Western element of culture which can quickly spread among Indian people is that of our music.

As a long-range project, Menuhin envisaged the foundation in India of an institution for the training of performers, instructors, and lecturers on Western music, who would serve the entire country, with branches in some of the larger centers. Simultaneously, a symphony orchestra was planned to function in close co-operation with the institution. When he repeated his visit to India in the spring of 1954, under the same auspices,

[6]"The Twain Shall Meet," by Yehudi Menuhin, in *The Saturday Review,* January 31, 1953.

he divided the proceeds between various charities and a fund for the foundation of a symphony orchestra in Bombay.

More immediately realizable were Menuhin's suggestions for an exchange of Western and Indian musicians and dancers. He was instrumental in presenting to U.S. television audiences Shanta Rao, the great dancer of India, and Ali Akhbar Khan, one of its leading musicians. On that occasion Menuhin appeared in the unaccustomed role of master of ceremonies for the programs those two artists presented on the Ford Foundation's "Omnibus" and at the Museum of Modern Art in New York.

Menuhin's visit had a most profound effect on all those who heard, saw, or met him in India. This reaction is best reflected in a letter written by Nehru on the eve of the Menuhins' departure for a week's holiday in Kashmir:

> *It was good to have both you and Diana here, and life has become the richer for it. Both of you have won our hearts and wherever you may be, we shall always remember you with affection and with a tinge of regret that you are far away.*
>
> *. . . I wish I were with you in Kashmir. I am happy that you are going there. It is not the beauty of the place that fills my mind, although there is beauty enough, but something intangible in the atmosphere which has some quality of enchantment about it. Most people perhaps do not feel it. I think you will.*

In a later letter, Nehru wrote:

> *Your visit to India was an event which none who saw or heard you is likely to forget. But, apart from other aspects, it was a delight to meet you and Diana and to find so much kinship of mind and spirit. Such a discovery lightens the gloom and makes one think a little more hopefully and generously of this world of ours.*

EIGHTEEN

"What's Past Is Prologue"

Menuhin the boy possessed the radiance of a mature, ideally integrated person whom human weaknesses and trials had by-passed as though by some divine dispensation. With the disappearance of his boyhood and childhood, along with the magic abandon they had given his music, and with the removal of the "glass shade" under which he had been kept, he was assailed by the thousand and one issues and harassments that plague all human beings. He did not shrink from the challenge, but the very foundations of his life were shaken, disturbing his emotional equilibrium and placing him on trial both as man and artist. His performances reflected the setbacks, as well as his triumphs, but enough greatness was visible in him at all times for the audiences and for most of the music critics not to lose faith in him; he was like a light tossed about in the wind but never extinguished.

Throughout it all, he kept himself open to the new experiences that came his way, were they his wartime work, the challenge of his art, Bartók's friendship and faith in him, the sorrows and the pride of being a Jew, his discovery of India, or the happiness that came in the wake of his love for Diana. Instinctively, he absorbed whatever was positive and wholesome in the experiences of those years and rejected the trivial and the unseemly, thus preserving that which makes him one of the small band of the eternally innocent and the pure in heart. It was indeed strange for me when, in rereading the notes I made in the course of my work on this narrative, I realized that nearly every one of the hundred-odd persons I had interviewed had actually remarked upon this quality in Yehudi, even to the point of using on occasion identical words and images. To pick at random, Bruno Walter said: "He has the innocence of a child and the creative maturity of a great artist. He is not spoiled because he cannot be spoiled, as a mountain stream cannot be muddied." (Walter used the more poetic German word *trüben*). And only a few days earlier, a French friend of Yehudi's, Mme. Gilberte Dreyfus, happened to say: "There is something of the child about him; he is a mountain stream bordered by grass." His own son, Gerard, aged four at the time, exclaimed: "Daddy's not a grownup, he's a boy!" And again, Patrick Leach of a London car-renting service, who never yields to any of his men the honor of driving Yehudi, put it in his own way: "Mr. Menuhin does not know how to be proud." One final illustration: when Winthrop Sargeant interviewed me while working on a profile of Yehudi for the *New Yorker,* he launched the discussion by exclaiming in mock desperation: "I cannot find a trace of the vulgar in him—is that possible?!"

Yehudi's art reflected the new era of happiness and fulfillment in his personal life just as it had the period of trial and suffering which was now over. As far back as 1946, some music critics, notably Louis Biancolli of the New York *World-Telegram* and Dwight Anderson of the Louisville *Courier-Journal,* took note of the beneficial change in his playing. Most critics were withholding judgment until Menuhin's Carnegie Hall recital of January 21, 1953. Howard Taubman wrote in the New York *Times:*

> *It is not too much to say that the Yehudi Menuhin who played in Carnegie Hall last night performed like an important new violinist. The importance lay in the thrust and personality Mr. Menuhin revealed as an interpreter. It was as though he had moved up to a higher level of accomplishment, a level one had expected him to achieve sooner. But maturity as an artist is not won easily.*

If it seems strange to speak of Menuhin in these terms, it is only because now, at 36, he can look back on a phenomenal history of public acclaim. He has been before the public as a performer for more than a quarter of a century. He was the golden boy of music in his childhood and boyhood. In recent years there has been indication of a struggle going on within him. Whatever private difficulties he has had with his art, he seemed to have conquered them.

The other critics wrote in a similar vein, including the music expert of *Newsweek* who summed up the general sentiment in a brief paragraph:

The fair-haired boy with gold in his fiddle has outlived his growing pains. The promise of tone and technique has been fulfilled and, at 36, a master musician has come of age.

In the same spirit, but approaching the sources of Menuhin's new felicity from a different angle, the New York *Herald Tribune* critic P. G.-H., wrote two years later:

The freshness and unique purity of his playing is exhilarating; no other violinist has such speaking eloquence in the tone alone, for it stems from a delicate poise of elements —conscious and subconscious, technical and intuitive, that is getting very rare in an age where, rather than risk the vulnerability of this intangible fusion, our young performers are settling for intellectual athleticism. Yet it is this very wholeness that enables Menuhin to speak intelligently from the heart and reach—as he ever has, the heart of audiences.

Being human, Menuhin has his off moments, as all artists do,[1] but the general level of his concerts has for years been witness that his faith, courage, doggedness, and God-given talent have overcome frustration and anxiety and have converted them into growth.

[1]Bruno Walter once said to me: "Show me an artist who is always in top form and I'll regard him with suspicion; I shall certainly not consider him a great artist."

The enormous pressures inherent in the profession of a concert artist, especially one of Menuhin's caliber, are so great that planning must be done far in advance. Since their marriage, he and Diana have flown or sailed across the Atlantic thirty-four times, and they have recently crossed the equator four times in one year, which meant packing for four summers and four winters. Their clothes are scattered all over the world, and the children's toys are divided between Alma, London, and Gstaad, in Switzerland. The mail pursues them relentlessly everywhere, from personal friends, concert managers, charity organizations or festival committees.

After the end of the war, Menuhin re-established and expanded his world-wide tours and soon found himself and his family flying incessantly, with hardly any respite between the last engagement on one continent and the first on the next. He often felt as though his energy were being dispersed in the air and that he needed to have his feet on the ground, both literally and figuratively. As a man, he missed his rest; as an artist, he felt the need for continually receiving impressions of new people and new places.

In the meantime, several of his colleagues had met with tragic death when the planes in which they were flying had crashed. Jacques Thibaud was killed near Nice; Ginette Neveu perished in the Azores, and the great American pianist William Kapell died not far from the Menuhin home near San Francisco. The same type of accident befell several of Yehudi's personal friends. The feeling of responsibility for his growing family and the longing for more restful journeys finally prompted him to decide in November 1953 not to fly any more, at least not until the hazards of blind flying were removed through the installation of radar equipment in all commercial aircraft.

As a rule, Menuhin spends about half the year in the U.S. and the rest abroad, mainly in Europe. When in the States, his family is based at Alma, where Diana finds great satisfaction in bringing a little of the serene landscaping of her own country to the beautiful, hilly acres. Together with Carl Coate, the caretaker, and his wife, the green-thumbed Ruth, she has cut trails through the bush, planted fruit trees, acacia, sycamores, and poplars, and gradually bordered the lovely lawns around the house and the guest cottages with rock gardens and flower beds.

Diana has completely transformed Alma, bringing to the task the sense of color and space that belong to the world of the ballet to which she had been dedicated. Surprised to find no paintings or exquisite *bibelots* in Yehudi's house, she made up for these deficiencies in the antique shops of London, the art exhibitions of Paris, the *souks* of Tunis and Marrakech, and the bazaars of Istanbul, returning home with swag which was as much a delight to the Menuhins as it was the despair of the customs officials. The walls of their home are now covered with paintings which reveal, as does the entire atmosphere of the house, an imaginative and catholic taste, ranging from a Corot, a Boudin, and a Breughel, chosen by Yehudi for Diana, to drawings given her by Derain, Kokoshka, and Marie Laurencin. There are Moshe Castels from Israel, Joenisches from Germany, and a Jewish wedding by Marc Chagall, among many others.

The once barren shelves of Alma (except for those in Yehudi's study, which have always spilled over with scores and books on music, philosophy, and science) are now populated with Diana's own collection of the classics, poetry, and works on the theater and the ballet.

The treasured days when the Menuhins are together at home are devoted in the main to a quiet family life interrupted by an occasional evening with friends and neighbors, and by the traditional Saturday night dinner with Yehudi's parents at Los Gatos. The two older children are at school in Switzerland, and Zamira spends her holidays with her family at Alma. With the birth of Diana's children, Gerard and Jeremy, a Swiss nurse, Schwester Marie, joined the Menuhin family to keep the home fires burning when Diana and Yehudi are away.

The golden-haired Gerard and Jeremy are equally charming but as different as two children can be. Gerard, nicknamed Smithy, was born in Edinburgh during the Festival in July, 1948. He is a sensitive child with an extraordinary flair and imagination, his large, brown eyes changing with every mood and thought. Although he is fond of music and plays with toys like any other little boy of his age, his chief preoccupation is with words and ideas ("Do you mind, Mummy? I love music but I prefer books."), and he has a poet's way with them ("The trees look as if they were pushing fingers through the skies"—this at the age of five, while contemplating trees silhouetted in moonlight). He is a very courteous child (admonishing a boy his own age: "Will you be so kind as not to be nasty to me?"), but he has little patience with Jeremy, his junior by slightly more than three years. Plump, earthy and self-assertive, Jeremy waddles into Smithy's room whenever the spirit moves him, and plays havoc with his brother's books and toys. Shouting, "You sin! You ashes! You evilness!" Smithy occasionally loses his patience with him, and when reproached, he cries out: "But Jeremy means so much unhelpfulness to me!"

Jeremy is full of appetites, desires, and charm, and always has both feet firmly planted on the ground, always that is, except when he listens to what he calls "musica." His plump baby face is then visited by unusual concentration, by a meaningfulness that is almost perception, and then it is his turn to be impatient with interruptions. Watching Jeremy as he listens to music, one's thoughts involuntarily go back to Yehudi the infant at his first concerts. When asked if he thinks Jeremy might follow in his footsteps, Menuhin replies: "It is too early to say," or "I shall not force anything," but one can practically see how, in his mind, he keeps his fingers crossed.

Yehudi has a deep sense of responsibility for his family, displaying in the performance of his duties all the solicitude of the proverbial devoted husband and father, especially in matters of health and diet. When at home, he spends as much time as possible with his children, reading to them and playing with them, enjoying their toys with an enthusiasm which they can hardly match. He has been reminded too of his own un-fulfilled childhood in ways which are less pleasant. He devel-oped the measles in Havana (caught from Krov in 1948), and the chickenpox in London (caught from Gerard during Christ-mas, 1954).

Paradoxical as it may seem, a touring artist's life provides little opportunity for listening to music and for making music with his colleagues. Menuhin's joy is all the greater, therefore, when in the course of a busy concert season he can attend a performance of Beethoven's Ninth Symphony or a violin re-cital by one of his colleagues. He is happy when he can go to a concert of Nathan Milstein or Zino Francescatti or play chamber music with Henry Temianka, David Oistrakh, Wil-liam Primrose, or Carleton Sprague Smith, or do the Bartók duos with Wolfgang Schneiderhahn, or bask in the beauty of Irmgard Seefried's singing. A particularly pleasant occasion was a concert at the 1953 Edinburgh Festival, at which Men-uhin played Vivaldi's *Concerto for Three Violins* with Gio-conda de Vito and Isaac Stern. The rehearsals provided no end of musical "scherzos" to mark the exceptional nature of the occasion.

Yehudi Menuhin has explored and expanded in many direc-tions. He is fascinated by the possibilities of the rapidly matur-ing medium of television, which is reaching into the homes and into the lives of most people. The first to televise a concerto with orchestra, as far back as 1950, Yehudi has since appeared on a number of television programs, most notably those of the Ford Foundation's Experimental TV Workshop.

Another nascent interest is teaching. Menuhin feels that he has reached a stage in his development when he can share his knowledge and experience with younger violinists, in the hope that he might help them to avoid the pitfalls which had exacted so high a price from him. As a matter of fact, he has already begun to systematize his findings, and in the summer of 1954 he had actually ventured into his first experiment in teaching, at Nadia Boulanger's American Academy at Fontainebleau. He has since accepted a repeat engagement at the Academy, as well as his first with the Accademia Chiggiana at Siena, Italy.

Menuhin's particular concern is the finding and presentation of new works for his medium. Ever since the great days of the violin in seventeenth and eighteenth century Italy, and until comparatively recently, most of the leading violinists were also composers who wrote for their instrument. Ysaye, Enesco, and Kreisler have extended that tradition into our own century, but for generations now the tendency has been toward a clear line of demarcation between the performer and the composer. The modern violinist is a specialist, a vehicle for interpretation, with little time, opportunity, or background for composition. The works written for his instrument are usually inspired or commissioned by him. This process, far from being new, is merely accentuated in our century. Brahms and Schumann wrote for Joseph Joachim; Mendelssohn for Ferdinand David; César Franck for Ysaye. More recently, Shostakovitch and Khatchaturian have written for David Oistrakh. It is in this same tradition that Béla Bartók, Ben Haim, Ernest Bloch, Georges Enesco, and William Walton have written for Yehudi Menuhin. He is continually in touch with American and European composers, in the hope of discovering and introducing new works by them.

While profoundly interested in contemporary music, Menuhin continues to devote much of his time and effort to the classics. Born in this young country and alive to its vital though necessarily eruptive creative processes, he is at the same time steeped in the unbroken historical traditions of Europe, where the music of the West originated and where it reached its highest peaks. One of the youngest among the major instrumentalists, Yehudi helps to prevent a historic and esthetic gap by bringing the hallowed values and traditions of the classics to a new generation of listeners. He feels strongly that the umbilical cord linking the old and the new must not be severed, secure in the knowledge that the faith and the dignity of the former can be absorbed without weakening the modern spirit of restlessness and search.

As man and artist, Yehudi Menuhin has fought for and won the right to the gifts which the gods bestowed upon him. At thirty-nine, he can look back at nearly a third of a century of hard work and universal recognition. He can also look ahead with anticipation into the unknown future, and with full confidence in the verity of Shakespeare's words which Willa Cather had once discovered for him: "What's past is prologue."

Recordings by Yehudi Menuhin

Released by the RCA Victor Company and His Master's Voice, the Gramophone Company. British record numbers are given in parentheses. The dates are of the recording of the performance.

La Romanesca, *Achron. Piano: Louis Persinger. 78 rpm: 6841 (DB 1267). March 15, 1928.*

Sierra Morena, *De Monasterio. Piano: Persinger. 78 rpm: 6841 (DB 1267). March 15, 1928.*

La Capricciosa, *Ries. Piano: Persinger. 78 rpm: 1329 (DA 1003). March 15, 1928.*

Allegro, *Fiocco. Piano: Persinger. 78 rpm: 1329 (DA 1003). Apr. 1, 1928.*

Nigun, *Bloch. Piano: Persinger. 78 rpm: 7108 (DB 1283). Feb. 12, 1929.*

Prayer from Te Deum, *Handel-Flesch. Piano: Persinger. 78 rpm: 6951 (DB 1284). Feb. 12, 1929.*

Sarabande & Tambourin, *Leclair-Sarasate. Piano: Persinger. 78 rpm: 7182 (DB 1295). Feb. 12, 1929.*

Adagio from Concerto in G, *Mozart. Piano: Persinger. 78 rpm: 7182 (DB 1295). Feb. 12, 1929.*

Scottish Pastorale, *Saenger. Piano: Persinger. 78 rpm: 6951 (DB 1284). Feb. 12, 1929.*

Canción del Olvido, *Serrano-Persinger. Piano: Persinger. 78 rpm: 7317 (DB 1301). Feb. 12, 1929.*

Chant d'Espagne, *Samazeuilh. Piano: Persinger. 78 rpm: 7317 (DB 1301). Feb. 12, 1929.*

Rondo, *Spohr-Persinger. Piano: Persinger. 78 rpm: 7317 (DB 1301). Feb. 12, 1929.*

Unaccompanied Sonata No. 5, in C, *Bach. 78 rpm: 7615-7 (DB 1368-70). Nov. 13, 1929.*

Sonata, opus 12, No. 1, *Beethoven. Piano: Hubert Giesen. 78 rpm: 7360-3 (DB 1365-7). Nov. 13, 1929.*

Sonata in C, K. 296, andante sostenuto, *Mozart. 78 rpm: (DB 1365-7). Nov. 13, 1929.*

La Folia, *Corelli. Piano: Hubert Giesen. 78 rpm:* (*DB 1501*). *Dec. 11, 1930.*

Rigaudon, *Monsigny-Franko. Piano: Giesen. 78 rpm:* (*DA 1196*). *Dec. 11, 1930.*

Perpetuum Mobile, *Nováček. Piano: Giesen. 78 rpm:* (*DA 1196*). *Dec. 11, 1930.*

Campanella, *Paganini. Piano: Giesen. 78 rpm: 7599* (*DB 1638*). *Dec. 11, 1930.*

Song of the Bride, from "The Tsar's Bride," *Rimsky-Korsakov–Franko. Piano: Giesen. 78 rpm:* (*DB 1638*). *Dec. 11, 1930.*

Concerto No. 1 in G minor, *Bruch. London Symphony Orchestra: Sir Landon Ronald. 78 rpm: 7509–11* (*DB 1611–3*). *Nov. 26, 1931.*

Guitarre, *Moszkowski-Sarasate. Piano: Artur Balsam. 78 rpm:* (*DA 1282*). *May 20, 1932.*

Devil's Trill Sonata, *Tartini-Kreisler. Piano: Balsam. 78 rpm:* (*DA 1786–7*). *May 20, 1932.*

Danse Espagnole, *De Falla-Kreisler. Piano: Balsam. 78 rpm:* (*DA 1280*). *May 23, 1932.*

Minstrels, *Debussy. Piano: Balsam. 78 rpm:* (*DA 1280*). *May 23, 1932.*

Flight of the Bumblebee, *Rimsky-Korsakov. Piano: Balsam. 78 rpm:* (*DA 1280*). *May 23, 1932.*

Sicilienne & Rigaudon, *Francœur-Kreisler. Piano: Balsam. 78 rpm:* (*DA 1282*). *May 23, 1932.*

Caprice No. 24, *Paganini-Kreisler. 78 rpm: 1650* (*DA 1281*). *May 23, 1932.*

Tzigane, *Ravel. Piano: Balsam. 78 rpm: 7810* (*DB 1785*). *May 23, 1932.*

Ave Maria, *Schubert-Wilhelm. Piano: Balsam. 78 rpm:* (*DB 1788*). *May 23, 1932.*

Scherzo Tarantelle, *Wieniawski. Piano: Balsam. 78 rpm:* (*DB 1788*). *May 23, 1932.*

Double Concerto in D minor, *Bach. Violin: Georges Enesco; orchestra: Pierre Monteux. 78 rpm: album DM 932* (*DB 1718*). *33 1/3: LCT 1120. June 4, 1932.*

Concerto No. 7 in D, K. 271, *Mozart. Orchestra: Enesco. 78 rpm: album M 231* (*DB 1735–8*). *June 4, 1932.*

Unaccompanied Sonata No 2, Andante, *Bach. 78 rpm: album M 231* (*DB 1738*). *June 4, 1932.*

Symphonie Espagnole, *Lalo. Orchestre Symphonique de Paris: Enesco. 78 rpm: album DM 136* (*DB 1999–2002*). *June 20, 1932.*

Caprice, opus 6, Recitative & Scherzo, *Kreisler. 78 rpm:* (DA 1786–7). *July 14, 1932.*

Concerto, opus 61, *Elgar. London Symphony Orchestra: Elgar. 78 rpm: 7747–52* (DB 1751–6). *July 15, 1932.*

Poème, *Chausson. Orchestre Symphonique de Paris: Enesco. 78 rpm: 7913–4* (DB 1961–2). *June 21, 1933.*

Concerto in E, *Bach. Orchestra: Enesco. 78 rpm: album DB 488, 8367–9* (DB 2003–5). *June 24, 1933.*

Unaccompanied Partita No. 1, Sarabande, *Bach. 78 rpm: album DM 488* (DB 2003–5). *June 24, 1933.*

Unaccompanied Sonata No. 1, in G minor, *Bach. 78 rpm: 8361–2* (DB 2007–8). *June 24, 1933.*

Sonata, K. 526, *Mozart. Piano: Hephzibah Menuhin. 78 rpm:* (DB 2057–8). *Sept. 29, 1933.*

Concerto in D ("Adelaide"), *Mozart. Paris Symphony Orchestra: Pierre Monteux. 78 rpm: album M 246, 8389–91* (DB 2268–70). *May 19, 1934.*

Unaccompanied Sonata No. 3, *Bach. 78 rpm: album DM 488* (DB 2284–6). *May 19, 1934.*

Perpetuum Mobile, *Nováček. Orchestre Symphonique de Paris: Monteux. 78 rpm: album DM 230* (DB 2279–83). *May 19, 1934.*

Concerto No. 1, *Paganini. Orchestre Symphonique de Paris: Monteux. 78 rpm: album DM 230* (DB 2279–83). *May 19, 1934.*

Unaccompanied Partita No. 2, in D minor, *Bach. 78 rpm: album DM 232* (DB 2287–90). *May 23, 1934.*

Sonata, opus 121, *Schumann. Piano: H. Menuhin. 78 rpm:* (DB 2264–7). *July 3, 1934.*

Ronde des Lutins, *Bazzini. Piano: Marcel Gazelle. 78 rpm:* 8695 (DB 2414). *Sept. 29, 1934.*

Moto Perpetuo, *Paganini. Piano: Gazelle. 78 rpm:* 8866 (DB 2414). *Sept. 29, 1934.*

Sonata No. 9 in A, opus 47, *Beethoven. Piano: H. Menuhin. 78 rpm: album DM 260* (DB 2409–12). *Nov. 28, 1934.*

Hungarian Dance No. 6, *Brahms-Joachim. Piano: Gazelle. 78 rpm:* 8866 (DB 2413). *Nov. 28, 1934.*

Romanza Andaluza, *Sarasate. Piano: Gazelle. 78 rpm:* 8695 (DB 2413). *Nov. 28, 1934.*

Unaccompanied Partita No. 1, in B minor, *Bach. 78 rpm: album DB 487, 16272–5, 15115–9* (DB 2816–8). *Dec. 19, 1935.*

Unaccompanied Sonata No. 1, in G minor, *Bach. 78 rpm:* (DB 2869–70). *Dec. 19, 1935.*

Concerto K. 216, *Mozart. Paris Symphony Orchestra: Enesco. 78 rpm: album DM 485* (DB 2729–31). *Dec. 19, 1935.*

La Fille aux Cheveux de Lin, *Debussy-Hartmann. Piano: Gazelle. 78 rpm: (DA 1499). Dec. 21, 1935.*

Songs My Mother Taught Me, *Dvořák-Persinger. Piano: Gazelle. 78 rpm: (DA 1499). Dec. 21, 1935.*

Negro Spiritual Melody from the New World Symphony, *Dvořák-Kreisler. Piano: Gazelle. 78 rpm: (DB 2856). Dec. 21, 1935.*

La Chasse, *Cartier-Kreisler. Piano: Gazelle. 78 rpm: (DA 1494). Dec. 21, 1935.*

Schön Rosmarin, *Kreisler. Piano: Gazelle. 78 rpm: (DA 1489). Dec. 21, 1935.*

Tambourin Chinois, *Kreisler. Piano: Gazelle. 78 rpm: (DA 1489). Dec. 21, 1935.*

Caprice Basque, opus 24, *Sarasate. Piano: Gazelle. 78 rpm: album DM 388 (DB 2856). Dec. 21, 1935.*

Habanera, opus 21, No. 2, *Sarasate. Piano: Gazelle. 78 rpm: 15823 (DB 2873). Dec. 21, 1935.*

Notturno, opus 28, No. 1, *Szymanowski. Piano: Gazelle. 78 rpm: 14383 (DB 2871). Dec. 21, 1935.*

Tarantella, opus 28, No. 2, *Szymanowski. Piano: Gazelle. 78 rpm: 14383 (DB 2871). Dec. 21, 1935.*

Souvenir de Moscou, *Wieniawski. Piano: Gazelle. 78 rpm: 14352 (DB 2872). Dec. 21, 1935.*

Sonata, opus 25, *Enesco. Piano: H. Menuhin. 78 rpm: 14107-9 (DB 2739-41). Jan. 6, 1936.*

Sonata No. 8 in G, opus 30, No. 3, Allegro Vivace, *Beethoven. 78 rpm: (DB 2832-34). Jan. 7, 1936.*

Turkish March, *Beethoven-Auer. Piano: Gazelle. 78 rpm: (DA 1494). Jan. 21, 1936.*

Hungarian Dance No. 1, *Brahms-Joachim. Piano: Gazelle. 78 rpm: 2010 (DA 1491). Jan. 21, 1936.*

Hungarian Dance No. 7, *Brahms-Joachim. Piano: Gazelle. 78 rpm: (DA 1482). Jan. 21, 1936.*

Hungarian Dance No. 17, *Brahms-Joachim. Piano: Gazelle. 78 rpm: (DA 1491). Jan. 21, 1936.*

Zapateado, *Sarasate. Piano: Gazelle. 78 rpm: (DA 1482). Jan. 21, 1936.*

Caprice No. 13 & 20, *Paganini-Kreisler. Piano: Gazelle. 78 rpm: (DA 1500). Jan. 21, 1936.*

Praeludium & Allegro, *Pugnani-Kreisler. Piano: Gazelle. 78 rpm: 1863 (DA 1490). Jan. 21, 1936.*

Unaccompanied Partita No. 3, *Bach. 78 rpm: 15124-6 (DB 2829-31). Feb. 3, 1936.*

Unaccompanied Sonata No. 2, *Bach. 78 rpm: (DB 2824-6). Feb. 3, 1936.*

Andante from Unaccompanied Sonata No. 2, *Bach. 78 rpm:* (*DB 1735–8*). *Feb. 3, 1936.*

Caprice in E, opus 1, No. 9, *Paganini. 78 rpm: album DM 451, 14228* (*DB 2829–31*). *Feb. 3, 1936.*

Caprice in E flat, opus 1, No. 23, *Paganini. 78 rpm: 7737* (*DB 2824–6*). *Feb. 3, 1936.*

Concerto No. 1 in A minor, *Bach. Symphony Orchestra: Enesco. 78 rpm: 14370–1* (*DB 2911–2*). *Feb. 21, 1936.*

Caprice, opus 1, No. 6, *Paganini-Enesco. Piano: Enesco. 78 rpm: 14228* (*DB 2838–41*). *Feb. 21, 1936.*

Slavonic Dance No. 1, *Dvořák-Kreisler. Piano: Gazelle. 78 rpm:* (*DA 1506*). *Feb. 22, 1936.*

Slavonic Dance No. 2, *Dvořák-Kreisler. Piano: Gazelle. 78 rpm:* (*DB 2922*). *Feb. 22, 1936.*

Hungarian Dance No. 4, *Brahms-Joachim. Piano: Gazelle. 78 rpm: 14905* (*DB 2922*). *Feb. 22, 1936.*

Caprice Viennois, *Kreisler. Piano: Gazelle. 78 rpm:* (*DA 1506*). *Feb. 22, 1936.*

Kaddisch, *Ravel-Garban. Piano: Gazelle. 78 rpm: 15887* (*DB 6139, DB 2873*). *Feb. 22, 1936.*

Concerto, opus 53, *Dvořák. Orchestre de la Société des Concerts du Conservatoire: Enesco. 78 rpm:* (*DB 2838–41*). *Feb. 28, 1936.*

Trio, opus 50, *Tchaikovsky. Piano: H. Menuhin; cello: Maurice Eisenberg. 78 rpm: album DM 388* (*DB 2887–92*). *March 4, 1936.*

Trio, opus 70, No. 1, *Beethoven. Piano: H. Menuhin; cello: Eisenberg. 78 rpm: DB 370* (*DB 2879–81*). *March 5, 1936.*

Sonata No. 3 in D minor, opus 108, *Brahms. Piano: H. Menuhin. 78 rpm:* (*DB 2832–4*). *July 1, 1936.*

Sonata in A, *Franck. Piano: H. Menuhin. 78 rpm:* (*DB 2742–5*). *Nov. 7, 1936.*

Concerto in D minor, *Schumann. New York Philharmonic Orchestra: John Barbirolli. 78 rpm: album DM 451, 14913–6. Feb. 9, 1938.*

Hungarian Dance No. 11, in D minor, *Brahms-Joachim. Piano: Ferguson Webster. 78 rpm:* (*DB 3500*). *March 21, 1938.*

Hungarian Dance No. 12 in D minor, *Brahms-Joachim. Piano: Webster. 78 rpm:* (*DA 1636*). *March 21, 1938.*

Spanish Dance, *Granados-Kreisler. Piano: Webster. 78 rpm:* (*DB 3500*). *March 21, 1938.*

Labyrinth, *Locatelli. Piano: Webster. 78 rpm:* (*DA 1636*). *March 21, 1938.*

"Moses" Fantasy, *Rossini-Paganini. Piano: Webster. 78 rpm:* (*DB 3499*). *March 21, 1938.*

Romance in A, opus 94, No. 2, *Schumann-Kreisler. Piano: Webster.*
78 rpm: (DB 3435–8). March 21, 1938.

Sonata in G, *Lekeu. Piano: H. Menuhin. 78 rpm: 15488–91 (DB*
3492–5). March 29, 1938.

Sonata in F, K. 376, *Mozart. Piano: H. Menuhin. 78 rpm: album*
DM 791 (DB 3552–3). March 29, 1938.

Sonata No. 3 in E, *Bach. Piano: H. Menuhin. 78 rpm: album DM*
887 (DB 3501–2). March 30, 1938.

Rondo in G, *Beethoven. Piano: H. Menuhin. 78 rpm: album DM*
1008 (DB 3503–6). March 30, 1938.

Sonata No. 7 in C minor, opus 30, No. 2, *Beethoven. Piano: H.*
Menuhin. 78 rpm: (DB 3503–6). March 30, 1938.

Concerto in E minor, opus 64, *Mendelssohn. Orchestre des Concerts*
Colonne: Enesco. 78 rpm: album DM 531 (DB 3555–8). May
2, 1938.

Légende, opus 17, *Wieniawski. Orchestre des Concerts Colonne:*
Enesco. 78 rpm: 15423 (DB 3653). May 2, 1938.

Sonata in A, *Pizzetti. Piano: H. Menuhin. 78 rpm: 15721–4 (DB*
2579–82). May 6, 1938.

Rondo in B minor, opus 70, *Schubert. Piano: H. Menuhin. 78 rpm:*
album DM 901 (DB 3583–4). May 6, 1938.

Sonata No. 10 in G, opus 96, *Beethoven. Piano: H. Menuhin. 78*
rpm: (DB 3585–7). May 7, 1938.

Allegro from Sonata in G, K. 301, *Mozart. Piano: H. Menuhin. 78*
rpm: 16106 (DB 3579–82). May 7, 1938.

Andantino sostenuto e cantabile from Sonata in B flat, K. 378,
Mozart. Piano: Yaltah Menuhin. 78 rpm: 16106 (DB 3555–8).
May 30, 1938.

Unaccompanied Partita No. 3, Praeludium, *Bach. 78 rpm: album*
DM 531 (DB 3555–8). May 30, 1938.

Malagueña, *Sarasate. Piano: Endt. 78 rpm: 15823 (DB 3782).*
March 13, 1939.

Abodah (God's Worship), *Bloch. Piano: Hendrick Endt. 78 rpm:*
15887 (DB 3782, DB 6139). March 14, 1939.

Hora Staccato, *Dinicu-Heifetz. Piano: Endt. 78 rpm: (DA 1685).*
March 14, 1939.

Sonata No. 6, *Handel. Piano: Endt. 78 rpm: 16450 (DB 3816).*
March 14, 1939.

Andalusa from Suite Espagnole, *Nin. Piano: Endt. 78 rpm: (DA*
1685). March 14, 1939.

Danse Nègre, *Scott-Kramer. Piano: Endt. 78 rpm: (DA 1685).*
March 14, 1939.

Sonata No. 1 in G, opus 78, *Brahms. Piano: H. Menuhin. 78 rpm:*
album DM 987, 11–8736–9. Sept. 18, 1940.

Concerto No. 4 in D, K. 218, *Mozart. Liverpool Philharmonic Orchestra: Malcolm Sargeant. 78 rpm:* (DB 6146–8). *March 31, 1943.*

Air from Suite No. 3 in D, *Bach. Piano: Gazelle. 78 rpm:* (DB 6156). *April 6, 1943.*

Praeludium from Unaccompanied Sonata No. 6 in E, *Bach. 78 rpm: album DM* 987 (DB 6156). *April 6, 1943.*

Negro Spiritual Melody from the New World Symphony, *Dvořák. Piano: Gazelle. 78 rpm:* (DB 6158). *April 6, 1943.*

Caprice Viennois, *Kreisler. Piano: Gazelle. 78 rpm:* (DA 1832). *April 6, 1943.*

Pièce en Forme de Habanera, *Ravel. Piano: Gazelle. 78 rpm:* (DA 1832). *April 6, 1943.*

Ave Maria, *Schubert-Menuhin. Piano: Gazelle. 78 rpm:* (DB 6158). *April 6, 1943.*

Sonata No. 4 in D, *Handel-Kauder. Piano: Gazelle. 78 rpm:* (DB 6175–6). *Sept. 25, 1944.*

Rumanian Folk Dances, *Bartók-Szekely. Piano: Gazelle. 78 rpm:* 12–1061 (DB 6178). *45 rpm:* 49–1796. *Sept. 30, 1944.*

Sonata No. 3 in E, *Bach. Harpsichord: Landowska. 78 rpm: album DM* 1035 (DB 6681–3). *33 1/3 rpm: LCT* 1120. *Dec. 28, 1944.*

La Fille aux Cheveux de Lin, *Debussy. Piano: Adolph Baller. 78 rpm:* 10–1020. *Dec. 28, 1944.*

Salut d'Amour, *Elgar. Piano: Baller. 78 rpm:* 10–1020. *Dec. 28, 1944.*

Concerto No. 1 in G minor, *Bruch. San Francisco Orchestra: Monteux. 78 rpm: album M* 1023. *Jan. 27, 1945.*

Minuet in D, *Mozart-Kross. Piano: Gerald Moore. 78 rpm:* 10–1459 (DA 1861). *Sept. 15, 1945.*

Romance based on a theme by Paganini. *Piano: Moore. 78 rpm:* 10–1459 (DA 1861). *Sept. 15, 1945.*

Violin Concerto, *Bartók. Dallas Symphony: Antal Dorati. 78 rpm: album DM* 1120 (DB 6361–5). *Jan. 15, 1946.*

Sonata No. 3 in D minor, opus 108, *Brahms. Piano: H. Menuhin. 78 rpm:* (DB 6441–3). *March 30, 1947.*

Sonata No. 10 in G, opus 96, *Beethoven. Piano: H. Menuhin. 78 rpm:* (DB 6495–7). *April 2, 1947.*

Symphonie Espagnole, *Lalo. Orchestre des Concerts Colonne: Jean Fournet. 78 rpm: album DM* 1207 (DB 6608–11). *33 1/3 rpm: LM* 1011. *April 4, 1947.*

Sonata for Violin Solo, *Bartók-Menuhin. 78 rpm: album DM* 1350 (DB 6533). *45 rpm: WDM* 1350. *33 1/3 rpm: LM* 1087. *June 2, 1947.*

Concerto in D, opus 61, *Beethoven. Lucerne Festival Orchestra: Wilhelm Furtwängler. 78 rpm: (DB 6574–9). Aug. 29, 1947.*

Habanera, opus 21, No. 2, *Sarasate. Piano: Moore. 78 rpm: (DB 6704). Nov. 1, 1947.*

Scherzo Tarantelle, opus 16, *Wieniawski. Piano: Moore. 78 rpm: (DB 6704). Nov. 1, 1947.*

Sonata for Violin and Piano, *Bartók. Piano: Baller. 78 rpm: album DM 1286. 33 1/3 rpm: LM 1009. Dec. 29, 1947.*

Sonata No. 1 for Violin and Piano, opus 80, *Prokofieff. Piano: Gazelle. 78 rpm: album DM 1403 (DB 6845). 45 rpm: WDM 1403. 33 1/3 rpm: LM 1087. Oct. 1, 1948.*

Concerto in D, opus 77, *Brahms. Lucerne Festival Orchestra: Furt-wängler. 78 rpm: album DM 1361 (DB 21000–4). 45 rpm: WDM 1361. 33 1/3 rpm: LM 1142. Oct. 7, 1949.*

Sonata in D, opus 137, No. 1, *Schubert. Piano: Baller. 45 rpm: WDM 1593. 33 1/3 rpm: LM 140. Nov. 11, 1949.*

Sonata in A ("Duo"), *Schubert. Piano: Baller. 45 rpm: WDM 1593. 33 1/3 rpm: LM 140. Nov. 11, 1949.*

Hungarian Dance No. 4, *Brahms. Piano: Theodore Saidenberg. 78 rpm: album DM 1361. 33 1/3 rpm: LM 1361. Dec. 30, 1949.*

Sonata for Violin and Piano, *Walton, Piano: Louis Kentner. 78 rpm: (DB 21156–8). 45 rpm: WHMV 1037. 33 1/3 rpm: LHMV 1037. May 8, 1950.*

Concerto No. 2 in B minor, opus 7, *Paganini. Philharmonia Orchestra: Anatole Fistoulari. 78 rpm: (DB 21245–8). 45 rpm: WHMV 1015. 33 1/3 rpm: LHMV 1015 (BLP 1018). Oct. 3, 1950.*

Concerto in G minor, opus 26, *Bruch. Boston Symphony: Charles Munch. 78 rpm: (DB 21415–7). 45 rpm: WDM 1547. 33 1/3 rpm: LM 1797. Jan. 18, 1951.*

Sonata No. 1 in B minor & No. 2 in A, *Bach. Piano: Kentner. 78 rpm: (DB 21292–3). 45 rpm: WHMV 1016. 33 1/3 rpm: LHMV 1016 (BLP 1026). Jan. 22, 1951.*

Sonata No. 3 in E, *Bach. Piano: Kentner. 78 rpm: (DB 21435–7). 45 rpm: WHMV 1016. 33 1/3 rpm: LHMV 1016 (ALP 1212). Jan. 23, 1951.*

Sonata No. 4 in C minor, *Bach. Piano: Kentner. 78 rpm: (DB 21514–5). 45 rpm: WHMV 1016. 33 1/3 rpm: LHMV 1016 (ALP 1212). May 5, 1951.*

Concerto No. 4 in D minor, opus 31, *Vieuxtemps. Philharmonia Orchestra: Walter Susskind. 78 rpm: (DB 21307–9). 45 rpm: WHMV 1015. 33 1/3 rpm: LHMV 1015 (BLP 1005). May 11, 1951.*

Concerto in D minor, *Mendelssohn. RCA Victor String Orchestra: Yehudi Menuhin. 45 rpm: WDM 1720. 33 1/3 rpm: LM 1720. Feb. 6, 1952.*

Sonata in D major, opus 12, No. 1, *Beethoven. Piano: Kentner. 45 rpm: WHMV 1037. 33 1/3 rpm: LHMV 1037 (ALP 1050). Feb. 16, 1952.*

Sonata in E flat, opus 12, No. 3, *Beethoven. Piano: Kentner. 33 1/3 rpm: (ALP 1050). Feb. 16, 1952.*

Poème, *Chausson. London Philharmonic Orchestra: Sir Adrian Boult. 78 rpm: (DB 21512–3). March 6, 1952.*

Concerto in E minor, opus 64, *Mendelssohn. Berlin Philharmonic Orchestra, Furtwängler. 45 rpm: WDM 1720. 33 1/3 rpm: LM 1720 (ALP 1135). May 26, 1952.*

Sonata No. 5 in F ("Spring"), *Beethoven. Piano: Kentner. 33 1/3 rpm: LHMV 1053 (ALP 1105). Sept. 22, 1952.*

Concerto for Violin and Orchestra, opus 33, *Nielsen. Danish State Broadcasting Orchestra: Mogens Wöldike. 33 1/3 rpm: LHMV 22 (BLP 1025). Sept. 28, 1952.*

Sonata in F, *Mendelssohn. Piano: Moore. 33 1/3 rpm: LHMV 1071 (ALP 1085). Oct. 8, 1952.*

La Fille aux Cheveux de Lin, *Debussy-Hartmann. Piano: Moore. 78 rpm: (DA 2023). 33 1/3 rpm: LHMV 22. Oct. 30, 1952.*

Spanish Dance from "La Vida Breve," *De Falla. Piano: Moore. 78 rpm: (DA 2023). 33 1/3 rpm: LHMV 22. Oct. 30, 1952.*

The Prayer, *Handel-Flesch. Piano: Moore. 78 rpm: (DA 2023). Oct. 30, 1952.*

Kaddisch, *Ravel. Piano: Moore. 78 rpm: (DA 2023). 33 1/3 rpm: LHMV 22. Oct. 30, 1952.*

Concerto in D minor, *Mendelssohn. Philharmonia Orchestra: Boult. 78 rpm: 11–8601–2. 33 1/3 rpm: (ALP 1085). April 2, 1953.*

Concerto in C ("Il Piacere"), *Vivaldi. Philharmonia Orchestra: Boult. 33 1/3 rpm: LHMV 16. April 2, 1953.*

Concerto in D, opus 61, *Beethoven. Philharmonia Orchestra: Furtwängler. 33 1/3 rpm: LHMV 1061 (ALP 1100). April 8, 1953.*

Romance No. 1 in G & No. 2 in F, *Beethoven. Philharmonia Orchestra: Furtwängler. 33 1/3 rpm: (ALP 1135). April 9, 1953.*

La Folia, *Corelli. Piano: Moore. 33 1/3 rpm: LHMV 10. July 1, 1953.*

Concerto No. 3, *Saint-Saëns. Philharmonia Orchestra: Gaston Poulet. 33 1/3 rpm: LHMV 1071. July 3, 1953.*

Malagueña, opus 21, No. 1, *Sarasate. Piano: Moore. 78 rpm: (DB 21595). 45 rpm: WDM 1742. 33 1/3 rpm: LM 1742. Aug. 31, 1953.*

Violin Concerto, *Bartók. Philharmonia Orchestra: Furtwängler.* 33 1/3 *rpm: LHMV* 3 (*ALP 1121*). *Sept. 13, 1953.*

Double Concerto in D minor, *Bach. Violin: Gioconda de Vito; Philharmonia Orchestra: Anthony Bernard.* 33 1/3 *rpm: LHMV* 16 (*BLP 1046*). *Sept. 15, 1953.*

Sonata No. 9 in A, opus 47, *Beethoven. Piano: Kentner.* 33 1/3 *rpm: LHMV* 10. *Sept. 17, 1953.*

Sonata, K. 454, *Mozart. Piano: Kentner.* 33 1/3 *rpm: LHMV* 1053. *Sept. 22, 1953.*

Sonata No. 10 in G, opus 96, *Beethoven. Piano: Kentner.* 33 1/3 *rpm:* (*ALP 1105*). *Oct. 9, 1953.*

Trio Sonata in D, *Handel. Violin: Gioconda de Bito; cello: John Shinebourne; harpsichord: George Malcolm.* 33 1/3 *rpm: LHMV* 16 (*BLP 1046*). *Oct. 11, 1953.*

Ave Maria, *Schubert-Menuhin. Piano: Moore.* 78 *rpm:* (*DB 21608*). *Dec. 1, 1953.*

Songs My Mother Taught Me, *Dvořák-Kreisler. Piano: Moore.* 78 *rpm:* (*DB 21608*). *Dec. 1, 1953.*

SCHEDULED FOR RELEASE IN DECEMBER 1955

Concerto No. 5, *Vieuxtemps. Philharmonia Orchestra: Anatole Fistoulari.* 33 1/3 *rpm: LHMV* 30. *Dec. 7, 1954.*

Concerto in D, opus 21, *Chausson. Piano: Kentner; string quartet: Quattuor Pascal de la Radiodiffusion Française.* 33 1/3 *rpm: LHMV* 30. *Jan. 28, 1955.*

INDEX

"Aba," *see* Menuhin, Moshe
Accademia Chiggiana, 296
"Alard," *see* Stradivarius violins
Aleutians, 225–27, 239–40
"Alma," 224, 259, 292; *see also* Villa Cherkess
Amati violin, 71
American Academy at Fontaine-bleau, 296
Anderson, Dwight, 290
Anker, Sigmund, 28, 30, 37, 39
Ashton, Frederick, 267
Asquith, Anthony, 261
Association Amicale des Prix de Violons du Conservatoire, 163

BBC, 256
BBC Symphony Orchestra, 206, 232, 234
Bach, Johann Sebastian, 77, 121, 135, 143–45, 178, 200, 207, 225, 230, 258, 277, 278; *Urtext* edition, 79, 143, 203; *Concerto in E Major* (violin), 44; *Double Concerto*, 165; *Italian Concerto*, 120; *Partita in D Minor* (violin), 13–16, 86, 87, 96, 100, 102, 179, 202, 210, 225; Sonatas (violin): *A Minor*, 145, 225; *C Major*, 257; *G Minor*, 43; *Six Sonatas & Partitas for Violin Alone*, 201–2; *Well-Tempered Clavichord*, 201–2
Balanchine, George, 267

Baller, Adolph, 223–24, 225, 239, 246, 256
Balsam, Arthur, 163, 172–73
Bartók, Bela, 254, 255–60, 289, 295, 296; *First Violin Sonata*, 256; *Sonata for Unaccompanied Violin*, 203, 257; *Violin Concerto*, 255
Bartók, Mrs. Bela, 259
Beethoven, Ludwig van, 47, 77, 123, 135, 152, 165, 174–76, 200, 203–4, 207, 225, 277, 278; *Concerto for Violin*, 45, 76, 77, 86, 87, 89, 92–94, 96, 233; *Minuet in G*, 39; *Sonata, op. 26*, 120; *"Kreutzer" Sonata*, 112, 165, 167; *Symphony #5*, 177; *Symphony #9*, 295
Belgian Order Leopold, 163
Ben Haim, Paul, 296; *Sonata in G*, 203
Bercovici, Konrad, 85
Berlin Philharmonic Orchestra, 40, 130, 174, 206, 270, 272–73, 277
Berlin State Opera House, 273
Bertaux, Félix and Pierre, 158–60, 219
"Betts," *see* Stradivarius violins
Biancolli, Louis, 290
Bloch, Ernest, 122, 191, 296; *Abodah*, 25, 122, 150, 203; *Macbeth*, 191; *Nigun*, 25, 122
Blochman, Louise, 222
Blockley, Judith, 79

Boccherini, Luigi, 112
Bohm, Jerome D., 206
Böhm, Joseph, 125
Boston Symphony Orchestra, 77
Boulanger, Nadia, 296
Boult, Sir Adrian, 232, 255
Bowles, Chester, 284, 287
Brahms, Johannes, 77, 135, 203–4, 207, 225, 277, 296; *Sonatas in A and D Minor* (violin), 112; *Violin Concerto*, 86, 91, 121, 127–28, 129–30
Britten, Benjamin, 269
Brooklyn *Eagle*, 97
Browning, Robert, 89-90
Bruch, Max, 112, 143; *Violin Concerto*, 149
Brunner Society, 161
Buber, Martin, 282
Busch, Adolph, 89, 125, 139, 141–46, 150, 153, 173, 175
Busch, Fritz, 86, 88-94, 123–24, 135, 137, 139, 142, 149, 153
Busch, Hans, 138
Busch Quartet, 139

California, University of, 110, 154
Cantacuzene, Prince, 74
Cantacuzene, Princess, 74, 84
Captain, Psyche, 284
Cardus, Neville, 171
Carnaval (ballet), 266
Carnegie Hall, 86, 92, 96–97, 121, 206, 256, 257, 290
Casals, Pablo, 233
Castel, Moshe, 293
Cathedral Oaks, 81, 115, 187, 189, 193, 194, 260
Cather, Willa, 154–55, 181–86, 192, 208, 217, 250, 296

Chagall, Marc, 293
Chaplin, Charlie, 122
Chausson, Ernest, 77; *Poème*, 86, 96
Chopin, Frederick, 203; *Fantasie Impromptu*, 120; *Valse in B Minor*, 30
Chotzinoff, Samuel, 96, 206, 207
Churchill, Winston, 228
Ciampi, Marcel, 79–80, 158
City Lights, 122
Cleveland Symphony Orchestra, 255
Coate, Mr. and Mrs. Karl, 292–93
Cohn, Eda, 135, 137–39
Cohn, Samuel, 109–10, 135
Coliseum (London), 266
Conservatoire Symphony Orchestra (Paris), 232
Coogan, Jackie, 88–89
Corelli, Arcangelo, *La Folia*, 86
Cortot, Alfred, 163
Crowthers, Dorothy, 56, 102, 111
Curran Theater (San Francisco), 26
Cushing, Edward, 97

Dailey, Gardner, 224
Dallas *Morning News*, 206
Damrosch, Walter, 88–89, 109-10
Dandelot, Maurice, 232
Dannenbaum, Raymond, 180
D'Aranyi, Jelly, 205–6
David, Ferdinand, 296
Da Vinci, Leonardo, 201; *Mona Lisa*, 81
De Basil, Col. W., 267

De Bériot, 44; *Concerto №9*, 39; *Scène de Ballet*, 51
Debs, Eugene, 107
Debussy, Claude, 203
De Havilland, Olivia, 227
De Mille, Agnes, *Dance to the Piper*, 265
Dennison, George, 80–81, 115, 189, 190–91, 222, 260
Derain, André, 293
Deuppel Center, 273
De Vito, Gioconda, 295
Diaghilev Ballet, 266
Diaghilev, Sergei, 266–67
"Dolphin," *see* Stradivarius violins
Dorati, Antal, 128, 248, 250, 258
Dorati, Klari, 250
Douglas Aircraft Corporation, 118
Dounis, *Technique of the Violin*, 243
Downes, Olin, 43–44, 94–95, 123, 206, 259
Dresden State Opera and Orchestra, 137
Dreyfus, Gilberte, 290
Dunn, Father, 193

"Edie" (Yehudi's aunt), 149–50, 163, 209, 260, 268
Ehrman, Esther, *see* Lazard, Esther Ehrman
Ehrman, Florence, 59, 62, 69, 103, 115, 139, 153
Ehrman, Sidney M., 54, 59–60, 62–63, 71, 103, 115–16, 135, 137, 139, 153, 177
Ehrman, Sidney, Jr., 115–16

Einstein, Albert, 137, 201, 277
Eisenberg, Maurice, 163
Elgar, Sir Edward, 168–71; *Violin Concerto*, 169, 171
Elliott, Madge, 267
Elman, Mischa, 49, 52, 123, 152
Elman, Sol, 57
Endt, Hendrick, 218, 220, 222
Enesco, Georges, 13–16, 50, 63, 65, 67, 68, 73–79, 81, 83, 84, 86, 101, 113–14, 128, 139, 142–45, 153, 157, 158, 163–64, 165, 175, 181, 185, 186, 191, 216, 219, 233, 296; *Oedipus*, 191; *Rumanian Rhapsodies*, 74
Engels, George, 88
Epstein, Jacob, 263
Ernst, Heinrich Wilhelm, 125
Evans, Maurice, 227–28
Evans and Salter, 88, 173

Fachiri, Adila, 205
Fairmont Hotel Gold Medal Contest, 39
Fauré, Gabriel, 74
Firestone, Nathan, 194
Fishbein, Captain, 273
Flagstad, Kirsten, 207
Fleg, Daniel, 191, 194–95, 219
Fleg, Edmond and Madeleine, 191, 219
Fleg, Maurice, 191, 219
Flesch, Karl, 243, 270, 277; *The Art of Violin Playing*, 243
Flesch, Mrs. Karl, 270, 277
Ford Foundation, 288; Experimental TV Workshop, 295
Français, Emile, 125
Francescatti, Zino, 295

Franck, César, 74, 75, 77, 86, 171, 296
Franko, Sam, 121, 135, 203
Fried, Alexander, 58–59
Furtwängler, Wilhelm, 174, 254, 270–73, 278, 279

Gabrilowitsch, Ossip, 49, 137
Gaisberg, Frederick, 169–70
Gandhi, Indira, 283, 284
Gandhi, Mahatma, 284
Garbat, Dr., 56, 123, 130, 131–32, 177, 180–81, 192
Garbat, Julian, 56
Garbat, Mania, 56, 131
Garbat, Rachael Lubarsky, 20, 56, 88, 123, 131–32, 180–81, 192
Garbo, Greta, 262
Gazelle, Marcel, 192, 229, 230–31, 233–34, 284
Gédalge, André, 74
Gehrig-Geisst, Justin, 141
Geismar, Berta, 270
Gerhardt, Elena, 131, 140
Giesen, Hubert, 141, 146, 149, 150, 163
Gillon, Mr. and Mrs. Baruch, 279–80
Gilman, Lawrence, 95–96
Glazunov, Aleksandr, 112
Godchaux, Rebecca, 61–62, 111–12
Godowsky, Leopold, 152
Goldman, Henry, 123–25, 130–31, 135, 137, 140, 177–78, 179, 180, 181, 222
Goldman, Mrs. Henry, 123–25, 130–31, 138, 140
Goldmark, Karl, 112

Goldschmann, Vladimir, 203, 206
Gould, Diana, *see* Menuhin, Diana Gould
Gould, Gerard and Gerard Jr., 260
Gould, Griselda, 260–61
Granger, Stewart, 261
Guadagnini violin, 115
Guarnierius violins, 65, 71, 126, 222
Gusikoff, Mr., 92

Hambourg, Mr. and Mrs. Jan, 71, 153, 154, 157, 212
Handel, George Frederick, *Sonata in E Minor* (violin), 57
Harcourt, Lady Evelyn Stuart Gould, 260–61, 268
Harcourt, Lord Cecil, 265
Harvard University, 153
Haskell, Arnold, 267
Hebrew University in Jerusalem, 282
Heifetz, Mr., 57
Heifetz, Jascha, 49, 108, 117, 125, 152
Heinsheimer, H. W., 257n.
Heinze, Sir Bernard, 210
Hekking, Gerard, 68, 71
Henderson, W. J., 175–76
Herrmann, Emil, 124–25, 126, 222
Hertz, Alfred, 27, 40, 51, 59, 62
Herzlia Gymnasium, 19
Hirschmann, Ira A., 271
His Master's Voice, 169
Hitler, Adolf, 150, 174, 185, 272n.

Hofmann, Josef, 152
Holt, Harold, 210, 228, 268
Honig, Dr. Camille, 282
Horowitz, Vladimir, 173
Huberman, Bronislaw, 125
Hyperion (Hölderlin), 158

"Imma," *see* Menuhin, Marutha Sher
Imperial Russian Ballet, 267
India, 254, 283–88, 289
Ingerson, Frank, 80–81, 115, 189, 190–91, 222, 260
Israeli Symphony Orchestra, 279, 282

Jacobowsky and the Colonel, 261
Janssen, Werner, 207
Jewish Community Center Hebrew School (New Jersey), 21
Joachim cadenza, *see* Beethoven, *Concerto for Violin*
Joachim, Joseph, 112, 125, 204–5, 296
Joenische, 293
"Jon" (Yehudi's cousin), 150
"Jonas of Lemberg," 273–76
Joseph of Lubavich, Rabbi, 17
Juilliard School of Music, *see* N. Y. Institute of Musical Art

Kafka, Franz, 159
Kapell, William, 292
Karsavina, Thamar, 267
Kavin, Natia, 23, 24, 33, 85
Kentner, Griselda, 268
Kentner, Louis, 128, 203, 268
Khan, Ali Akhbar, 288

Khatchaturian, Aran, 296
Kokoshka, Oskar, 293
"Königen Louise," *see* Wolff, Louise
Koos, Dr. de, 178
Koshland, Mrs., 80
Koussevitsky, Serge, 77, 171
Kreisler, 49, 56–57, 108, 123, 125, 152, 248–49, 296
Krindler, Sarah, 39
Kshessinskaya, Matilde, 267
Kubelik, Ján, 152
Kulenkampff, Georg, 206

La Bruyère, Jean de, 113
Lalo, Edouard Victor, *Symphonie Espagnole*, 57, 65, 71, 209, 233
Lamoureux Symphony Orchestra, 71, 72
Langer, Dr. Samuel, 53–54, 59, 60, 71–72, 79
Laurencin, Marie, 293
Law, Prime Minister, 169
Lazard, Claude, 154
Lazard, Esther Ehrman, 59, 62, 63, 103, 115–17, 139–40, 153, 154, 197
Leach, Patrick, 290
Leda and the Swan (ballet), 267
Légion d'Honneur, 163
Lener, Jenö, 246
Lener String Quartet, 246
Lester, Keith, 267
Leuschner, Mark Hindricks, 272
Leventritt, Rosalie, 179–80, 192, 194, 195, 196–97
Leventritt, Victor, 194, 195
Lewis, Edith, 182, 250

Lipinsky, 44
Locatelli, *Labyrinth,* 210
London *Evening News,* 209
London Symphony Orchestra, 149, 268
Louisville *Courier-Journal,* 290
Louvre, the, 81
Lubarsky, Mr., 19
Lubarsky, Rachael, *see* Garbat, Rachael Lubarsky
Lysistrata (ballet), 267

MacLeish, Archibald, 228
McCloy, John J., 276
Magic Bow, The, 261
Mahler, Gustav, 73
Mangeot, André, 101n.
Manhattan Opera House, 57–58, 89
Mann, Heinrich, 159
Mann, Thomas, 159
Marantz, Sam, 21–22, 23, 55, 57, 154
Marie, Queen of Rumania, 79, 83, 84
Mariposa, S. S., 217
Markova–Dolin Ballet Company, 267
Marseillaise, the, 233
Marsick, Martin, 74
Mason, Redford, 39, 51, 59, 172
Massenet, Jules, 74
Massine, Leonide, 267
Melbourne Symphony Orchestra, 210
Mendelssohn-Bartholdy, Felix, 44, 45, 152, 174, 225, 296; *Violin Concerto in D Minor,* 203, 233
Mengelberg, Willem, 122–23

Menuhin, Benjamin, 17–18
Menuhin, Diana Gould (Yehudi's present wife), 254, 260–68, 269, 280, 282, 284, 288, 289, 292–93
Menuhin, Gerard (Yehudi's son), 290, 293–94, 295
Menuhin, Hephzibah (Yehudi's sister), 29, 54, 62, 69–71, 79–80, 81–86, 100, 103–6, 110, 111, 113, 115–16, 117–18, 119, 120, 130, 131, 139, 141, 146–47, 154, 156, 158, 161–65, 179, 182, 183–84, 186, 187, 189–90, 194, 195, 196–97, 198, 203, 208, 211, 212, 213, 217, 221, 236–38, 250, 262, 279–82; first recital, 120; Paris debut, 165–66; joint concerts with Yehudi, 165–68; marriage to Lindsay Nicholas, 216
Menuhin, Jeremy (Yehudi's son), 293-94
Menuhin, Krov (Yehudi's son), 222, 295
Menuhin, Marutha Sher (Yehudi's mother), 19, 20–23, 24, 26–28, 29–31, 33–36, 37, 43, 44, 45–46, 48, 49, 52, 53, 54–55, 57–58, 59–62, 63, 65–66, 69–71, 74, 80, 81–86, 88, 92, 97–98, 99–100, 102–7, 109, 111, 119, 120, 125, 126, 130–32, 135, 138, 139, 140, 141, 146–47, 153, 154, 155–56, 157, 158, 159, 161–63, 164, 165, 167, 169, 172, 173, 176, 177, 179, 180–82, 187, 190, 192, 193, 194, 195–96, 198,

210, 212, 213, 215, 221, 241, 260, 293

Menuhin, Moshe (Yehudi's father), 13, 14, 17–23, 24, 25, 26–27, 29, 33–36, 44, 46, 52, 54, 56, 57–58, 59–60, 61, 62, 63, 68, 69–71, 74–75, 78, 79–80, 81–86, 87–88, 90–92, 97–98, 99–100, 101, 102–5, 109, 111, 118, 122, 125, 126–27, 130–32, 135, 138, 139, 141, 142, 146, 149, 150, 151, 152–53, 154, 156–57, 162, 169, 172, 173, 177, 179, 187, 190–91, 192–93, 195, 208, 212, 218–21, 260, 293

Menuhin, Nola Ruby Nicholas (Yehudi's first wife), 190, 210–15, 217–22, 234–36, 238, 249, 250, 264

Menuhin, Yaltah (Yehudi's sister), 29, 54, 62, 69–71, 79–80, 81–86, 100, 103–6, 110, 113, 115–16, 117–18, 119, 120, 130, 131, 139, 141, 146, 154, 158, 161–63, 164, 179, 182, 183–84, 189–90, 194, 195, 196–97, 198, 208, 211–12, 213, 222, 236; marriage to Wm. Stix, 216; marriage to Benjamin Rolfe, 221

Menuhin, Yehudi, 13ff.; birth, 21; move to West Coast, 23; first lessons, 28; first public appearance, 39; lessons with Persinger, 40–48, 58; first professional performance, 51; New York debut, 57; in Paris, 65–81, 155ff., 191ff.; meeting with Ysaye, 65–67; lessons with Enesco, 13–16, 68, 74–79, 157, 158; first Carnegie Hall concerts, 87–97; San Francisco homecoming concert, 116; first U. S. tour, 121–30; Berlin concerts, 135–37, 139; lessons with Adolph Busch, 141–46, 153; friendship with Willa Cather, 154–55, 181–86, 192, 208, 250; concerts with Hephzibah, 165–67; concerts with Elgar, 169–71; concerts with Toscanini, 172–77; first marriage, 210–15, 238; World War II concerts, 223–34, 239–40; friendship with Bartók, 255–60; second marriage, 260–69, 293ff.; defense of Furtwängler, 273–78; Tel Aviv concert, 280–82; in India, 283–88; present family life, 293ff.; books read by, 111, 155, 158, 160–61, 184–85; on discovering new music, 296–97; on Mozart, 47–48; on musical analysis, 200–2; on musical memory, 128–30; recordings by, 299–308; on violin literature, 243–44; violins owned by, 56, 71, 115, 124–25, 126, 222; on violin technique, 242–45

Menuhin, Zamira (Yehudi's daughter), 179, 221, 222, 293

Merry Widow, 267

"Messiah," *see* Stradivarius violins

Metropolitan Opera House, 166

Michael, King of Rumania, 83

Millay, Edna St. Vincent, 111
Milstein, Nathan, 173, 295
Minneapolis *Evening Tribune,* 127n.
Minneapolis Symphony Orchestra, 127, 255
Miracle, The (ballet), 267
Mitropoulos, Dimitri, 128, 255
Molinari, Bernardino, 173
Monteux, Pierre, 163
Moore, Grace, 207
Moser, Andreas, 205
Mozart, Wolfgang Amadeus, 47–48, 77, 112, 152, 166, 196, 207, 278; *A-Major Concerto* (violin), 45, 86, 87–88; *"Adelaide" Concerto* (violin), 203; *Concerto ♯7 in D Major,* 86, 96; *Sonata in A* (K. 526) (violin), 165
Munch, Charles, 232, 233
Murphy, Robert, 272–73, 276
Museum of Modern Art, 288
Musical America (pub.), 57, 102
Musical Courier (pub.), 125, 137
Mussolini, Benito, 173, 185

Nation, the (pub.), 111
Nazis, 142, 150, 159, 161, 206, 223, 233, 270–71, 274–75, 277
Nehru, Pandit and Mme., 283–84, 288
Neveu, Ginette, 292
New Friends of Music, 271
Newman, Ernest, 171
Newsweek (pub.), 291
Newton, Ivor, 169

New York *Evening World,* 96, 97
New York *Herald Tribune,* 95, 206, 291
New York Institute of Musical Art, 55, 102
New York *Journal,* 96
New York Philharmonic Society, 216
New York Philharmonic Symphony Orchestra, 122
New York *Post,* 206
New York *Sun,* 175–76
New York Symphony Orchestra, 86, 88
New York *Times,* the, 43–44, 94, 102n., 240, 290
New York *World-Telegram,* 290
New Yorker, the (pub.), 290
Nicholas, George, 211, 212, 214, 217
Nicholas, Lindsay, 190, 210–12, 214, 216, 217
Nicholas, Nola Ruby, *see* Menuhin, Nola Ruby Nicholas
Nijinska, Bronislava, 267
Ninotchka, 262
Nürnberg trials, 271

Office of War Information, 228–29
Oistrakh, David, 295, 296
"Omnibus," 288
Orient Express, 82, 88

"P.G.-H." (critic), 291
Pacific Hebrew Orphan Asylum, 53
Pacific Musical Society, 39

Paderewski, Ignace, 152
Paganini, Nicolò, *Caprices*, 77; *Moses variations*, 210; *Violin Concerto in D Major*, 44, 57, 261
Palais des Beaux Arts (Antwerp, 231
Pallanza, 177; *see also* Toscanini
Paray, Paul, 71, 72–73, 135
Paris Conservatoire, 163
Paris Opera House, 232, 233, 234
Pashkus, Theodore and Alice, 251
Paterson, John, 110, 112, 194
Pavane (ballet), 267
Pavlova, Anna, 267
Peisach, Mr. and Mrs. Fritz, 132–33, 135, 137
Perera, Mrs. Lionello, 256
Perera, Lydia, 179, 191, 192
Persinger, Louis, 27, 28, 40–48, 54, 57, 60, 61, 63–64, 65, 86, 90, 92, 94, 96, 111, 114, 117, 124–25, 146, 175, 242, 243
Persinger String Quartet, 40, 54, 56
Perstein, Arnold, 110–11
Piastro, Michel, 242–43
Piatigorsky, Gregor, 173
"Pistol-Packing Momma," 225
Pons, Lily, 207
Popov, Professor, 125
Prasad, Sri Rajendro, 284
Primrose, William, 295
"Prince Khevenhüller" violin, 124–25, 126, 177, 199, 222, 232
Prix de Rome, 152

Prussian State Library (Berlin), 205, 206

"Queen Louise," *see* Wolff, Louise
Queen Marie's Fairytales, 84
Queen's Hall (London), 165

Rambert, Marie, 266, 267
Rao, Shanta, 288
Ravel, Maurice, 78; *Kaddisch*, 25
Recordings, list of Menuhin's, 299–308
Redgrave, Michael, 261, 268
Reinhardt, Max, 136, 267
Rejto, Gabor, 246
Rethberg, Elizabeth, 110
Rice, Diana, 101–2
Rilke, Rainer Maria, 159
Rinder, Cantor Reuben, 27, 28, 33, 39, 40, 53–54, 58
Ritchard, Cyril, 267, 268
Rodzinski, Artur, 255
Rogers, Will, 111
Rolfe, Benjamin, 221
Rolfe, Yaltah Menuhin, *see* Menuhin, Yaltah
Ronald, Sir Landon, 149
Roosevelt, Eleanor, 229, 284
Roosevelt, Franklin D., 229
Rosen, Max, 57
Rosenfield, John, Jr., 206
Royal Albert Hall (London), 149, 169, 171, 209

Sacco and Vanzetti, 107
Sacred Heart Novitiate, 193
St. Louis Symphony Orchestra, 203, 206

Saint-Saëns, Camille, 152; *Violin Concerto in B Minor*, 128
Salle Pleyel (Paris), 165
Salomons, Jacqueline, 163
Sandburg, Carl, 111
San Francisco *Chronicle*, 39
San Francisco Civic Auditorium, 116
San Francisco *News*, 120, 198
San Francisco Symphony Orchestra, 26–8, 40, 51, 112, 242
Sarasate, Pablo, 44; *Gypsy Airs*, 39
Sargeant, Elizabeth Shepley, 183n.
Sargeant, Winthrop, 290
Scheherazade (ballet), 266
Schneiderhahn, Wolfgang, 295
Schott Publishers, 203–4
Schubert, 278; *Ave Maria*, 117
Schumann, Clara, 204–5
Schumann, Robert, 77, 204–5, 207, 296; *Kinderszenen*, 80; "Lost" concerto, 203–6; *Phantasie*, 203, 204; *Sonata in D Minor*, 165
Schurman, Ambassador, 136
Schwartzschild, Rabbi, 277
Scottish Rite Hall (San Francisco), 51, 59
Seefried, Irmgard, 295
Serkin, Rudolf, 142
Shadows on the Rock (Cather), 154
Shapeero, Ezra, 52–53
Shaw, G. B., 282–83
Sher, Marutha, *see* Menuhin, Marutha Sher
Shorr, Lev, 79, 120

Shostakovitch, Dimitri, 296
Sinding, Christian, 112
Singakademie, 139
Smith, Carleton Sprague, 295
Société Gastronomique, 71
"Soil," *see* Stradivarius violins
"Sonia" (Yehudi's cousin), 150, 163, 179
Spalding, Albert, 76
Spivakovsky, Tossy, 255
Spohr, Louis, 44
Starr, Roger, 229
Stern, Isaac, 295
Stix, William, 194, 212, 216
Stokes, Richard, 97
Stokowski, Leopold, 207
Stradivarius violins, 124–25, 126, 232, 239
Stuart, Evelyn, *see* Harcourt, Lady Evelyn Stuart Gould
"Swan," *see* Stradivarius violins
Swarthout, Gladys, 207
Swift, Curran D., 120
Szell, George, 128
Szigetti, Joseph, 243

Tait, Mr., 187
Tansman, Alexander, *La Nuit Kurde*, 123
Tartini, Giuseppe, *Devil's Trill Sonata*, 85, 96, 209; Sonatas, 86
Taubman, Howard, 240, 290–91
Taylor, Deems, 111
Tchaikovsky, Pëtr, 123, 171; *Sérénade Mélancolique*, 108; *Violin Concerto*, 44, 72, 117, 121, 122

Temianka, Henry, 295
Temple Emmanu-El (San Francisco), 80
Thibaud, Jacques, 67, 163, 232, 292
Thomson, *Outline of Science,* 119, 132
Toscanini, Arturo, 128, 151, 168, 172–77, 191, 214, 219, 278
Toscanini, Mme., 174
Totenberg, Roman, 246
Town Hall (New York), 165, 168, 191
Tudor, Anthony, 267
Twain, Mark, 49

U.S.S.R., 121
Ur-texts, 142–43; *see also* Bach, Johann Sebastian

Vanda, Poppoea, 267
Verbrugghen, Henri, 127–28
Verdi, Giuseppe, *Requiem,* 214
Vian, M. and Mme., 156
Vienna Conservatoire, 152
Vienna Philharmonic Orchestra, 73
Vieuxtemps, Henri, 74, 102, 112
Villa Cherkess, 189, 190, 191, 192–93, 194, 215, 218, 222, 224; *see also* "Alma"
Villa Luminish, 13, 81, 84, 87
Ville d'Avray, 153, 155, 161–63, 186, 194
Violin technique, 38, 78, 242–45, 251
Vivaldi, Antonio, 112, 203; *Concerto in G Minor, op. 4*
(violin), 203; *Concerto for Three Violins,* 295

Wagner, Friedelind, 272n.
Walter, Bruno, 136, 137, 174, 248, 290, 291
Walton, William, 296
Wasserman, Jakob, 159
Weber, Karl Maria von, *Perpetual Motion,* 120; *Rondo Brilliante,* 79, 120
Webster, Beveridge, 194
Webster, Ferguson, 206, 210
Weil, Irving, 96
Weinhold, Kurt, 110
Weiss, Arthur, 26
Weizmann, Mr. and Mrs. Chaim, 279, 282
Weldon, George, 268
Werff, Tineke van der, 178–79
White, Theodore, 159n.
Wieniawski, Henri, 44, 112; *Souvenir de Moscou,* 96
Wilk, Maurice, 246
Williams, Air Vice-Marshal, 119
Williams, Paul, 189
Wolff, Herman, Agency, 135
Wolff, Louise, 135–36
World War II, 223–34
Wood, Charles Erskine Scott, 189, 216; *Heavenly Discourse,* 160, 189; *The Poet in the Desert,* 189

Yoga, 247, 283, 284
Ysaye, Eugène, 40, 60, 61, 65–67, 71, 74, 75, 77, 97, 125, 127, 199, 296

Zimbalist, Efrem, 124–25
Zirato, Bruno, 216

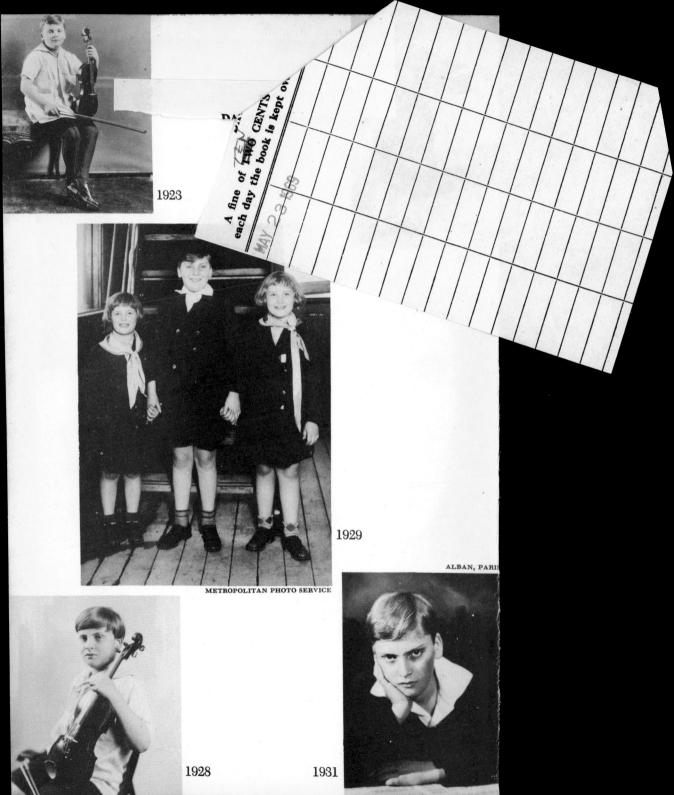

1923

1929

METROPOLITAN PHOTO SERVICE

ALBAN, PARIS

1928   1931